THE MEMORY CODE

THE
MEMORY
CODE

The Secrets of Stonehenge, Easter Island,
and Other Ancient Monuments

DR. LYNNE KELLY

PEGASUS BOOKS
NEW YORK LONDON

THE MEMORY CODE

Pegasus Books Ltd
148 West 37th Street, 13th Floor
New York, NY 10018

First Pegasus Books hardcover edition February 2017

ISBN: 978-1-68177-325-4

10 9 8 7 6 5 4 3 2 1

Printed in the United States of America
Distributed by W. W. Norton & Company, Inc.

For Damian Kelly,
Leah, Abigail and Rebecca Heitbaum

CONTENTS

||||||||||||||||||||||||||||||||||||||||||||||

CONTENTS

PREFACE

I had no idea that indigenous animal stories from around the world would lead me to a new theory for Stonehenge. I had a PhD scholarship as a science writer and was looking forward to three years of gentle research leading to a natural history book about animal behaviour and indigenous stories. Eight tumultuous years later and that book is now in your hands, bearing only scant resemblance to the confident outline that started my journey.

It was only weeks into the PhD in the English program at La Trobe University that I glimpsed the complexity of Australian Aboriginal elders' knowledge, the first group of cultures I explored in depth. They memorised a vast amount of information about animals, their identification and behaviour, habitats and uses. A huge number of species of birds, mammals, reptiles and invertebrates were accurately described in stories, even when they had no apparent practical use. I realised that the elders could identify all the animals across a wide landscape, when I was struggling with just the birds in my local area. I had a field guide; they had only memory.

I started asking the question which soon became an obsession: how could they remember so much stuff?

At our second meeting, my PhD supervisor, Professor Sue Martin, named a list of suggested resources, casually adding 'and it might be worth looking at Ong on morality'. I dutifully wrote down 'Ong' and 'morality', wondering if it was something about my ethics that was giving her concern. I found Ong's book in the library. The title was *Orality and Literacy*.

Orality, I soon discovered, was about making knowledge memorable. It was about using song, story, dance and mythology to help retain vast stores of factual information when the culture had no recourse to writing. It was the first step to understanding how they could remember so much stuff. The definition of 'stuff' was growing rapidly to include not only the animal knowledge I was researching, but also the names and uses of plants; resource access and land management; laws and ethics; geology and astronomy; genealogies, to ensure they knew their rights and relatives; navigation, to ensure they could travel long distances when there were no roads or maps; ideas about where they had come from; and, of course, what they believed. Indigenous cultures memorised everything on which their survival—physically and culturally—depended.

I wasn't far into my research when I began to understand that songlines were key to the way Indigenous Australians organised this vast store of information so that it would not be forgotten. Songlines are sung narratives of the landscape, singing tracks that weave across the country and enable every significant place to be known. At each location, rituals are performed that enact the knowledge associated with that specific place. In this context, rituals are repeated acts and no more should be implied by that word. The degree to which they are religious ceremonies depends entirely on the specific ritual. One elder explained to me how singing the names of the sacred sites along the songlines created a set of subheadings to the entire knowledge base, a place for knowing about every animal, plant and person. The songlines could be sung when moving through the space in reality or in imagination.

By repeating the stories of the mythological beings through songs and dances at sacred landscape sites, information could be memorised, even if it was not used for tens, hundreds or thousands of years. Songs are far more memorable than prose. Dances can depict animal behaviour and tactics for the hunt in a way no words can do. Mythological characters can act out a vivid set of stories that are unforgettable.

I recognised that Aboriginal elders were using their songlines in a similar way to the ancient Greek orators who mentally walked through their buildings and streetscapes from location to location to help them memorise their speeches. They called it 'the method of loci'. Modern memory champions memorise shuffled decks of cards using the same method, walking through their homes or churches, grand buildings or public spaces in their imaginations as they recall each card. They call them memory palaces.

A few months later, I travelled to England with my husband, Damian. He had also returned to university, in his case to study archaeology. My goal was to spend time at museums looking for representations of animals among indigenous collections to frame my book. Damian was off to visit archaeological sites. The downpour on the day he'd planned to go to Stonehenge was so intense that he decided not to stop on his journey to Cornwall. On a fine day, he wanted to try again. I just wanted to get to Bath and indulge in Jane Austen. Dutifully, I walked around Stonehenge, tourist earphones providing commentary. At that early stage of my newly acquired obsession, I was so immersed in my subject that I naively expected orality and memory to be the focus of every commentary. The disembodied voice with the perfect English accent told me about the various theories but didn't mention orality or memory or anything about the builders' system of knowledge. There was a great deal of very important information, but I was immune to it, listening only for my pet topic.

Stonehenge was initially a simple stone circle built at the very start of the transition from a mobile hunting and gathering lifestyle to settling and farming. What would happen, I asked myself on Salisbury Plain that day, to the knowledge that these people had acquired over thousands of years and embedded in the landscape? Farming doesn't happen rapidly. The transition takes time. How would the settlers avoid forgetting all their songs and stories and knowledge of the animals and plants if they were no longer visiting the memory locations their ancestors had spread across the broad countryside? How clever of them, I decided. They've replicated a series of landscape sacred places in their local environment. What could be more perfect than a circle of stones, each stone representing a former sacred location, each stone acting as a memory aid? I didn't realise that this had never been suggested before.

As we were funnelled out through the gift shop, I started checking the indexes of books for 'orality', having by this stage forgotten that I'd never heard the term until a few months before. I searched every book for any mention of 'orality' or 'memory' and found nothing. I bought the most recent book I could find written by a bona fide archaeologist. Flicking through it, the word 'illiterate' caught my attention. In the field of orality, the word 'illiterate' is used for those who cannot read or write within a literate culture, while those with no contact at all with writing are referred to as 'non-literate' or 'oral'. Was it possible that the body of sociological research on the way oral cultures memorise information had not crossed into the archaeological interpretation of monuments built by oral cultures? Could I be so lucky?

I was online as soon as I could and found only one reference linking Stonehenge to orality. An American sociologist, Carl Couch, had written a paper titled 'Oral technologies: Cornerstones of ancient civilisations?' It was an obscure paper and I was unable to access it until I returned home. I could find nothing else. I became wildly excited. Maybe no one had actually suggested this before. Maybe I had an original theory for the purpose of Stonehenge. Surely not.

A few days later I was a guest at a small dinner. I started enthusing about my theory. The first of my fellow diners to respond told me it sounded like rubbish but he was willing to be convinced if I could provide the evidence. It took me five years to convince him. The second response was that it sounded like rubbish, and 'What on earth would they need to memorise anyway?' That question had to be answered before there was any point in going on. It takes the first chapter of this book. A third guest asked how I would know if I was not self-deluded? Wasn't I just seeing my beloved orality and memory everywhere I looked? That question became a profoundly difficult one.

I was soon back at university, half-jokingly telling Sue Martin that I thought I had solved the mystery of Stonehenge. Any normal supervisor would have pointed out that I had a PhD scholarship for my original topic and a publisher interested in publishing it. To abandon all that to chase some wild idea when I didn't even have a background in archaeology was clearly foolhardy. Sue Martin, however, was not a normal supervisor. She wanted the idea evaluated so I would not be constantly distracted by my latest enthusiasm. We talked about how I could know that I was not self-deluded, just seeing orality and memory everywhere

I looked. We decided it required external checking by somebody quite dispassionate about my research. Being so early in the PhD process, she suggested that I run my two themes parallel—keep reading on animals in indigenous stories and take six months to see whether there was any validity to my claims about Stonehenge.

The librarian attached to our faculty, Lisa Donnelly, did numerous convoluted searches, the sort that only academic librarians know how to do. She constantly checked my sources and searched for anything which could indicate that the theory had been proposed before and been rejected for fairly obvious archaeological reasons. At the end of six months she reported that the theory appeared to be totally original and all my sources sound.

I approached three archaeologists at the university, only to be dismissed by each of them. I could understand. For an archaeologist, someone from the English program with a new theory for Stonehenge must represent a stereotypical nightmare. Sue asked me to outline the theory in writing. She sent the dozen or so pages to the archaeology department explaining that we were perfectly happy for this to be dismissed, but could we please have the reasons why. It was only then that I would be able to get back on track with my gentle PhD topic.

The response was rapid. In essence it said the archaeology appeared sound, the theory appeared original, and the anonymous archaeologist wanted nothing to do with me. I was devastated. I needed help. I needed to sit down and talk about my ideas with somebody who would be able to guide me in the archaeology. Over the next few months, we approached two other members of the faculty, to no avail.

The question posed by the third guest at the dinner party haunted me. I was starting to believe that I was self-deluded in seeing my theory everywhere. Logic told me that if these ideas explained

Stonehenge and all the stone circles of the British Neolithic, then I should be able to see similar patterns in any archaeological site in the world that represented the early stages of settlement. The list of archaeological sites matching the pattern was growing daily. Two in particular had attracted my attention: Chaco Canyon in New Mexico and Poverty Point in Louisiana. I gained a university travel grant to visit these sites, which included funding for two days to hire American archaeologist Larry Baker to take me to Chaco Canyon and the surrounding Ancestral Puebloan sites. I had a captive archaeologist at last; he was stuck in a car with me for two whole days. He loved the theory.

I submitted articles to journals. An archaeology journal said it was too much anthropology for them. An anthropological journal said it was much more about archaeology. An interdisciplinary journal rejected it within twelve hours. The niggling voice in my head started to yell that there was no way someone as ordinary as me should be trying to solve one of the world's great mysteries.

By 2010, I was becoming more and more stressed keeping two PhD topics running. I just needed to pinpoint exactly what was wrong with the Stonehenge theory so I could return to my straight-forward thesis about animal behaviour and indigenous stories. I was struggling to sleep and my health was deteriorating.

Damian announced that psychiatric bills would be far more expensive than a trip to England and he was booking flights. I was to make contact with a British Neolithic archaeologist, gain time for an interview, and then we would fly there and settle the matter. Dr Rosamund Cleal is lead editor and contributing author of English Heritage's seminal book *Stonehenge in its Landscape*. I imagined that she would do all she could to avoid yet another Stonehenge theory. She offered an hour. It stretched to four, followed by an invitation to return the next day. A few more hours' discussion finished with

Dr Cleal stating that I could quote her publicly saying 'This theory is well worth pursuing.' After that encouragement, nothing was going to stop me.

It was to be another three years before the thesis was formally assessed by archaeologists and passed. After further review, it was published as a book for Cambridge University Press.

During those years I started implementing in my everyday life the memory methods that I had learnt from indigenous cultures. I was creating songlines in my own neighbourhood and linking to them vast amounts of information about every country in the world, about all of prehistory and history. At the same time, I was copying an African memory board to encode the more than four hundred birds found in my state, and assigning the hundred native mammals to a wooden post. As somebody who struggled to remember what others would consider general knowledge, I was rapidly gaining an encyclopaedic knowledge base beyond anything I could have imagined possible.

With the doctorate finished, I invested more and more time into these memory experiments, adding knowledge daily as I walked the dog. It was fun, and nothing like the stressful memory work required for exams in the past. Why hadn't I been taught these methods at school? After a year or so, I was starting to see patterns in the information even though I was not actively searching for them. I found my stories starting to take on the form of the indigenous stories I'd read from all over the world. I was seeing familiar knowledge in a different way—vivid, visual and emotional. I gained insight and pleasure from the process.

This book is about indigenous memory, about Stonehenge and archaeological sites all over the world, and about a journey I took from the moment I stumbled across a simple idea standing on Salisbury Plain. Stonehenge was a memory space. The world is full of ancient memory spaces. My world is now full of contemporary memory spaces and so much the richer for it.

CHAPTER 1

Encyclopaedic memories of the elders

IIIIIIIIIIIIIIIIIIIIIIIIIIIIIIIIIIIIIIIIIIIIIII

It is only recently that the depth and complexity of oral traditions has been acknowledged. Archaeologists have long recognised that the Neolithic Britons had the same brains and the same intellectual potential as you and me. Modern humans have been around for tens of thousands of years. Yet for far too long, indigenous cultures were seen as intellectually inferior and primitive. It is only a hundred years ago that the hugely influential Sigmund Freud wrote: 'I shall select as the basis of this comparison the tribes which have been described by anthropologists as the most backward and miserable of savages, the aborigines of Australia.'[1]

It is these very 'aborigines of Australia' who enabled me to glimpse the complexity of their information systems and the extraordinary range of memory methods they used—and started me on the journey that led to this book.

If I was to argue that Stonehenge was primarily about memory methods, then I had to demonstrate that non-literate cultures memorised a great deal of information. I wasn't talking about simply remembering what they had seen, done and been shown out on the daily gather and hunt. I wasn't saying that the ancient stones were simple reminders, much as a statue of Darwin at a museum reminds us of the great man.

I was talking about formally memorising information—learning, studying and repeating it. I was saying that the stone circles were part of a structured system for memorising vast amounts of rational information. I had come to believe that Australian Aboriginal songlines, Native American trails, Inca ceques and many other landscape paths created by indigenous cultures were the result of training their memories. In years of research, I found no indigenous culture that relied on casual memory and chatter around the campfire to store the knowledge of their environment and culture.

As my fellow dinner guest had asked only days after I had first formulated my ideas about Stonehenge: what on earth would they need to memorise anyway?

Indigenous knowledge of animals

When researching my book *Crocodile: Evolution's greatest survivor* I became aware of how indigenous stories spelt out the specific characteristics of all 23 crocodilian species. Stories and songs from around the world recorded behaviour specific to each species, for example, the ability of the saltwater crocodile (*Crocodylus porosus*) to swim thousands of miles in the ocean. Crocodiles are deadly predators, haunting the rivers and oceans on which many people depend for water and food. Elders told stories of the way crocodiles' eyes shine at night in the light of torches, of their ability to wait and note human habits, how to know if they had detected human presence, when their eggs would be ready to collect, and how to retrieve these precious sources of protein in the face of an aggressive mother.

Australian Aboriginal stories distinguish clearly between the potentially deadly saltwater crocodile and the relatively harmless freshwater crocodile (*Crocodylus johnstoni*), while Papuan stories distinguish between the saltwater crocodile and the smaller, harmless New Guinea crocodile (*Crocodylus novaeguineae*).

At the most obvious level, there is a need to know all the plants and animals in a tribal territory, often encompassing many different environments. If I mention hunter-gatherers, I conjure up the image of a hunter chasing a crocodile, kangaroo, mammoth or buffalo, but the vast majority of the creatures with which indigenous people interact are fish, small reptiles and, critically, invertebrates; there are thousands of insects, spiders, scorpions, worms, crustaceans and other little creatures in every landscape. It is necessary to know which ones can be eaten, which can be used for other products and which must be avoided. Every environment houses animals that bite, sting or maul, and some are deadly.

As Indigenous Australian Eileen McDinny of the Yanyuwa people of the Gulf of Carpentaria in Australia's Northern Territory explained: 'Everything got a song, no matter how little, it's in the song—name of plant, birds, animal, country, people, everything got a song.'[2]

The North American Navajo, for example, named and classified over 700 species of insect for zoologists a few decades ago, recording names, sounds, behaviour and habitats in myths, songs and dry sand paintings.[3] Only one is eaten (the cicada) while some are bothersome (lice, gnats, mosquitoes, sheep ticks, flies). The vast majority of the 700 insects, the Navajo elders told the scientists, are classified because the Navajo love to categorise. And that study only included insects. All people, literate and non-literate, possess curiosity, intellect and a love of knowledge for knowledge's sake. But beyond simply identifying the species, a knowledge of animals and plants is often important because of what they indicate about seasonal cycles, and they often feature in stories that contain lessons about human ethics and behaviour.

Despite being active in natural history groups, I know no one today who could identify all the insects they may encounter even with a guide book, let alone all animal species. Yet, that is common practice among indigenous people.

In oral traditions, dance acts as a complementary memory cue to the sung narratives. Not only do the dances entertain but information can also be encoded in dance that defies clear expression in words. As a natural history writer, I doubt I could accurately describe details of the movement of a kangaroo—the flick of an ear, the subtle change in stance as it detects an approaching human—despite having observed them for most of my life. Australian Aboriginal dancers can represent this behaviour in a matter of moments.

Rituals performed before a hunt are often referred to as 'hunting magic', the word 'magic' implying that they are simply superstitious acts performed in the belief that they increase the fortune of the hunt through a call to supernatural beings. A little more invest-igation shows otherwise. Many of the songs reinforce details of animal behaviour, such as indicators that the animal may be aware of the hunters, or the way in which a mob of animals may disperse in fleeing. These rituals confirm planned hunting strategies and so, exactly as claimed, enhance the likely success of the hunt. When I discussed 'hunting magic' informally with Australian Aboriginals and Native Americans, they indicated that they were well aware of this rational link. The songs, for them, combine practical and magical aspects.

Anthropologist T.G.H. Strehlow recorded hunting songs from Central Australia which not only included detailed behaviour for each of the three species of macropods likely to be encountered, but replicated the sounds made by the animals in various phases of activity. They also included descriptions of foot and tail prints for tracking and nutritional information for butchering, in particular the location of fat deposits and how to ensure these were exploited to the full.

I have heard Australian Aboriginal songs about birds that capture their call exquisitely. I've heard skilled didgeridoo players mimic the sounds of animals with extraordinary accuracy. Singing the songs of bird calls accurately before heading out to sea can mean the difference between life and death. Fishers across a wide area of the northern hemisphere rely on the behaviour of a fairly insignificant-looking aquatic diving bird known as a loon or diver (genus *Gavia*) to reach land if they get into difficulties. Unlike pelagic birds, which spend most of their life out at sea, loons always return to land at night. They have a piercing call that can be heard from a distance. In the case of bad weather and loss of visibility, the fisher who can identify the loon call among all the others will be able to follow it back to land. The Tlingit are an indigenous culture of the Pacific Northwest Coast of North America. They have a totem pole known as the loon pole because the bird is so important in their oral tradition.

In the New Guinea Highlands, the 'spells' recited when planting taro include a range of knowledge about taro crop cultivation, but are often simply described as 'rituals'. Native American Pueblo 'magic' performed before raiding parties included the call and behaviour of a wading plover, the killdeer (*Charadrius vociferus*), which lets out a shrill cry when anyone approaches. By camping near killdeer, the warriors utilised the birds as sentinels to warn them of an approaching war party. The killdeer behaviour is encoded in the songs, dancing and mythology of the associated kachina, the mythological beings who perform much of the Pueblo oral tradition. The songs and dances tell the stories of mythological characters who act out the highly memorable narratives. Mythology is the perfect medium for storing critical knowledge because it makes the information so vivid and so memorable.

Does 'magic' work? Yes. Is the belief in it justified? Yes, empirical evidence has proven it so and there are rational reasons why this is the case. Rituals can be pragmatic and rational as well as spiritual. Trying to separate indigenous practical knowledge from mythology is a process doomed from the start. The two are intricately interwoven. Rituals in non-literate cultures need to be considered on their own terms without trying to find an equivalent in literate cultures. Such an equivalent does not exist.

It was a fortuitous day when I met the Aboriginal woman who taught me a great deal and became a dear friend. Nungarrayi, to use her Warlpiri title, described the catalogue of sounds which are encoded as far more extensive than just the calls of birds and other animals. For example, she described the way her people were able to identify trees and bushes and grasses by the sound in a breeze. I found this hard to believe, but was assured that if I gave it a try I would discover that it is possible. That afternoon I sat in the bush and listened. What I would have described as silence, on a day with very little wind, was anything but. I became aware of the bird sounds fairly quickly, but before long I became aware of the sounds of the plants. The eucalypt to my left, the acacias in front, and the grasses to the right all made distinctly different sounds. I could not accurately convey these sounds in writing. In subsequent sessions, I've been able to distinguish between different species of eucalypt, although my skills are too primitive to keep those differences in memory. The experience convinced me that the sound of plants, animals, moving water, rock types when struck and many other aspects of the environment can be taught through song in a way that is impossible in writing.

Nungarrayi constantly reminded me that 'the elders were pragmatic old buggers. We wouldn't have survived if they weren't.' It became my mantra.

Indigenous knowledge of plants

Plant species usually greatly outnumber the animals and are well known by indigenous cultures, partly because they are a critical source of food and materials for a wide range of applications. The African Dogon systematically classify about 300 vegetables. Again, however, researchers have shown that indigenous knowledge is far more extensive than just the plants they use. The Hanunóo in the Philippines, for example, named many more plants for the region than did Western science when botanists worked with them in the middle of the twentieth century. They classified 1625 plants into 890 categories of which over 500 species were edible and around 400 species were used purely for medicinal purposes.

The Matsés peoples of Brazil and Peru have recently documented their traditional medicine in a 500-page encyclopaedia to ensure the information is not lost. Before it was written down, their entire corpus of Amazonian plant knowledge was stored in memory. A great deal of traditional medicine is already part of conventional medicine, or has been discarded as ineffective compared with other treatments; but Western science is still learning from traditional knowledge.

Healers in traditional societies are powerful and highly respected individuals who specialise in knowing the details of useful plants. Their work may sound like superstition and spells, partly because of the way the information is memorised through mythology, as will be described in the following chapter. The use of plants may also seem to be more magical than practical. For example, various species in the Datura genus are used in spiritual and recreational activities because of their hallucinogenic properties. Search a little deeper and you will find that Pueblo Zuni doctors from New Mexico use Datura as an anaesthetic for operations and as a powdered antiseptic for wounds; again the methods for preparation and use are retained in myth.

It is not only essential to be able to identify the plants and animals that are used in some way, but also those that are not. The latter is the vast majority, but constantly testing all the available resources is a logistical impossibility. All plants and animals need to be named, known and recalled regularly.

Imagine the situation where the tribe finds itself in a severe drought. Many decades ago, their forebears had survived a similar drought. As the stories of the drought recorded, without water the plants in their territory would offer only minimal sustenance, not enough for survival. However, the bush with the red leaf tips was safe even though they would never normally eat it. They wouldn't like the taste, the stories warned, but if they boiled and dried it then it was palatable and would keep them alive. The bush with the orange leaf tips was deadly no matter how it was treated. No one had eaten either bush since that last drought when the tribe had survived near starvation through processing and eating the bush with the red leaf tips. What chance is there that natural memory would distinguish the red from the orange after such a long time in which the bush was of no interest? What chance is there that they could determine that fact by testing all the plants that were still alive through the drought? If that information, however, is stored in songs performed regularly at rituals that are restricted to the elders who ensure the songs are sung accurately, then the knowledge will endure. The tribes who respect these rituals and store the knowledge in restricted forms will survive. Those who don't will die out at the first severe stress on resources.

Restricting information is a trait found across all non-literate cultures and serves two fundamental purposes. Restricting knowledge affords power to those who have been taught and deemed competent by the elders who control that information. But there is another critical purpose. It is all to do with what is inappropriately referred to as 'the Chinese-whispers effect'. Lots of people repeating the information in an uncontrolled way will inevitably lead to corruption of the facts stored within the songs. Distortion cannot be tolerated in information such as the navigation to a waterhole on a long-distance route, identification of poisonous plants, timing to ensure optimal access to seasonal foods, genealogies, details of treaty agreements on resource rights and so many other parts of the information system. This knowledge is not varied. It is sacred. Consequently a large portion of songs, paintings and other aids to memory are restricted and repetition of them carefully monitored by elders.

People would only occasionally experience extreme resource stresses. The last severe drought, say, may be long before living memory. Elders store the knowledge needed to optimise the chance of surviving extreme drought, floods, failed crops or other disasters in the highest levels of restricted knowledge. For example, the Nunamiut and Tareumiut of Northwest Alaska depended on the availability of caribou and whale respectively, both animal populations being subject to unpredictable seasonal fluctuations. The survival of Nunamiut or Tareumiut, when they had insufficient animals for food, depended on the elaborate feasts that were held to secure inter-village relationships and formal agreements to support each other when resource crises occurred. The elders memorised the sacred knowledge through song-poetry that taught crucial survival strategies. These included complex relationships with critical trading partners, methods for long-term storage, pooling of labour, utilising kinship ties, setting community responsibilities, the use of secondary resources, inter-community marriages and feasts, exploring resource potential of other habitats or even moving there, trading with people in alternative habitats and learning to handle unfamiliar resources through social contact. Oral tradition about past hardships, seasonality, climatic change, famines, starvation and death were all recorded within the song-poetry as lessons for future events.

Whenever an attempt is made to convey indigenous knowledge in writing, a great deal of the original genre is lost. In documenting the songs containing extensive knowledge of over a hundred plants used by the Australian Yankunytjatjara people from the remote northwest of South Australia, the translator noted that 'in written form the stories lack the performance quality that was so much a part of the way they were told'.[4] Collecting the plant information required a team of seven Yankunytjatjara elders, a linguist and a botanist. It is not surprising that most ethnographic studies do not address scientific knowledge.

Performed and restricted knowledge

We outsiders are not initiated. We will not be taught the songs nor told the stories that encode the critical information. In books of indigenous stories written for outsiders, engaging characters enact childlike stories. The reason these stories appear simplistic is that they are usually the version told to children. As the children are initiated into higher and higher levels of the society, they are taught more details built on those first stories. The stories serve as a structure on which to base their future learning. Information that has to be maintained accurately is restricted so that it is only talked about in controlled situations. Secrecy is both a way of maintaining power and a method for ensuring the accuracy of practical knowledge. Taking the public indigenous stories as indicative of the depth of knowledge is equivalent to judging Western society solely by the texts found in the children's section of the bookshop.

We must also be wary of the mistake many early ethnographers made when describing ceremonies they witnessed as religious rituals. They saw only superstitious actions intended to appease gods. Imagine yourself at a regular community ceremony of a tribe that you have just 'discovered'. There are leaders in distinctive costumes, some with elaborate headdresses. There will be singing and chants, but you have no idea what the words mean, although you can recognise that some are repetitive. Unfamiliar items will be held and displayed. Statues and painted images are around (probably various gods), a woman with a baby (probably a fertility goddess), a man being tortured on a cross. Some kind of herb may be burnt in circular containers strung from a chain, producing an intoxicating aroma. Some of the people will leave their seats, move to the front of the performance space and kneel before the leader who will give them a small amount of a liquid known to have hallucinogenic effects, and a token amount of some kind of prepared food. People make monetary offerings, supposedly to their gods. The people in the costumes process down the aisle and out of the building. The community emerge and each perform a ritual where opposing hands are clasped and ritual words are exchanged. Afterwards food is served, probably of animals sacrificed for the ceremony. How would you interpret this service if you were not familiar with Western churches?

In order to share the knowledge, huge gatherings are usually a part of the annual cycle for traditional societies. These gatherings serve the need for trade and to find marriage partners, as well as being for pure pleasure. Gatherings are also the forums to teach and trade knowledge through ceremony. To attend ceremonies, native peoples the world over often travelled large distances with no charts and no roads. The Australian Aboriginal cultures, between them, could navigate the entire continent, teaching travellers passing through their territory the navigational routes even when those travellers didn't share their language. Without accurate knowledge of the location of waterholes, crossing Australia's parched inland would soon prove fatal. The Pacific navigators could cross thousands of kilometres of open ocean, not only visiting neighbouring islands but enabling them to reach remote places like Hawaii and Easter Island. The Inuit could navigate on moving ice with almost no landmarks, and get home safely again no matter how bad the weather. None of the navigators depended entirely on the stars or they would have been limited to travelling only on clear nights. They were all far more sophisticated than that.

The songs, poetry and rhythmic chants of oral cultures are not simply exotic rituals to be compared with hymn singing and religious rituals in literate cultures. Songs in traditional cultures are a matter of survival. An Aboriginal elder may know a thousand songs. Songs must encode every landscape feature and every resource, not just the plants and animals. Elders need to know where to find flint and obsidian, salt and ochre, while the ability to navigate across terrain with no roads, that often appears the same in all directions, is critical to collecting these resources and to trading them.

The landscape, and all within it, changes over the seasons. It would be impossible to survive a hunter-gatherer or farming lifestyle without maintaining a calendar. Mobile and settled peoples use the movements of sun and stars, the appearance of migratory birds, the flowering of plants, the behaviour of insects and a vast range of weather patterns as indicators of the availability of seasonal resources or the time to plant crops. All cultures maintain calendars, the timekeepers being highly respected and powerful members of the community. Those calendars serve both the subsistence and ceremonial cycles, the two being intricately interwoven.

Songlines

I first glimpsed the ideas that were to consolidate on Salisbury Plain a few months later when I listened to Indigenous Australians talking about songlines. By singing the landscape, they could navigate from one sacred location to the next, taking in waterholes, sheltering places and sources of food and materials. Passing through a neighbouring tribe's territory, they could be taught the next phase of their journey if they had not travelled that way before. As elders are usually able to speak the languages of those who live in adjoining territories, the knowledge can be conveyed.

Zoologist Sue Churchill described her extraordinary experience of navigation by songline in 1983, when searching for cave-dwelling ghost bats.

> We travelled, different old men from different communities, and ourselves in an old Landcruiser. There were no maps and most of the caves had not been visited for many years. One involved a 100-kilometre drive crosscountry through sand dunes to a cave that couldn't be seen if you stood more than 3 metres from its small vertical entrance. The old men who guided us were navigating by the shape of the sand dunes. They would stop every now and then and sing a long song to help them remember the landmarks of the journey. At each new locality the old men would try to tell us

(there were some serious language barriers) the Dreamtime story of the Ghost bat, or explain some of the standing stones that were in rings not far from the cave mouths, and sing the songs that they learned as young men.[5]

Songlines, or Dreaming Tracks, are pathways through the landscape connecting a large number of significant locations in a fixed order—rocky outcrops, springs, mountains, valleys, caves, waterholes. When performed, a songline is sung as a long sequence of short verses, which together form a sung chart of the ancestral being's creative journey or origin story. Some songlines crossed hundreds of kilometres and several tribal territories. The ritual cycle ensured that sites were visited regularly, the knowledge performed and associated sacred paintings retouched, a further aid to memory.

Sadly, there are few elders left now who can sing their clan's songlines, despite Australia having more than 300 distinct language groups before European arrival. In the past, the elders took children along the songlines to teach the stories, singing the songs of the sites and schooling them in a mental map of Country, as the term is used in Australian Indigenous contexts. With age and initiation, the content of the stories became more complex. Initiates were taken to sacred sites at night and chanted the relevant lines over and over until they were word perfect.

I found the concept of singing the road map, with paintings and sand drawings to help visualise it, mightily impressive, but I had yet to glimpse the power of the songlines. They were so much more than navigational tools. At each sacred place along the route, songs were sung and rituals performed. Rituals, by definition, are simply acts that are repeatedly performed. Those performances include the songs and dances that encode knowledge of a wide range of the practical subjects I was exploring, not just the navigational routes.

What intrigued me was the way the songlines acted as an organiser, a table of contents to so much of the knowledge.

Each location acted as a subheading for the knowledge encoded in the ritual performed at that location. Vivid stories at each of these sacred sites told of the mythological ancestors who created the landscape, the animals, plants and everything in Country. Everything was linked. Everything had a place and was named and known. The traditional Aboriginal landscape is a memory space on a grand scale.

Non-Indigenous observers have mentioned their surprise at the depth of the emotional response in a singer when chanting a set of placenames, a seemingly unemotional task. Within the singer's mind are all the associated stories. I have set up a series of 'songlines', a few kilometres of locations to which I have encoded information such as countries of the world, history and families of birds. When I list the locations, my head is full of all these associations, vivid images, funny stories and a precious store of knowledge. But even more than that, my songlines are now so familiar and so much a part of everyday life, I am extraordinarily fond of them. I have an emotional response as well as an intellectual one when I think of my songlines. I could not have understood this had I not done it myself. For elders with their entire culture tied to the knowledge embedded in the landscape, the effect must be extraordinarily intense.

An easily visualised mythological landscape is that which encircles the massive natural Central Australian monolith, Uluru (see Plate 1.1). The base of the massive rock is nearly nine kilometres in perimeter. The many crevices and indentations around the base are each linked with stories. Walking around the rock stimulates the stories to be recalled in sequence. The Anangu traditional owners describe Uluru as part of their knowledge system, *Tjukurpa*, which they explain has many deep, complex meanings, including the law for caring for each other and Country, the relationships between people, plants and animals, and the physical features of the land, the past, the present and the future. It is not necessary for the Anangu knowledge specialists to be walking the rock to recall the stories. The sequence of sites is so well known after years of learning that they can travel any part of the perimeter in their memories whenever they want.

Anthropologist John Bradley has mapped over 800 kilometres of songlines in a three-decade-long association with the Yanyuwa people of Carpentaria.[6] The songlines are referred to by the Yanyuwa as *kujika* and described by them as a 'Yanyuwa way of knowing' and the 'key to rich, complex and intricately related knowledge systems'. For one *kujika*, Bradley recorded over 230 verses, with knowledge stored in layer upon layer, the more complex knowledge gained with initiation into higher levels. He also described the way that discussions between elders complement the verses learnt and provide commentaries on the stories. When reading transcripts of indigenous songs and stories, there is often little to be gleaned from them as the commentaries are not there.

Bradley wrote about the experience of learning a Yanyuwa *kujika*.

> So much knowledge was being presented to me, at many levels and intricately interrelated. I was struggling to find words for much of the material as it was deeply encoded and dependent on other knowledge.
>
> There were many verses describing the myriad species—fish, sharks, birds and other animals and plants, whose names in Yanyuwa were so familiar to my informants that I had yet to identify in English . . .

I was amazed by the detail of this *kujika*, especially of the different species of sea turtles, their life cycle and habitats; it was a biology lesson in sung form.[7]

The following extract from the Rrumburriyi tiger shark *kujika* shows the way the songline acts as a set of subheadings telling the elders what songs to sing at each location.

We sing the spring waters there in the north and we come ashore at Yulbarra. We come ashore and we sing the people at Yulbarra. We sing the paperbarks swamp and then onwards and northwards we sing the messmate trees and then we climb up onto the stone-ridge country and we sing the cabbage palms, and then we come to that place called Rruwaliyarra and we are singing the blue-tongued lizards and then the spotted nightjar, the quoll and the death adder, and we sing that one remains alone—the rock wallaby—we are singing her, and then we sing the messmate trees.[8]

Bradley also described a singing track of Yanyuwa elders which led to a stone quarry.[9] The songs linked to the songline detailed specific stone tool technology along with names of the land, people, winds, seasonal events, objects, the correct way to hunt and forage, process food and make tools and various groups' rights to Country. At the stone quarry, elder Jerry Ngarn-awak-ajarra sung verses that told of the technology that matched the flakes scattered at the location, a technology that had not been used for a hundred years. It was over 50 years since Ngarn-awak-ajarra had last travelled there.

The use of landscape locations to form a memory space is far from uniquely Australian. Indigenous cultures all over the world have experienced their homelands this way. Anthropologist Keith

17

Basso described the way Native American trails served to link every event in the past to a specific location. The associated knowledge was performed and dramatised in ceremonies; the storytelling becoming a form of theatre. Basso described listening for over ten minutes to an Apache quietly reciting a list of placenames. One well-documented path is a pilgrimage trail covering hundreds of kilometres that connects one of the Pueblo language groups, the Zuni, with a location in the Bandelier National Monument in New Mexico. The names of the shrines along the trail are still recited in narratives restricted to the initiated, which describe the ancient migration routes.

Archaeologist Gertrude Bell described her experiences at the beginning of the twentieth century riding with Arab horsemen in the Middle East. Every feature was named, no matter how insignificant it seemed in what she described as an almost featureless landscape. The abundant Arab nomenclature and the ability for them to describe what had happened there in the past explains why the 'pre-Mohammadan poems are so full of names'.[10]

The songlines of Australian cultures, the Native American trails, the sung tracts of land all over the world act as an organising system for the songs, a set of subheadings to all the knowledge of the culture. Songs are located in the landscape and recalled when that landscape is walked in reality or in imagination. Indigenous elders sing their list of locations, visualising them in memory and recalling the information associated with each place.

Memory spaces and ancient Greeks

For most of human history there was no writing. There was no other way to record all that people knew than to memorise it. The memory method being invoked in the songlines is a complex version of the technique usually associated with the classical orators.

The ancient Greek and Roman cultures flourished from around 800 BCE, the time of Homer. Without books, the memories of the great orators served as the encyclopaedias for the entire population. Even as writing became more widespread, as orality gave way to literacy, the power of the orator continued. Cicero and Quintilian, around the time of Christ, and later Augustine of Hippo, were the pop stars of their time. Their lengthy speeches and dramatisations captivated audiences. All of them relied on formal memory training without which they simply couldn't have performed their incredible feats.

The ancient Greeks made a clear distinction between 'natural memory' and 'artificial memory', a differentiation that is fundamental to thinking about memory as presented in this book. Everyone remembers events of their life and interesting snippets of information fed to them in the daily round of chatter, observation and reading. That is your natural memory. That is not what this book is about.

Ancient Greek texts describe artificial memory training using the 'method of loci'. The method consisted of memorising a sequence of locations so you could move through them in your imagination with ease, just as indigenous cultures do with their landscape. The classical orators would create journeys through streetscapes or buildings. In medieval and Renaissance Europe, more and more elaborate buildings, churches and theatres were used, sometimes existing only in the imagination of the user. This is why these memory spaces, real and imagined, became known as memory palaces.

All modern memory champions use the same method, as no more effective method has been found. Eight times world memory champion, Dominic O'Brien, developed the same technique independently, claiming his powers of concentration were greatly enhanced, along with his memory. He called it 'the journey method', which is a lovely description of the way it feels as you walk through memory palaces in reality or simply in your imagination. Joshua Foer is a science journalist who investigated the world of modern memory champions by spending a year intensely training and then winning the 2006 United States Memory Championship. He set a new US record by memorising a shuffled deck of 52 cards in one minute and 40 seconds. To achieve this feat, Foer trained in his basement with earmuffs and goggles to reduce distraction. Foer talks about how much he enjoyed getting better and better at dreaming up bizarre, weird, raunchy, funny and violent images to store in his memory spaces.[11]

My training is not as intense. I could not deal with the pressure of competition or memorise at high speed. Joshua Foer trained by having fun in his silent basement. I went out and walked the dog. We were both dreaming up bizarre, weird, raunchy, funny and violent images to store in our memory spaces. I had read that hundreds, if not thousands, of locations were used by the memory champions and the Greco-Roman scholars. I thought that such claims were fanciful and grossly exaggerated but I now have thousands of locations in active use myself. I may use a different landscape, and my memory spaces serve a different purpose than those of the memory champions, the orators and the indigenous elders, but the methods I use are just the same. I integrate both the landscape and smaller portable spaces as indigenous cultures do. I refer to them collectively as memory spaces. In the following chapters, I shall explain exactly how my memory spaces work.

Foer and I dream up our own vivid characters to populate our memory palaces. For indigenous cultures the mythological narratives have been taught to them by previous generations, each generation adapting the stories, adding new information and letting things that are no longer relevant drop from their library. The stories, however, are ancient and sacred and may have been part of their culture for thousands of years. The basic structure survives because it is defined by the rivers and mountains, rocky outcrops and ravines as narrated in the origin stories. These describe the ancestral beings as they travelled the landscape creating every hill and valley, every cliff and beach, the animals and plants, the heavens and the weather. The ancestors created humans and defined the relations and rules by which those humans live.

The sequence does not need to be memorised; the landscape itself fixes the order and acts as a constant reminder of the action which took place there. At each waypoint songs are sung that are directly related to that sacred site. These songs often recall the stories of the ancestors, both forebears and mythological beings. People can remember stories of lively, dynamic, bizarre and often violent characters and encounters much more easily than they can remember lists of facts. Encoding practical information in vibrant stories is the ideal way to ensure the information is recalled. Indigenous people are perfectly able to extract the practical knowledge they need for any specific occasion from the mythology. The degree to which the stories are believed literally almost certainly differs with the stories, the context and the individual.

There is ample evidence that indigenous people distinguish imaginary folklore from reality within myths, even describing the way in which mythology may be generated. Hamilton A. Tyler described the performance of the Hilili-Eagle dance, introduced into Zuni from another Pueblo culture, Acoma-Laguna, around 1892. Various aspects of the dance had been added, so much so that a number of elements were slowly gathered to form a new ceremony. Significantly, he described the way mythology emerged almost immediately to account for parts of the new Zuni dance. Tyler concluded that myths can have secular origins but can acquire religious meaning when the dance becomes significant and is added to the ceremonial calendar. The ceremony was then restricted to the control of one of the societies, and required initiation to participate.[12]

Similarly, a historical affray between the Hopi, another of the Pueblo language groups, and the Navajo led to a division of land between them. Traced over the following 80 years, the narration of the events started to gain mythological characteristics. The event is now recalled as an important part of Hopi history and serves to record the location of the tribal border through oral tradition.[13]

Mythology certainly reflects spiritual beliefs, but what is pertinent to the story being told in this book is that it also encodes a vast store of practical information and rational knowledge of the world. Mythology, in this context, is an incredibly effective memory aid.

If the story carries knowledge about a particular plant, for example, then the plant will often be cast as an animated character. The plant-character will have human-style adventures and experiences, setbacks, difficulties and successes, acting as a metaphor for the events of a normal life. The character or personality of a medicinal plant, say, will be easily remembered while often telling a moral tale as well. If a plant is poisonous, then the story will involve its deathly quality. Realising that mythological stories are memory aids is not a revelation from Western researchers. Non-literate people are well aware of the role of story. Inuit elder Hubert Amkrualik explained:

> Stars were well known and they were named so that they could
> be easily identified whenever it was clear. They were used for
> directional purposes as well as to tell time ... stars could be

remembered by the legends associated with them. The people before us had no writing system so they had legends in order to remember.[14]

Traditional peoples would not have survived had they been, as so often portrayed, living in a fog of superstition and irrational thinking. Indigenous mythology is a complex concept that encompasses stories that are known to be fanciful, content that is known to be factual from everyday experience, and spiritual content that is firmly believed. All facets are interwoven through the vibrant stories to create a whole, which Western culture refers to as oral tradition.

Ceremonies serve a multiplicity of purposes

Indigenous ceremonies almost invariably served a multiplicity of purposes. At a single gathering, people would not only attend to spiritual practices but seek marital partners, resolve disputes, be entertained and trade material goods. Indigenous Australians put a great deal of effort into preparing for their gatherings, which would often involve a few hundred or even thousands of people. Critically, the transmission of practical knowledge occurred in the ceremonies.

Some 174 songs were analysed from the corroborees of the Dyirbal language group of northeast Queensland. A significant proportion dealt with hunting, fishing, or the behaviour of animals, or with natural phenomena such as the moon or king tides. A handful of the songs related to the behaviour of white people, four or five with an emotional message of happiness or grief, and about twenty related to religious topics, such as how to avoid a particular evil spirit.[15]

Australian Indigenous ceremonies often involved restricted performance sites for 'women's business' and a separate restricted location for 'men's business'. The bora ceremony involved the construction of circles and arrangements of stones for the large public gatherings and smaller areas for initiation into the restricted knowledge. It was through initiation rites that the restricted songs and dances were taught. Geometric designs were carved into trees at the bora grounds—circles, spirals, concentric lozenges and diamonds—with other objects, designs and sand drawings created to represent ancestral beings and their stories. The trees, objects and sand served to augment the landscape as memory spaces.

The Australian Yolngu of northeast Arnhem Land have collaborated with filmmakers since 1966 to enable documentation of one of their most important ceremonies, the Djungguwan. The Yolngu talk of the songs, dances, paintings and sacred objects as their clan's *mardayin*, which is translated by them as 'history law', 'sacred law', or simply 'law'. The performances and representations derive from the actions of the *wangarr*, the ancestral beings who created the land and the order of the world.[16]

One problem with trying to understand something as critical as the *wangarr* is that we have no equivalent in Western culture and no appropriate words to describe the concept. A viewer who watches the three long films, a number of short films and listens to the narrative about the Djungguwan learns that there is nothing in the *wangarr* that can be called a god. The mythological ancestors are not worshipped nor are they the objects of prayers. Their stories are told and through those stories cultural knowledge is imparted and cultural values sustained. It is simplest to accept the term and describe, granted in simplistic terms, that the *wangarr* are those who travelled through the land, creating the landscape, plants, animals and people. The *wangarr* gave the Yolngu languages, ceremonies, sacred designs and laws and, critically, the songs, dances and stories that encode all the knowledge and beliefs of the culture.

As is the case with Australian gatherings, Pueblo ceremonies serve a multiplicity of purposes, including redistributing food, trade, socialising, feasting and conveying practical knowledge. Pueblo ceremonies are also known for their bawdy and comic songs, often repeated from ceremonies at other villages for enjoyment and gossip. Some Pueblo enact their social commentary in the form of clown burlesque dances that mock Catholic rituals such as a mass, baptism or wedding, while also ridiculing government officials, missionaries, tourists and modern devices like the telephone. Performances also include grotesque and exaggerated caricatures of other tribes such as the Apache, Navajo, Mojave, Comanche and Sioux.

Native American Pueblo peoples are divided among a number of language groups living in New Mexico and Arizona. Of these, writings by and about Hopi, Zuni and Tewa speakers were paramount in my understanding of their rich culture. One of the major Pueblo writers, himself Tewa born and raised, Alfonso Ortiz wrote that burlesque and caricature serves to show what 'the pueblos find serious or absurd, baffling or wrong, fearful or comical about life and about other people'.[17] Pueblo ceremonies tend to be very elaborate, while ceremonies surrounding birth, puberty, marriage and death are fairly insignificant by comparison.[18]

When exploring archaeological sites built by small-scale non-literate cultures, as I shall be doing for most of this book, Ortiz's observations about the priorities within Pueblo ceremonies are worth noting. Like the Pueblo, many indigenous cultures do not make a fuss over burials. Others do. Many cultures include burial practices with other ceremonies. All grieve; they are human. Not all make a point of constructing cemeteries.

All cultures do, however, make a fuss about maintaining a calendar. In all non-literate cultures, timekeepers were revered members of the community, as they ran the ceremonial calendar and ensured that everyone had been notified of upcoming events. Similarly, if the tribe was to collect the eggs of emu or hunt migrating deer, they needed to know when to leave one resource to exploit another. An agricultural community would be even more dependent on advanced timing. If the seeds were not in the ground at the right time, then the harvest would be compromised, if it germinated at all.

Indigenous people who needed to travel for days or weeks to any gathering had to know when to leave in order to arrive on time. Each year, huge gatherings were organised in southeastern Australia when the protein-rich Bogong moths massed in vast numbers and so provided food for the gathering. Other ceremonies were timed for when a particular fish was flooding into the fish traps.

Knowledge was imparted at ceremonies, but not always for free. In our contemporary education system, knowledge is traded. Books are sold and teachers paid. The same is true in non-literate cultures. Songs, stories and entire ceremonies have been traded for material goods. One Australian Aboriginal ceremonial dance appeared on the Great Australian Bight only 25 years after it was first 'exchanged' in northwestern Queensland, over 1600 kilometres to the north. An entire ceremony has been traced from Alice Springs in Central Australia to Port Augusta over 1000 kilometres to the south. Women who had purchased the ceremony could give very detailed information about all the places named in the song series despite not having been there.

Songs aren't only performed in ceremonies. Archaeologist Peter R. Schmidt described the way sexually explicit rhythms and movements in the songs of the Haya, in northwestern Tanzania, served to dictate every phase of iron production, controlling the timing while indicating the actions to be taken at each stage. The trained iron workers sung the ritual chants in obscure language in order to mystify the process to such a degree that they maintained power and economic advantage through secrecy.

The West African Lo Dagaa myth, known as the Black Bagre, also acts as a memory aid to iron working along with brewing beer. Interwoven with the technical processes are stories about human behaviour, such as procreation and origin stories. The companion myth, the White Bagre, is essentially an outline, a schedule for each of the ceremonies. It also includes details of how the various staple crops in the area were first discovered and what natural events dictate the sequence of harvesting. Re-enactments are scheduled throughout the season, teaching how to harvest and prepare each crop. To learn the White and Black Bagre, neophytes were shut for hours in a long-room while the elders repeatedly recited the lengthy 'myth'.

I was able to find the same pattern in cultures all over the world. Many rituals among non-literate cultures were an essential repetition of critical knowledge at times when the knowledge was specifically required. Often these rituals had been perfected over hundreds, if not thousands of years. I have no doubt that the mechanisms described above, supplemented by those described in the next chapter, are robust enough to store information over millennia. I believe that it would be only certain genres of information that would survive reasonably intact. The landscape is the basic structuring system for many indigenous cultures, so it is to be expected that records of landscape features would be the most enduring of all traditional knowledge. Consequently, I am very comfortable accepting the long-term records quoted in the following pages that relate to changes in the landscape. Although the content of stories may vary, what will survive longest is the base structure, a description of Country.

Longevity of stories

Many researchers argue that oral tradition is not a reliable source for information on historical events. I have no reason to doubt their research. Historical events are less critical to survival than the practical knowledge of plants, animals, the environment and the laws and expectations which bind the community. The natural sciences cannot be so readily adapted. Reality acts as an audit on the knowledge stored. As with all cultures, literate and oral, history is adapted to the political will of the powerbrokers who tell the stories.

There are some cultures that recall hundreds of years of historical data. In many Pacific villages, hereditary lines of the chiefs were used as a basic organising structure for the knowledge system. Some Māori can recite an 800-year genealogy dating from when their ancestors first reached New Zealand. In Africa, the king lists for Rwanda were structured by their reign and the quality of their kingship, which in turn acted as a set of subheadings for the many different anecdotes associated with their reign. The Fang of Gabon and Cameroon were able to recite genealogies of up to 30 generations in depth, recalling associated events from centuries ago. However, it is the landscape that offers the best examples of robust, long-term oral tradition.

The Dyirbal language group has lived in northeast Queensland for at least 10,000 years. One myth describes a volcanic eruption and the consequent origin of the three volcanic crater lakes which were formed at least 10,000 years ago: Yidyam (Lake Eacham), Barany (Lake Barrine) and Ngimun (Lake Euramoo). It describes the very different terrain in that time. Only recently, scientists were surprised to discover that the rainforest in that area is only about 7600 years old. Another Dyirbal storyteller told of how in the past it was possible to walk across the islands, including Palm and Hinchinbrook islands. Geographers have since concluded that the sea level was low enough for this to be the case at the end of the last ice age.[19]

Similarly, the Boon Wurrung and Kurnai people from Victoria, Australia, gave evidence to a select committee of the Legislative Council in 1858 detailing the landforms in Port Phillip Bay, including the path of the Yarra River. These details have since been verified by scientific mapping of the bay floor. It is debated whether the bay was last dry at the end of the last ice age, about 10,000 years ago, or had possibly dried out again, about 1000 years ago. At the very least, the geographical knowledge has been passed down accurately within oral tradition for a thousand years.[20] Examples like these are being published regularly as geographers explore indigenous stories as scientific records.

Integrated knowledge systems

Many of the examples I have discussed in this chapter imply that a particular genre of information is known in isolation from the rest of the knowledge system. We store our books in neat categories: science on one side of the library, ethics on the other and mythology somewhere else. These silos of generic information are an artefact of literacy, where so much is written and research is so focused that much of the interconnectedness of the human experience is lost. The extraordinary depth within each genre has come at the cost of the integrated format of oral tradition.

A Dreaming story of an Australian Aboriginal culture, for example, may tell of the creation of the landscape, the natural history of an animal species and the expectations of the people who claim that animal as their totem, while entertaining and teaching moral codes. Interwoven themes are apparent in a great number of the stories I have read from indigenous cultures across the world. In reading traditional stories in fairly accurate translations, I became aware of my inability to understand the purpose of a great deal of what was being said. We all use metaphor. When I say that someone 'met their Waterloo', that expression has meaning for those with some knowledge of Western history. It is meaningless outside that community. Oral tradition had to record a great deal of information in memorised stories so, not surprisingly, it was encoded with many metaphors. A few words can convey an entire concept.

For the West African Kpelle, the mere mention of the tree pangolin, a scaly anteater, will conjure up in a Kpelle mind a person who wantonly reveals secrets. The tree pangolin is covered with tough scales except for its belly which is soft and white. When threatened, it rolls up in a ball to protect its vulnerable underside with the tough outer scales. One Kpelle folktale describes how the foolish tree pangolin reveals to a hungry leopard the secret of its soft belly. No longer daunted by the tough scales, the leopard proceeds to eat the tree pangolin by unrolling the animal ball. Powerful elders must not be tree pangolins. They must be able to keep secret any information that would aid their enemies. In stories about elders, for example, the tree pangolin folktale is not repeated. The animal is simply named and the implication is understood.

Until quite recently, very few anthropologists looked for science within oral tradition. Too often only the most simplistic level of a story's meaning is considered by non-indigenous writers. Almost everything I have read about the Ifá cult of the Yoruba of West Africa refers to their 'priests' performing divination and superstitious acts. A more considered study showed that the 'priests' or babaláwo memorised 260 sets of ordered verses of oral literature. Known as the Odù Corpus, the verses included acute observation of animal behaviour, plant properties (including a pharmacopoeia), navigational information about the rivers, historical records, election processes, and a body of law giving precedence and administration guidelines for almost every conceivable situation.[21]

Who were those who memorised all the knowledge? And what riches did all that work grant them? There is no sign of individual wealth in the cultures I have been talking about. In small-scale non-literate cultures such as the Australian Yolngu hunter-gatherers, the North American Pueblo agriculturalists and a wide range of other traditional societies around the world, people appeared to be absolutely equal because no one had more material goods than anyone else. There was no sign of a hierarchy that forced those lower in the structure to obey the elders. These cultures are usually referred to as 'egalitarian', but they were only egalitarian in terms of material possessions. There is no such thing as a truly egalitarian society when knowledge is added into the mix.

The evidence from indigenous peoples around the world is unequivocal: in small-scale oral cultures with no individually wealthy leaders, control of knowledge is the major source of power.

The traditional knowledge specialists are referred to by different names in each culture, such as the 'clever men' of Australian cultures. In Africa there are the *n/om k"ausi* of the !Kung San and the *!gi:ten* of the /Xam, the *Xhosa imbongi*, the *bulaam* of the Kuba, the Haya *embandwa*, the Yoruba *babaláwo* and the *griot* of West Africa. There are the *noajdde* of Scandinavia and the *towosi* of the Trobriand Islands. Similar roles exist in larger societies, but they don't necessarily hold absolute power and may control only part of the knowledge system, such as the *bangara* ('Big Man' and calendar-keeper) of the Solomon Islands, the Inca 'Rememberers', the Shoshonean 'talker', the Pueblo 'sun chief' or 'sun-watcher', the *Bumbudye* secret society of the African Luba with their 'men of memory'. Power and esoteric knowledge are closely tied to the North

American 'medicine societies' and the African 'secret societies'. The list goes on and on. In fact, it didn't take long in reading anthropological reports to identify knowledge keepers and recognise the power associated with their role. They are always elders within their communities, so that is the general term I choose to use.

The elders have always had to work at acquiring knowledge. They worked hard. Too often it is claimed that indigenous peoples just know their landscape or ocean through some kind of paranormal link to the earth which Westerners don't have, as is so popular with those who prefer a romanticised version of indigenous reality. The implication is that this knowledge is just handed on from father to son, mother to daughter, around the campfire or out on the daily gather and hunt, apparently with no need to actually work at learning. There is no society I could find that operated this way. In all cases, knowledge was formally taught over many years through the levels of initiation within the tribe.

In Australian Aboriginal cultures, it took on average 30 to 40 years for initiates to learn the full song cycles and dances, and to know all the sacred sites, objects and designs. Initiates were often removed from the community for an intensive period of instruction in the songs, mythology and dances that formed the integrated system of sacred, social, artistic and practical knowledge.

Māori in New Zealand attended traditional schools where they studied from dawn until midnight for five months of the year. The Baktaman of New Guinea were trained from childhood for over twenty years through seven degrees of initiation. The intense study regimes of the Poro of Sierra Leone and Liberia, the Yoruba diviners of southwestern Nigeria and the central African Luba have all been documented. Students of the Luba secret society, the *Bumbudye,* paid fees at each level of initiation and were formally examined before being initiated at that level.

The members of the Ojibwa Midewiwin, or Grand Medicine Society, of North America and Canada were thoroughly examined in the songs at the end of each of the levels of initiation. They were particularly thoroughly examined on the origin-migration songs, which were central to their oral tradition. Over one thousand songs were known to be used in the rituals, covering topics that included animal, plant and other natural history themes, medicine, history and cultural laws. Although there were public songs known to all the tribe, the *mide* training was sacred knowledge, strictly restricted to the initiated. Only those initiated knew how to read the abstract markings on the sacred birchbark scrolls used as memory aids. Should a *mide,* as the initiated society members were known, lack suitable initiated heirs when he died, then his scrolls and ritual paraphernalia would be burnt to ensure that they did not get into the hands of the uninitiated.

It was only as societies settled and population centres grew large that hierarchies became established, with those at the top becoming wealthy and their world protected using guards, soldiers and warriors. It is from this time that individual burials with grave goods appear in the archaeological record. The knowledge specialists became the servants of the chiefs. From then until today, the power of knowledge was subjugated by the power of wealth and violence.

CHAPTER 2

Memory spaces, large and small

||||||||||||||||||||||||||||||||||||||||||||||||

A fter a year of research, I had become wildly enthusiastic about the extraordinary ability of elders in oral cultures across the world to memorise vast amounts of information. They were using a range of memory aids, from the landscape and skyscape to totem poles and an array of handheld objects. Devices carved from wood or stone operated in a similar way to the landscape of memory locations, just on a smaller scale. I was finding memory spaces everywhere, in every culture. It seemed that these mnemonic technologies explained the purpose of many ancient monuments, from the way stone and timber circles were constructed to mysterious inscribed objects found associated with them.

I started to worry that I was deluding myself. I simply couldn't believe that these memory techniques were powerful enough to enable the elders to recall the equivalent of a swag of field guides, an atlas of road maps, entire law books and massively complicated family trees. I found it hard to believe that the landscape along with a few decorated objects would provide the robust memory technologies that my research implied and my theory demanded. I simply didn't believe my own conclusions.

The only solution was to experience the memory methods for myself. I started experimenting. I categorised all the methods I found from indigenous cultures, the subject of this chapter. As described in the next two chapters, I created songlines through my local landscape, stories in the skyscape, a totem pole and an array of handheld decorated objects. I experimented with them all. I am now totally and utterly convinced of the power of the memory spaces, both large and small. What astonishes me is that these memory skills were allowed to fade from the Western education system during the Renaissance and are today used only by a smattering of people keen to memorise the order of shuffled decks of cards for competitions.

Once I had been experimenting for a year or so, I found my mind started working in a totally unfamiliar way. I had become, almost without noticing, very strongly attached to the landscape around my home. My neighbourhood became alive with imagined characters and their stories. I can walk that landscape and engage with them or not, as my mood takes me. But they are always there, rooted in the memory locations or travelling with me. The songlines around my home enable me to imagine a walk through every space on earth, through every country and across every continent and ocean. I can walk through time, firstly through all of prehistory and then through history. Each time I walk one of the journeys I add a little more detail to the picture. Every event, every person, every country, town and lake, ocean and river, every book and war and glacier and human triumph has, theoretically, a place in my landscape. I just haven't put them all in yet and of course never can. Memory spaces are infinitely expandable.

Every one of the thousand or so locations has a story associated with it. Some remain skeletal. Others are being fleshed out each time I add more information. My stories have started to take on the structure of indigenous stories without me ever consciously intending this to be the case. Initially, I structured my stories with a beginning, middle and a conclusion. Gradually the stories seemed to form themselves, their narratives no longer dependent on a beginning nor needing an ending. Initially, my animals were animals and my people were people. Even characters I created as part animal, part human, retained that form throughout the story. Gradually, characters would take on different forms depending on the purpose of the story at any given moment. They were shape-shifting in a way I then recognised in the indigenous stories. If I was identifying the bird, the characters in the bird stories would be more feathered and flighty, yet if I was just enjoying the story and repeating the ritual, then the bird would be more human and the moral of the tale would take precedence.

It must be close to impossible for indigenous cultures to convey their knowledge to us literates because we ask for it in the way we would write it down, in neat linear sequences. That is not how they know their stories.

On that most memorable of days on Salisbury Plain, I realised that my ideas on non-literate knowledge systems may also apply in interpretation of sites such as Stonehenge. Archaeology works by interpreting the physical remains in a site. Songs, dances, stories told about mythological characters—none of these leave any imprint in the archaeological record. The people who walked the landscape in its natural state may well have recognised rocky outcrops, riverbeds and caves as sacred sites, but the archaeologists will only see natural features. But what happened when they started to spend more time in one location? What happened when they stopped moving around the landscape following resources over the annual cycle and started to farm? They couldn't afford to lose their memory aids—there was just too much essential information associated with them. I believe that is why they built monuments designed to replicate the landscape. They built them alongside the earliest settlements and so created memory spaces for the elders to continue their essential role.

In later chapters, I look at the stone circles of Neolithic Britain and the stone rows of Neolithic France, the great houses of the Ancestral Pueblo, the statues of Easter Island, mounds and pyramids the length of the Americas and lines inscribed by the Nasca in the deserts of Peru that I believe were all constructed primarily to serve the memory needs of the elders. They were memory spaces. Associated with these landscapes, archaeologists have found many mysterious objects marked with abstract or representational motifs which seemed to serve no practical purpose. They are usually labelled as ritual objects and left at that. Many of them are just like the memory devices used by non-literate cultures across the world.

It was only through experiencing a multitude of memory spaces that I came to know that the ancient sites were memory spaces and that the techniques the elders used to memorise their knowledge of their natural world, culture and beliefs were every bit as powerful as my theory required.

Skyscapes of memory

Both landscape and skyscape are used in a complex, interwoven oral tradition by indigenous cultures across the world. Unlike the landscape, the heavens move regularly over the day and over the annual cycle, so stories of the characters seen in the night sky often relate to the seasons and the passage of time.

The Australian Boorong people of southern Australia tell the story of the Spirit Being, Marpeankurrk, the personification of the most spectacular individual star in the winter sky, Alfa Bootis. The story tells where to find the pupae of the wood ant or termite, a staple item of diet, rich in protein. The position of the star is used to indicate the beginning and end of the pupae stage in the months of August and September. As winter is a time of limited food sources, the accuracy of this timing is critical. Harvest too early and the protein supply is reduced. Harvest too late and the pupae will have transformed into a nymph. The Yolngu in northern Australia used the appearance of Scorpius to indicate that their trading partners from Indonesia, the Macassans, would soon arrive. They were also well aware of the relationship between the phases of the moon and the tides, which were so much a part of their life on the sea border.

The heavens do far more than provide a reliable synchronisation device. Australian language groups name a huge number of stars, including many small and seemingly insignificant ones. By relating stories to the star patterns, a feedback loop is in effect. The stories aid memory of the sky patterns while the stars aid memory of the stories and their encoded content.

Like the mobile Australian cultures, the farming Pueblo societies are primarily concerned with time in terms of the annual subsistence and ceremonial cycles. The movements of the sun are mapped against named points on the horizon. One Pueblo Hopi ritual, for example, consists of a recitation of twenty verses naming the rising or setting points of the sun on the horizon and linking these to the timing of planting as well as the ceremonial cycle. Of course, such precious and valuable information is linked to power. Pueblo sun-watchers are extremely powerful members of their communities.

The impressive, almost uncanny, ability of most Inuit hunters to find their way accurately over vast areas of frozen, seemingly featureless, terrain in virtually any weather has long amazed and puzzled European visitors to the Arctic. Reliable 'wayfinding' was, and still is, an essential element of Inuit culture. Survival depended not only on locating and killing animals but also on returning safely home with the product of the hunt. Consequently, Inuit placed an exceptionally high value on the skills that enabled them to move efficiently around their territory.

Inuit used the stars as one of their navigation tools, making periodic adjustments for the star's apparent movement. Their calculations involved a thorough knowledge of star and constellation positions in relation to their seasonal and nocturnal cycles. However, depending entirely on observing the stars would be totally impractical as the stars were frequently obscured by cloud, fog or blowing snow. For almost five months a year, the stars could not be observed at all due to the extremely long days. Consequently, stellar observations were used as one aspect of the navigational methods along with wind direction, the set of snowdrifts, landmarks, sea currents and floating seaweed, cloud formations and movement, and atmospheric effects. While often travelling on moving sea ice, wayfinders modified their direction allowing for the movement of the ice and their own passage over it. The hunters also drew navigational insight from the behaviour of their sled dogs and other animals such as walruses and birds, including the loons described in the previous chapter.

In the New Guinea Highlands, the Kalam used the movement of the sunrise along a mountain range as their calendar. However, their solar calendar was then moderated by the behaviour of the bee-eater or rainbow bird (*Merops ornatus*) from Australia. Stories of the behaviour of the *byblaw*, as it is called by the Kalam, explained how to use the arrival of this migratory bird as an indicator of probable rainfall and when to harvest crops. The *byblaw* first appears in April, but flies very high, where it is heard but cannot be seen. Responding to environmental conditions three or four weeks later, the *byblaw* starts flying close to the ground. This was used as an indicator for the start of the dry season, a time of good hunting and plentiful harvest. The term 'spells' is often used when talking about the chants of the New Guinea Highlanders when starting various phases of their cultivation cycle for their staple food source, the taro. In fact, these spells encapsulated a range of knowledge about the cultivation of the crop at each stage, knowledge that was restricted to the elders through using archaic language for the chants.

A similar pattern can be found in the Trobriand Islands off the east coast of New Guinea. Garden 'magic' is the domain of the *towosi*, a very powerful elder within the community. Magic and practical work were inseparable in Trobriand Islander life, but never confused. The ritual sequence determined where the garden was to be made, who would cultivate each plot and when the work would commence. Each stage of practical work in the gardens was ushered in by the appropriate ceremony, such as a ritual for careful selection of the best tubers for propagation.

The *towosi* constantly studied the state of each garden and the weather, after which he made decisions on when to perform the rites that enabled the next stage of gardening to proceed. Yet the literature on the Trobriands uses the term 'magician' liberally, which to Western readers implies that his role was based on superstition, not studied understanding of the natural sciences. Timekeeping was a complex affair. Running parallel to the thirteen months based on moon cycles and five wind seasons was a naming system for Trobriand history. By naming every division of garden land, Trobriand Islanders were able to associate a past event with the name of the two or three fields that were put under cultivation in any given year.

Miniature memory spaces

Archaeologists are forever digging up small decorated objects for which they can see no practical purpose. Around the world, indigenous cultures have used similar objects covered with abstract motifs as memory aids. Again, my own experiments convinced me just how effective these simple devices can be. I found the same psychological processes were stimulated using these objects as when using my landscape and skyscape memory spaces. I concluded that these abstract decorated objects were simply memory spaces in miniature.

Almost every natural medium that can bear an image is used in some form by indigenous cultures as a memory space. By far the most familiar surfaces painted by ancient cultures are rocks and caves. We know that Indigenous Australians used rock art painted shelters and caves to represent their stories and songs, hence turning them into memory spaces.

This brings us to the problematic term 'art'. In the Western context, the primary measure of art is aesthetic. In non-literate contexts, the primary motivation is didactic. I am confident in making such a grand statement because indigenous people have told me that it is so. My Warlpiri colleague Nungarrayi explained that traditional Aboriginal art is always to help remember Country, the stories and the knowledge. Aboriginal people gain a great deal of pleasure out of the aesthetics of their art, she explained, but it is never the primary purpose. In traditional Australian societies, designs were owned. To reproduce them an individual had to be initiated into the knowledge represented. Many artworks depict the mythological beings and events that created the land, while also offering a map of the physical land forms and how to navigate through them. Aboriginal art acts as a miniature memory space, the locations represented encoded in song.

In describing Australian Yolngu art, anthropologist Howard Morphy[1] explained the way abstract designs were used to represent the animals and their tracks, nests, burrows and methods to exploit the resource, such as how to dig the nests of honey ants. Within a single artwork, each of the design elements may encode a multiplicity of meanings; a circle can represent a waterhole or a campsite, a mat or a campfire, eggs, holes left by maggots, nuts—it all depends on the storyteller, their gender, the level of initiation of those present and the context in which the story is being told.

Bark paintings constitute a major component of the array of art forms used to tell the traditional stories. The Yolngu live in Arnhem Land in country that embraces both fresh- and saltwater environs. They have written about their art to explain it to non-Indigenous readers.

> Together the bark paintings form a comprehensive map of the saltwater country ... whilst documenting Yolngu culture, knowledge systems, Indigenous rights, law, history, Indonesian contact, animals, fishing, oceanography and climate ...
>
> Aboriginal bark paintings are more than just ochres on bark: they represent a social history; an encyclopaedia of the environment; a place; a site; a season; a being; a song; a dance; a ritual; an ancestral story and a personal history.[2]

Along with bark paintings and rock art, Yolngu use the surfaces of digging sticks, breast girdles, canoes, paddles and sacred sticks as memory aids, which they cover with motifs to represent the ancestral events re-created in performance.

When reading books on ancient rock art, it is often the representational images that are emphasised because of their beauty, while the abstract motifs are merely mentioned in passing. It is highly likely that for those who created the work, those abstract symbols were as important, if not more so, than the representational ones. Research across a wide range of cultures indicated that the most restricted art is likely to include a high proportion of geometric designs, while the representative art is more likely to be accessible publicly. If you or I, or, more importantly, an uninitiated ethnographer asked about the meanings of the symbols known only to elders, we would simply not be told.

Knowledge of the artworks is often gender specific. Consequently, a male ethnographer would gain the impression that there was no 'women's business' because the male ethnographer would be told nothing of women's restricted information. As most early anthropological works were written by men, the women's role in intellectual affairs was not acknowledged.

Some inscribed objects are so restricted that it would be inappropriate to show a photograph of one in a book for the general public. For example, the highly restricted Australian tjuringa (also spelt churinga) is still used by a few language groups. Tjuringa are made of wood or stone. They tend to be flat, ranging in size from about twenty centimetres to ten times that length. The patterns incised on them are usually abstract, although some are clearly identifiable as animal tracks. These designs include circles, concentric circles, dots, grooves, double grooves, small arcs, U-shapes, zigzags, parallel lines and animal tracks of mammals, reptiles and birds. Elders would retrieve their tjuringa from hiding places at sacred sites, which were visited on journeys to ceremonial grounds. When used, the tjuringa was held by male elders sitting on the ground, touching the various design elements as they chanted the associated songs.

I saw a photograph of Aboriginal elders using a tjuringa taken by anthropologist Charles Mountford. It was inappropriately on display in a museum. The elders were sitting with the tjuringa in a very familiar pose. It was almost identical to a photograph of an African Luba *Bumbudye*, or 'man of memory', using a memory board, a lukasa (see Plates 2.1 and 2.2). Like the tjuringa, the lukasa is a memory space, a miniature landscape on which is encoded multiple layers of information.

The Luba Kingdom once flourished in what is now the Democratic Republic of the Congo in central Africa. The wooden memory board, the lukasa, is an extremely complex device, encrusted with beads and shells in what seems to be, at first glance, a random arrangement.

Lukasa measure 20 to 25 centimetres in length and about 13 centimetres in width, a perfect size to be hand held. The elite *Bumbudye* who used the lukasa were members of the powerful secret society, the Mbudye. The walls of the society building, the lukala, were covered with maps, the location of local chiefs and a pantheon of deceased rulers. All were located in landscape places and represented on genealogy staffs. Although not to scale, the maps showed territory over 300 kilometres away, including major lakes and rivers.

Like the abstract symbols of Australian Aboriginal art, the *Bumbudye* could read each bead or shell on the lukasa in multiple ways depending on the context. In this way, vast amounts of oral literature and other information was encoded onto the memory board. Touching the beads, each of which symbolised an episode of the story, the narrator recounted mythological stories. The major river, the Zaire (now the Congo River) was represented on one lukasa by a ridge in the wood, its reeds by green beads, its birds by white. A battle between a column of ants and termites was represented by two rows of tiny beads and used to discuss battle strategies. The 'men of memory' could recite the Luba Epic as well as genealogies and king lists; migration stories; royal political practices and etiquette; techniques for hunting, smelting, blacksmithing and other critical technologies; knowledge of the movement of the sun, moon and certain stars; cultural heroes and social protocols; behavioural expectations; deities and ancestral spirits—all encoded into performances linked to the lukasa. The *Bumbudye* were essentially the tribal encyclopaedia and were highly respected for their role.

The lukasa was not only a representation of the subheadings of knowledge, but also acted as an index to *Bumbudye* ceremonies and the complex set of initiations required to progress through the society. This initiation sequence was likened to a journey, walking through the maze of beads on the lukasa as you would walk through a landscape imbued with memory locations.

The lukasa, tjuringa or any other of the portable memory spaces could not be read like writing. The oral tradition itself is retained in the memory of the owner, the device being an aid to that memory. The knowledge encoded in the lukasa was slowly taught to initiates through numerous stage of initiation with payment of fees at every level. The *Bumbudye* were not only a cultural elite, but also an economic power base, paying substantial amounts to chiefs in exchange for privileges.

The patron animal of the *Bumbudye* was the tortoise. A design representing a stylised tortoiseshell is found on the reverse side of all nkasa (the plural of lukasa) as well as on royal canes. Surprisingly, each striated triangle or square acts as a mnemonic to an esoteric piece of information, despite its regular pattern making each triangle very similar to the next. The complex symbolism of the lukasa is linked to other Luba memory devices, such as stools, staffs and headbands, among many other forms.

Luba sculpture is highly valued in the Western art world for its elegance and exquisite execution. Many carvings feature naked women. Ethnographers who have worked closely with the Luba have written that: 'As is too often the case with other African art objects, Luba works have been labelled simplistically as "fertility figures" due to their nudity, or "ancestor figures" because of what is interpreted as ethereal spirituality, without an accurate sense of what they were intended to mean for the people who originally made, owned and used them.'[3] One iconic Luba figure is of a female holding her breasts. This has been readily identified as a fertility figure. The Luba explain that the figure is indicating that only a woman is strong enough to guard the profound secrets of royalty and it is on the breasts that sacred kingship depends. Similarly, in contemporary Pueblo tradition, a common figurine depicts a woman with many children. With no further explanation, it could also be identified as a fertility symbol. The figurine is the Storyteller, her presence emphasising the critical role story has in Pueblo life. Without the oral component, interpretation of indigenous 'art', historic or from the distant past, is speculative at best.

I found it difficult to believe the claims being made for the lukasa—that such a vast amount of information could be reliably encoded onto such a small memory space. As I will describe in more detail in the next chapter, one of my favourite objects is my own version of a lukasa. I took a piece of wood and attached beads and shells to it without paying any attention to the arrangement. It is very comfortable to hold in one hand. Once I started using it, I had no trouble finding structure in what appeared to be a random arrangement of beads, shells and wood grain. I found it remarkably easy to attach various levels of information to the ever more familiar spaces the beads and shells created.

I love holding it. As I recite the information I have encoded I naturally touch each part of the board, the feel of the shells, beads and their position on the wood aids to make each unique. This is reminiscent of the way elders using the lukasa or tjuringa are described, carefully touching the objects or designs as they chant. Over a few months, I became so familiar with the look and feel of each bead that I could trace the board in memory without having it with me. I sometimes drew it on paper, singing the songs I had attached to it as I went. I then threw away the drawing. It was the process that mattered, not the product. I gradually understood why so many indigenous 'art' works were simply erased or left to rot after ceremonies and rituals. They had already served their purpose by the very fact that they were made.

The Native American Ojibwa, also referred to as the Chippewa, create the most beautiful scrolls from lengths of bark from birch trees, a number of which I was able to study at the Peabody Museum of Archaeology and Ethnology at Harvard (see Figure 2.1). The oral specialists, the Midewiwin, inscribed the scrolls to help them chant the origin–migration songs that form the basis of their oral tradition. Each pictograph stood for a single song. The scrolls were designed as memory aids for performances. They not only signal

FIGURE 2.1 Ojibwa birchbark scroll, as drawn from one of the smaller scrolls at the Peabody Museum of Archaeology and Ethnology, Harvard. (LYNNE KELLY)

the content but also changes in rhythm, tempo and the divisions between song sequences. The performances were accompanied by drums and rattles. Along with the scrolls, the Ojibwa used other memory aids. Within their Medicine Lodges, for example, they enshrined carved trees and large sacred stones.

I was intrigued by the delicacy of an elaborately carved song board also at the Peabody Museum (see Figure 2.2). Native American Winnebago (now known as the Ho-Chunk) used wooden planks in the same way the Ojibwa used their scrolls. Initiated men, women and children in the Dance Society used the boards to recite the myths at ceremonies and sing the knowledge of their culture. The Evenki of Siberia used a notched stick to keep track of a series of around 700 songs performed at feasts. In so many cultures, decorated objects were used by elders to help recall hundreds of songs.

Some Native American cultures use belts made of coloured beads to record information and document treaties. These are known as wampum belts. The conventions of the designs within the beads were known to anyone who had been taught to read them, even if they spoke different languages. Some of the belts were quite simple in design, while those known as storytelling belts could be extremely ornate, incorporating thousands of beads over a few metres of length. Like all forms of knowledge, wampum belts were traded and highly valued.

FIGURE 2.2 This Native American Winnebago song board is nearly 50 centimetres long and was created some time before 1871. Drawn from a cast held at the Peabody Museum of Archaeology and Ethnology, Harvard. (LYNNE KELLY)

FIGURE 2.3   An Aboriginal message stick held at the Castlemaine Art Gallery and Historical Museum. (LYNNE KELLY)

Sometimes a decorated object was used to encode a small amount of information. If there is to be a gathering, large or small, how do participants know when to leave for the ceremonial grounds, a trip which may take days or even weeks? Like indigenous cultures across the world, Australian Aboriginals sent envoys with message sticks (see Figure 2.3) containing details of when and where the tribes were to meet and who was being invited. These message sticks were lengths of wood or bone, usually marked with abstract designs. The message was meaningless without the memory of the bearer who linked the various notches and marks on the stick to the message to be conveyed. The message stick also acted as an identifier to enable the carrier to pass across territory beyond that of his own clan.

Not all mnemonic etching and painting is placed on objects that are used solely for that purpose. Mobile cultures in particular need to limit the number of objects they carry, so it is not surprising that the surfaces of utilitarian objects are used for symbolic cues to information. I have been granted custodianship of a coolamon (see Plate 2.3) through Nungarrayi, my Warlpiri friend, who explained:

> The coolamon is from the Western Desert and it is unknown which Western Desert language/tribal group it came from. It is very old (over 100 years) and so its makers and traditional owners have long gone ... The coolamon is a child's coolamon and would have been used by a little girl to collect bush foods as she imitated her mother and female relatives. The symbols on the coolamon

are a 'message stick' and represent messages only known by those who carved them. As coolamons were carried from place to place, the symbols reminded people of meetings, places, stories, events and travels across the landscape's Dreaming tracks, in the footsteps of the ancestors and creation spirits. Such symbols also had levels of meaning according to who read them. Initiated women would know the deeper meanings. Coolamons were used by women as the gatherers and nurturers to carry food, water, small animals and lizards, honey ants, sugar bag (wild bush honey), medicine leaves and plants and even babies! The coolamons were extremely important possessions. They supported life and carried messages.

Although many indigenous cultures show little interest in accurate chronological history, some are very particular about recording their past. Native Americans create winter counts, which often take the form of small images recorded on buffalo skin. The keeper of the winter count adds an image of the most significant event of the previous year at the time of the first snowfall of the winter, the start of the new year. Other events, such as births, marriages and sociopolitical occurrences, are stored in stories linked to the event depicted on the hide or wood. I was stunned by the aesthetic beauty of Lone Dog's winter count on display at the National Museum of the American Indian in Washington DC. It was created by the Nakota, one of the Sioux language groups. The 1833 record, for example, shows the Leonid meteor shower, while 1840–41 depicts the Nakota making peace with the Cheyennes.

The winter count is named for the last keeper, in this case Lone Dog. These objects were so precious that a number of copies were maintained by the tribe. Another example of Lone Dog's winter count is held by the Museum of Native American History in Bentonville, Arkansas (see Plate 2.4).

I mimicked Lone Dog's winter count by depicting one symbol for each event since 1900 on a piece of leather. The symbols spiral outward. I have found it an extraordinarily easy memory device to use because I have drawn tiny symbols that are instantly memorable for me. Having explained the winter count to others, I find symbols that to me seem obvious are meaningless to them unless I disclose the event represented.

Strings: twisted, turned and knotted

A large number of cultures use string to aid memory. String games accompany stories, the actions ensuring the narrative unfolds in the correct order. Native peoples from Polynesia, New Zealand, North America, Africa, Asia and Inuit territories have all demonstrated the way they tell stories through complex and remarkably artistic manipulations of a simple piece of string.

Sometimes, the string is knotted and kept in a fixed format. By far the best-known knotted cord device is the khipu (also spelt quipu) used by Andean cultures to record information. The khipu specialist held a single main cord horizontally and let the attached cords hang vertically. Some khipu I have seen in museums had only a dozen or so cords, while others had hundreds.

Until recently, it was thought that the khipu was primarily a device for keeping financial records. Researchers now consider the khipu as a far more complicated device which was used as a memory aid for a wide variety of information, including narratives, laws, rituals and histories, along with demographic data, tributes and as a form of calendar. *Quipucamayos* were experts in creating and reading khipus, giving them a powerful role within Inca society. As a khipu was a memory device, not a written one, a *quipucamayo* was able to read his own khipu, but some of the information is thought to have been undecipherable to others unless they were specifically taught by him. Consequently, the information was restricted to the initiated few. In Chapter 11 I will explain why it was the khipu along with the set of locations along the landscape paths, the ceques, which gave the Inca the ability to create the most extensive non-literate culture in the Americas, if not the world.

It is unlikely that strings and cords would survive in the archaeological record, but it is highly likely they have been used throughout human prehistory.

Bundles of non-utilitarian objects

What are often found in archaeological contexts are bundles of objects. Superficial interpretations describe them as belonging to shamans and rituals, and ask no more of the objects. The knowledge specialists from a wide range of different cultures use bundles of objects, each of which acts as a memory aid to a particular song or group of songs. It is equivalent to a repertoire of music being carried for a performance. Members of the Blackfoot Confederacy of the Great Plains area, for example, use a bundle of objects to provide what is effectively a running sheet for the ceremony. Some Blackfoot ceremonial bundles contain over 160 items.

West African Mende healing specialists carry a bag of stones, each representing a particular illness, which are manipulated as the elder asks the patient questions to lead to the diagnosis and treatment. I have experimented with a medicine bag and add to it an object representing each disease as I learn about it, a stone for kidney stones, a tiny doll for issues of pregnancy and conception. I grouped the objects according to symptoms, which is enabling me to see links between different genres of illness. I have found it a highly effective method of remembering.

The bundles of objects are just like memory spaces if, and only if, the objects have a specific order associated with them. In some descriptions, it is implied there is a specified sequence either to dictate the ritual order of the songs or to eliminate diseases through a rational link to a list of symptoms. This method is extremely simple to implement.

I am struggling more to implement the sophisticated use of a bundle of objects as found in many West African divination systems. These bundles contain sets of identical objects, such as seeds or cowrie shells. Songs are sung depending on the outcome of tossing the objects and noting how many of each fall in a particular way. Seven cowrie shells face up, for example, invokes the recitation of different verses from those which result from eight shells landing face up. I have found it very difficult to rapidly recall the mythology I have constructed, which provides the sequence needed to recall the information associated with each outcome. My attempts at this method are based on the well-documented example of the Yoruba diviners. In the simplest version, the Yoruba diviner would toss a set of sixteen cowries onto a basketry tray. The number of shells facing mouth up were counted giving seventeen possible outcomes. Each outcome was associated with the mythological ancestor that fits into a hierarchy. The song-poetry associated with this system takes 305 pages to print and represented all the verses memorised by a single sixteen–cowrie diviner.[4]

A more complex Yoruba system, known as Ifá divination, is based on the oral specialist, the *babaláwo*, tossing sixteen palm nuts twice.[5] There are 240 different combinations possible with two tosses. Sixteen possible outcomes with only one toss are also included, giving 256 different possible readings. Each outcome is associated with stories, some of which are mythological and some of which are the narrative of real events. A *babaláwo* was recorded as being able to recite over 1200 verses at the most basic level. The corpus of verses encodes a body of knowledge, including, among other things, knowledge of animals, plants and a pharmacopoeia, how to protect against smallpox infection, navigation instructions, rules for trading, guidelines for the use of power and authority, cultural history, social and legal precedents, and methods for resolving disputes.

Among their many roles, the *babaláwo* were considered to be healers. Much of their knowledge is recognised as efficacious in Western medicine. Calcium was advised for bones, antimony for eye diseases, laudanum for sleep and for mental illnesses, *rinrin* was used as an anti-convulsive, *tètè*—a kind of spinach—was used for anaemia. Often patients were advised to get a great deal of sleep as part of the treatment. Sound dietary advice was given in verse. Prescribed diets for some diseases included banana, now known as an excellent source of potassium, while medically sound advice was given for dealing with issues of menstruation and childbirth. The *babaláwo* advised precautions against the spread of infection such as separating defecation pits for each member of the family of an infected person, covering waste and washing afterwards. Mental diseases were also discussed. For paying sitters, the *babaláwo* also divined the future, but there was a strong rational component in the advice given.

In a method remarkably similar to the use of divining cowries and palm nuts of the West African Yoruba, divining seeds are still used by the Highland Maya. The seeds are not tossed but arranged in various patterns. Some Highland Maya, unlike the Lowland Maya, still maintain their complex calendar in the ancient oral tradition. Barbara Tedlock was formally trained by contemporary Quiché-speaking people of Highland Guatemala and initiated in August of 1976. She described how all the information had to be memorised, none was written down.

Each prescribed arrangement of numerous seeds has a specific meaning. Tedlock wrote that during training 'the student observes, over and over again, the teacher's method of mixing, dividing, arranging, and counting the seeds . . . [The teacher] goes more slowly than he normally would, repeating himself over and over and setting aside divining seeds as mnemonic devices to help the student follow the complex summation'.[6]

Tedlock became a daykeeper, known in Quiché as *ajk'ij*, one of a large group of specialists who maintain a solar 365-day calendar which dictates civil activities. They also retain a 260-day sacred calendar. The two calendars combine to produce what is called the 'Calendar Round'. Tedlock described the increasingly complex recitations and range of memory devices used to retain the knowledge associated with the calendars. Stories included creation myths with reference to animals, plants and constellations along with history, religion and long genealogies.

Physical pathways in the landscape were also used as memory spaces. Tedlock described the Mayan pilgrimages to cairns, referred to as 'shrines', which are visited in an order according to the calendar. One pilgrimage took 40 days. At each shrine, the Quiché speakers would chant. Tedlock wrote that the shrines were described by one priest-shaman as 'like a book where everything—all births, marriages, deaths, successes, and failures—is written down'.[7] As there is no equivalent in Western cultures, there is no suitable word in English so the inappropriate term 'shrine' is applied.

The word 'divination' is used to describe the complex rituals associated with the Yoruba and Mayan systems. The term implies that the complex rituals are purely superstitious. Detailed studies, such as those described above, indicate that a vast store of practical information is encoded in the songs. The public version performed for the non-initiated within the culture or from outside, contains much which sounds superficially like fortune telling. This leads to a simplistic interpretation of the practices.

Representation of mythological ancestors

Modern memory champions populate their memory spaces with vivid characters to make the information more memorable. This is akin to the way mythological characters make oral tradition so much more memorable. Obviously, there is a much more complex and spiritual significance in indigenous cultures, but the way in which these characters serve to bring information to life is essentially the same.

Representations of mythological beings are commonplace in the art of traditional cultures and can be seen as another memory aid. Because of their supreme importance in oral tradition, mythological characters are represented in art on every possible medium and as figurines. Stories of the mythological beings encode a significant proportion of the formal knowledge system, while ceremonies act out their stories in performances organised according to the ceremonial calendar.

When discussing these dances with indigenous people both in Australia and in the United States, I was told the dancer becomes the mythological ancestor when they put on the mask and costume. The most common term I heard was that the dancers then tell the stories of the ancestors. This is often an origin story in which the ancestors create the plants and animals, the landscape and humans. In telling the story the details of the environment are revealed. Consequently, masks and costumes are an essential aid to the knowledge system and should be interpreted as such in the archaeological record.

I was intrigued and inspired by the Pueblo Indian cultures and their kachinas (also spelt katcina, katchina or katsina), many of which are still active today. These supernatural beings live on mountains, including the San Francisco Peaks in Arizona. The Pueblo tell stories about the 250 or so kachinas, each of which only appear at ceremonies at certain times of the year. In both public and restricted ceremonies, the various kachinas dance their stories which are told in song accompanied by drums and gourd rattles. Men dance both the male and female kachinas. They describe the experience as being taken over by the spirit of the kachina when they put on the mask and costume.

New kachinas are created while others gradually fade from the pantheon through lack of appearances. In this way the knowledge system adapts to new information. Occasionally, highly respected people who have died are represented by a new kachina.

Pueblo are initiated into various restricted societies, each taking responsibility for the knowledge and activities of some aspect of the culture. Kachinas are associated with each of these societies performing in restricted, often subterranean, ceremonial rooms known as kiva. The kachinas also perform in the plazas in public ceremonies, in groups of identical kachinas or in a mixture of kachinas wearing different masks and costumes. Clown kachinas amuse the audience during intervals of serious ceremonies, while other kachinas visit the village at night exacting punishments for misdemeanours, enforcing the legal system.

Kachinas are also represented by dolls, but these are not children's playthings (see Plate 2.5). They are figurines to aid children in learning the names of the kachinas and are used when they start to be educated in the knowledge system.

When in Albuquerque, I was shown a priest killer kachina doll who represents the beheading of a priest during the Pueblo Revolt of 1680, an uprising against the Catholic Church in an effort to retain the Pueblo traditional religion. Other kachinas are represented in rock art dating back thousands of years. One of these is the hunch-backed flute player, Kokopelli/Kokopele, a vibrant, active kachina associated with erotic and fertility themes. Kokopelli is described as entering the kiva with an erect penis (made of a gourd) in hand and lunging at the spectators, particularly the women, causing great hilarity. Kokopelli's performances were considered obscene by early European observers and his appearances were suppressed by the authorities.

Not all Pueblo dances are kachina dances or restricted. The buffalo dance, which I watched at the Indian Pueblo Cultural Center in Albuquerque, is a public dance often performed for non-Puebloan audiences.

As will be clear by now, ancestors may be actual forebears. More often they are mythological beings, be they human, animal, or some combination of the two. They may be fantastic creatures that bear no resemblance to anything known to roam the land.

I have yet to find an indigenous culture that did not wrap their knowledge in wondrous stories of ancestors of all sorts. It would be presumptuous of me to even attempt to experience the spiritual connection any of these peoples have to their ancestors. I dare say it varies as greatly as do the cultures themselves. But I felt certain that I could experience the impact a set of ancestral characters could have within a memory space. As I describe in the next chapter, I have created a set of ancestors from the history of my own culture and assigned them to decks of cards to give them a structure and order. Their stories enhance my life.

Pueblo corn stories: mythology and science

When I first read the Pueblo stories of the corn mothers and corn maidens, I saw no relationship between the mythology and the practicalities of ensuring a viable annual crop of the food on which the Pueblo are dependent. The corn kachinas, and the rituals they dictate, are essential for the survival of the Pueblo. It takes the rare combination of an indigenous expert and a skilled scientist working together to demonstrate how hugely differing ways of understanding can lead to the same outcome. It was only through reading the writings of Alfonso Ortiz, the Tewa-speaking Pueblo anthropologist, and Richard I. Ford, a Western ethnobotanist, together, as they both suggest you do, that I started to understand.[8]

Unlike our familiar yellow corn, Pueblo corn is grown a range of colours, each associated with one of the sacred directions: blue for north, yellow for west, red for south, white for east, black for the zenith, and all-coloured for the nadir. The corn mothers and maidens are named for the colours of the corn.

The Pueblo have two chiefs, each taking control for half the year. The agricultural cycle starts when the Summer Chief takes over from the Winter Chief. From a Pueblo perspective, each family in the village takes a basket of seed grain to the new chief to be blessed before planting. Through this ritual, the Summer Chief guides the selection of seed for each of the colours and provides rules for planting. The format of the ritual is encoded in the stories of the corn mothers and the corn maidens. From a scientific perspective, the Summer Chief, when blessing baskets of seed corn, rejects any cobs that do not conform to the optimum for each colour. When the corn is husked, sorted and stored, perfect ears are selected for ritual and for seed. Non-perfect ears are then used in daily life, different colours serving different purposes. This careful selection ensures the varieties remain as pure as possible.

Corn cross-pollinates very easily, so Pueblo farmers in each village are guided to plant each colour in a separate field, with fields scattered and bordered with other crops as a buffer. They also stagger the time of planting. Natural events will affect the yield of the various colours differently. There are many variables that impact on the corn yields, including weather, grasshoppers, birds, skunks, deer and diseases. Planting different coloured varieties reduces the risk of total loss that could occur with a monoculture. Such a loss would mean starvation for the entire village. By following their rituals religiously, the Pueblo farmers have managed the extraordinary feat of keeping all the varieties pure for hundreds of years, if not a very much longer time.

The outcome, whether viewed from a Pueblo perspective or scientifically, is exactly the same: the Pueblo can rely on their corn harvest in a harsh environment. They will survive.

It is not just their domestic products that are critical to the Pueblo way of life. The Pueblo retain a detailed understanding of numerous mammals, birds, reptiles, amphibians, fish, spiders and insects in mythology, which is relayed through ritual. The stories help elders recall accurately how to use migratory birds as calendrical indicators, the optimum timing of hunting and fishing expeditions, how to ensure that sufficient breeding stock of non-domesticated species are left in the wild, how snake venom is stored in the snake and the impact when it is injected into humans. One Tewa ethno-zoological study from the beginning of the twentieth century included details of molluscs and corals that were not found in Tewa territory. Seventeen long-extinct bird species were described while the insect list included many unknown to science at that time. Curiosity and the desire for knowledge for knowledge's sake is a human trait, not a Western one.

Genealogies and totems

There is one area of indigenous knowledge that I have failed miserably to replicate other than superficially. Genealogies are recognised as one of the most complicated data sets maintained in memory by oral cultures, recalled through song and a wide range of designs. Somehow, complex networks of relationships within tribes and between them are known. Every person belongs within the network and every kinship is understood. I have seen diagrams from studies done within Australian language groups where every member of the family is identified, from close relatives to those who are only distant kin. The lines crisscross the diagram, which the ethnographer described as a simplified schematic. I cannot imagine how memorising this tapestry is possible.

The research is indisputable—elders the world over do memorise intricate family ties. I know that part of the system involves objects decorated with patterns reflecting clan affiliations, such as the Australian Aboriginal weapons carved with geometric patterns that denote relationships and symbolise the ownership of specific tracts of land. Kinships serve to define land ownership, resource rights and, in some hierarchical societies, status. The genealogies also dictate who an individual may or may not marry, with most cultures banning close blood ties as marriage partners.

Simple lineages in hierarchical societies are often represented by notched sticks, where each notch or knob is touched as the generation is named. Genealogy staves are found right across Polynesia but also in totally unrelated cultures in Africa and the Americas. These I have been able to imitate and use as a very effective memory aid.

The Fang of Gabon and Cameroon memorise up to 30 generations. They then associate historical events with the appropriate generation, giving a chronological history. A 'learned man' of the Iatmul in the Sepik River area of New Guinea may remember between 10,000 and 20,000 multisyllabic names. In some African cultures, there are full-time oral poets who study for years to memorise genealogies. In West Africa, these specialists are known as *griot* (male) or *griotte* (female). Their role is to maintain the ruling hereditary line, sing praises, comment on social and political issues and chronicle the tribal history in sung narratives which take hours, if not days, to perform. They continue to hold elite positions in their villages today.

Genealogies, when memorised and not written, can be adapted to contemporary political needs; unwelcome ancestors forgotten, desirable ones emphasised. History is not only written by the victors—before writing, it was memorised by them.

Closely related to the association with a clan's ancestors is the difficult and highly varied concept of totems. The Australian Gunditjmara culture, for example, has two totemic moieties, the red-tailed black cockatoo and the sulphur-crested white cockatoo. Each family and individual belongs to either black or white cockatoo moiety. Within each moiety, a person also belongs to one of seven or eight other totems. There are also five different marriage totems. Associated with all totems are complex laws guiding marriage. Somehow, elders manage to navigate this web of relationships between every person they are likely to meet. And they do it entirely from memory.

Totem poles of the indigenous peoples of the Pacific Northwest Coast are best known for their role as mortuary poles that represent the genealogies of people and their totems. Mortuary poles are also well known in Australian Aboriginal cultures. Decorated posts and poles are a feature of indigenous performance spaces around the world and are used to store information well beyond genealogies. A carved pole is a dramatic and semipermanent way of representing oral tradition. Images are presented sequentially, up or down the pole, which allows the songs and stories to be performed in order. Totem poles act on human memory in exactly the same way as other forms of memory space.

Many of the American Indian and Canadian First Peoples use totem poles as a memory aid to knowledge such as the behaviour of terrestrial and marine animals, restrictions on rights to specific hunting grounds, resource rights, quarrels, murders, debts, events in the recent history of the tribe, how to construct a bow and arrow safely, and how to best hunt with it. The stories associated with totem poles are often restricted through ownership by a particular clan.

One of the most famous of the totem poles of the Tlingit, from the Pacific Northwest Coast of America and Canada, represents the story of Raven. With the frog as his guide, Raven visited the ocean and learnt about each of the marine animals and how to utilise the food provided by the sea. He then returned to teach the Tlingit all that he had learnt through story. At feasts, or *potlatches*, costumed Tlingit performers sing the histories and mythological events symbolised on a totem pole.

If timber posts have served the knowledge system so effectively across the indigenous world, is it not likely that the many post holes excavated by archaeologists around the world are the remnants of poles that served exactly the same purpose? Similarly, shouldn't objects with abstract designs also be found among the artefacts left by ancient cultures around the world, from the Neolithic Britons who built Stonehenge to the mound and pyramid builders of the Americas? If I could find these smaller objects in the reports of archaeologists, then I had more evidence that the monuments served as memory spaces. If not, then I had to question my theory. I could not have been more delighted when I first read about the Stonehenge chalk plaques and Scottish Neolithic carved stone balls. My search for portable memory devices in the archaeological reports of monumental sites had just begun.

Before we can explore the archaeological records for memory spaces, both large and small, it is worth understanding exactly how these memory technologies work. The most effective way is to experience them yourself, as I have done. It has been a revelation to learn to think differently. It has also been the most wonderful fun.

CHAPTER 3

Memory spaces in a modern world

||||||||||||||||||||||||||||||||||||||||||||||||

Just how much can a person remember? I now believe that an ordinary person with a normal, fallible memory will never reach the limit if they use the memory methods of the experts—the indigenous elders for whom memory was the only way they could retain all the information of their culture.

World memory champions memorise deck after deck of randomly shuffled cards, while others learn the digits of pi to thousands of decimal places. Memory books often teach how to memorise shopping lists, phone numbers and appointments. None I found gave me methods to memorise information which would enable me to grasp a much bigger picture of my world and therefore to be able to analyse and play with the information. I wanted to memorise knowledge in a way that would enhance my everyday life.

I have instigated over twenty experiments mimicking indigenous memory systems. The various techniques integrate, mish and mash together, and feed each other to create an unbelievably effective way of memorising almost anything. My thinking becomes more dependent on images and emotions and less on words. It is weird and wonderful and close to impossible to describe in writing. Of course, that won't stop me trying.

The indigenous peoples of this world walked their timelines, their stories of origin from the moment the first ancestors emerged from the earth or descended from the mountains. The stories of their origins bring to life the landscape and all that is within it. I wanted to do the same. Obviously, I cannot replicate a lifetime of immersion in a landscape filled with the stories known since childhood, constantly enhanced with learning, but I could certainly replicate the concept and see how it felt. I had no idea how precious my landscape journeys would become, how emotionally attached I would be to them, and how the effectiveness would work at a much more complex level than the simple recording of facts, which was my original intention.

In my imagination I can walk through every space on earth. In reality, I am walking my home, garden and neighbourhood. Into those spaces I have encoded every country and all of time. Each time I walk one of the songlines I add a little more detail.

The more I let my imagination go wild, the more fun and the more memorable the knowledge becomes. The methods described here can be adapted to almost any topic.

The landscape as a memory space

I believe the method of loci—creating songlines—is by far the most effective memorisation method ever devised and it has been used by all non-literate cultures for that reason. From indigenous songs of the landscape to the memory palaces of the classical Greek and Roman orators, and the mnemonic journeys of all modern world memory champions, the method is essentially the same. A sequence of physical locations is defined in space. Information is associated with each point on that journey. When walking that journey again, in reality or in your imagination, the information is recalled easily through the associations with that location.

Memory champions race around their palaces, embedding or withdrawing a card and running on to the next location. Indigenous people occasionally walk their sung trails during pilgrimages, but more often sing their songlines or simply withdraw knowledge as it is required. They discuss them at length, adding commentary to every sacred site. I stroll my memory journey, often with the dog, embedding new information and examining what is already there. I ponder connections and patterns I had never seen before and ramble around the journey again in my imagination.

The memory journey that is constantly in use, every time I watch the news or meet someone from another land, is my Countries Journey. I have associated every one of the 198 countries and 53 dependencies in the world to a location. The numbers vary with dynamic world politics, but the method is so flexible that any changes can be added in easily. I start in the studio where I write, wander around the garden and into the house. I have divided each room and every garden segment into ten locations as is suggested in the anonymous ancient Greek textbook on the topic, the *Rhetorica ad Herennium*, used in Greek and Roman schools and then rediscovered and revered in the Middle Ages and even into the Renaissance. Every fifth location is marked in some way, as was also the Greek advice. Within the house, it is a window. In the garden, something I can sit on. That ensures that nothing is missed as there must always be four locations between a marked spot.

The first 120 countries fit into the garden and house. The rest I have encoded to a house or shop, road or tree along the route I walk daily to the bakery. The countries are in population order, with China just behind the desk where I write, and the tiny Pitcairn Islands at the last house I pass with the aroma of the fresh bread demanding it be eaten. I add some mnemonic at every fifth location, giving me the approximate population so I can estimate the number of people in every country.

As I walk through the countries, the populations gradually reducing, questions arise. China, India, the United States, Indonesia, Brazil, Pakistan, Nigeria, Bangladesh . . . Bangladesh? Why, with its massive population, wasn't I coming across Bangladesh far more in the history of the world when Russia, with approximately the same population, was a constant player? Was it something to do with Bangladeshi history or geography, or was it to do with the bias in my education? I suddenly became very interested in Bangladesh.

My mind had deviated into questions about the past, and that is encoded in another songline, my Journey Through Time. It starts at 4600 million years ago. I then walk around the neighbourhood, in my mind walking through all of time until the present. This songline forms the basis of the next chapter, but what is of interest here is that questions about specific countries may relate to their geography or to their history. Information may be in either of the songlines. It doesn't matter. The links started happening from my first ventures into creating the songlines. The term I had used so often when talking about indigenous cultures was emerging. I was creating an 'integrated knowledge system'.

Most of the countries I couldn't place geographically so I started making up songs. First was Africa. I sang the countries in geographic order around the mainland and then back via the islands to the tune of 'Meet me in St Louis'. I have no idea why that melody seemed right at the time, but it did. I can't add more detail to a song once it is composed without ruining the rhythm of the song, so I add further information to the location in my home or garden, house or shop that represents that country.

In my head is a map of Africa, another of the Caribbean, then Asia and the Pacific and so on. Each has a song. The map helps me to remember the song. The song recalls the map. It is no longer clear which dominates; they work together. Australian Aboriginal paintings are so often of their landscape; the designs recall the songs while the songs recall the landscape and the designs that represent it.

So enthused was I about making up new songs that I neglected to repeat the old ones and they faded. I needed to ensure that I repeated the songs regularly; I copied the indigenous cultures. I started a ceremonial cycle. I sing my country songs in the shower, one or two a night. I sing the bird families encoded to my lukasa as I walk the dogs for the RSPCA once a week. As my singing is painful for others to hear, these times work well. Loud and clear, I sing my knowledge.

Throughout this whole process, my motivation to learn has soared. Any country mentioned on the news has a place, even the little dependencies I had never heard of before I started this process. I want to know more about the countries that are just names and spaces on the map. They are now familiar and have their own place in my personal scheme of things.

Using multiple memory spaces should lead to confusion. For example, should I put the famous australopithecine skeleton nicknamed Lucy in Ethiopia in the Countries Journey or meet with her in the Pliocene in my Journey Through Time? There aren't rules. I just seem to know where it will fit best and my brain makes the links between different songlines seamlessly. She is in the Pliocene. Ethiopia, a small garden near the studio, is above a stone wall, which reminds me of the country's critical role in paleo-anthropology. The Manchu Dynasty is over in the next block at 1644 and continuing into the garden to 1911. The two songlines overlap by this stage. Here in the corner of the studio where I write is China. My brain has no trouble extracting information from either songline and linking them, nor does the overlap confuse me. When I add new information, it just seems natural which location provides the right hook. The Manchu Dynasty is now referred to as the Qing Dynasty, so a link to that fact is added to the story over at 1644. The more I play with these memory spaces, the more the whole system becomes an integrated whole of many mnemonic parts.

The songlines discussed here and the range of portable devices I will describe all meld naturally into a system which is far more complex to describe than it is to use. I don't understand why I am never confused by drawing information from a whole range of memory spaces, but I am not. After a few years of adding data and commentary, stories and mythological characters, I cannot explain it to friends when they ask. It is too like hypertext and too little like the linear flow of a book. I can only explain small portions of it.

When I talked about my understanding of Australian Aboriginal memory methods to Daryl Pappin, a Mutthi Mutthi friend from northern Victoria, he said that what I was saying was all true, but that he had never thought about it that way. He just knew it. Then I tried to explain how the knowledge system works in my literate world. I couldn't. I've never thought about it. I just know it.

I walk through time when I walk the dog and through space when I do the shopping or sing in the shower. Each day, I choose to either recall what has already been encoded or add something new. There is no hurry. No additional time has to be allocated to the study; it just blends in naturally with my normal life. Like the oral cultures I write about, the mundane and the sacred are not separate domains. The pragmatic and the mythological, the utilitarian and the emotional, they all just meld into a complex whole. And I enjoy it thoroughly.

Skyscapes as a memory space

All cultures, whether they are oral or literate, see patterns among the stars, and all cultures create mythological characters from those patterns. Just as groups of stars have been given names familiar in our society—Orion, Aries, Scorpio and so on—indigenous cultures also name bright stars and planets, groups of stars and often the dark spaces between them. They note the patterns within the movement of the sun and the appearance of the moon. Astronomy is a critical science for all peoples. Western cultures store that information in books; indigenous cultures encode it in mythology.

Indigenous cultures use their skyscapes much as they do landscape memory spaces; the constellations are memory locations encoded in mythology. They use stories of characters moving across the space to represent the way this memory space moves while the landscape stays still. A moving memory space adds another dimension to mimicking indigenous methods. Obviously I can use the skyscape as a calendar, but I wanted to try something with narrative. I am using the constellations to encode the story of physics—the history and, through that, the science itself.

My physicists follow each other through time and across the sky. To add in more physicists and their discoveries, I incorporate the nearby stars and spaces. I taught physics for many years, but by adding historical context I am populating my physics more than I have ever done before. I am using a chronological structure rather than separating the sub-disciplines: mechanics from light and electricity from gravity. In doing so, I am seeing the subject very differently from teaching the regular curriculum. I am not sure it is a better way to know physics than the more traditional way it is taught and applied as technology, but it is revealing. My physicists no longer calmly make their discoveries as I create the vivid stories so critical to the memory arts. Newton's apple has never smashed so vividly nor Nikola Tesla's fight with Thomas Edison been quite so violent before. Physics has really come to life in my imagination. Not surprisingly, I have found that the heavenly bodies combine superbly to form a memory space.

The landscapes and skyscape just get richer and richer as more knowledge is encoded into them. They form structures that will last a lifetime of learning.

Decks of cards as memory spaces

Contemporary memory champions memorise the order of random shuffled decks of cards by giving each card a character. They then create a narrative linking these characters in the order of the shuffled deck. I have no desire to memorise the order of a shuffled deck of cards. I realised that this method in some ways mimics the mythological characters of indigenous cultures. Often these are represented by figurines or in art on a wide range of media. A pantheon of characters is used in these wildly differing scenarios to aid memory. I have been fascinated by the kachina of the Pueblo cultures and even started collecting kachina made by contemporary artists. I decided that I would like my own pantheon of ancestors who have influenced my contemporary life but that a portable media would best suit my needs.

I chose two different decks of cards to represent my ancestors, one normal deck and one tarot deck giving me 130 cards to represent 130 ancestors. I chose significant people from history and listed them in chronological order. I assigned each to a card in order. I start with Homer and go to Oliver Cromwell on the standard card deck and then from Blaise Pascal to Linus Torvalds, the creator of Linux, by the end of my tarot deck.

I memorised the character-cards through stories linking the character to the card value. As I strolled my Journey Through Time with the dog, my ancestors attached themselves to objects at the right time in history. The cards and the Journey Through Time put them in order. Sometimes it was the walk that gave me the order, sometimes the cards told me who to look for next as we ambled around the block. The two systems meshed.

The walk doesn't suit adding too many details to the plethora of people and events that are ever increasingly filling its space. I see links to the cards. The jack of spades holds a staff, reminding me of Cicero and his oratory. The horizontal line on the seven of hearts is, in my imagination, now that little curly sign called a tilde. Combined with the heart, I know this card as Tilda the Honey. I doubt Attila the Hun would be impressed.

As each card gained a character, I started adding more and more details about each historical person to the stories. Birthplaces and family members, achievements and struggles, colleagues and contributions all entered the stories, sometimes in a fantastical, exaggerated narrative and sometimes reflecting reality. The ancestor's deeds and doings just became part of the vivid story of the card. For months, I carried my cards with me in a pouch, pondering over one or two each day when I was out walking or waiting in a queue. Slowly, each story grew as I became hugely motivated to find out more about those who were little more than names. Some of my ancestors are now the protagonists of long vivid narratives and some are still mere hints of the stories they will become. It all takes time.

So many indigenous devices are used to memorise multiple levels of information in widely varying genres. To see if this was possible in my system I decided to encode my medieval tarot deck with another genre of information entirely. I need to be able to recall the details of archaeological sites all over the world when talking about this book, many of which I have not written about here. Given my very poor natural memory, I would never have attempted this before. I would have carried reams of notes with me everywhere I went. Instead I now use the tarot deck to represent 78 key archaeological sites around the world. I use the different suits and the arcana for regions, and then order the sites chronologically within the geographic areas. It works a treat. As I chat to people, I am seeing cards that feed me information as if I had a screen which called up the image I need at the mere thought of the site.

I expected to be confused with the ancestors and the unrelated archaeological sites on the same cards. At first I tried to separate them. Then I gave up. My ancestors wanted to be involved with archaeology. The four of swords has the image of a man on an island. That man is Sigmund Freud. The card also refers to the Cave of Lascaux where, in my imagination, Freud is psychoanalysing the Stone Age artists from their glorious paintings. The story I have created is highly memorable and, for me, very funny. I never confuse the Lascaux images with those from Altamira, say, as only the Lascaux cave art has Sigmund Freud as my guide.

Miniature memory spaces

But it isn't only large spaces, the sky and landscape, and representations of ancestors that are used by non-literate cultures to act as memory aids. The portable memory devices described in the previous chapter work as miniature memory spaces. My brain deals with my contemporary versions of them in a very similar way to the landscapes and skyscape, except that I can also use touch. The way each bead or incision or knotted cord feels adds to the other sensations which make the attached stories memorable.

I am using a range of carved wooden objects to explore the reason memory boards are used so widely in non-literate cultures. I am not pretentious enough to suggest that I have managed the depth and spiritual associations which pervade their ancient crafts but I am experiencing the extraordinary effectiveness of these devices and the way my mind works very differently when using them than when learning from written notes. I am convinced that the combination of methods of learning would be invaluable in contemporary education.

My favourite is a memory board in the style of the Luba lukasa: a piece of wood fifteen centimetres long, covered in beads and shells (see Plate 3.1). I use my lukasa to act as a field guide to the birds of my state, Victoria. I was initially daunted by the task of memorising 408 birds in 82 families, their classification, identification, distribution and other features. Slowly, the apparently random beads gained an order and structure in my imagination. I don't need my lukasa physically with me anymore, I know it so well.

I found memorising the 82 scientific names for the families very difficult. I started using puns as some non-literate cultures do. The sandpiper family, for example, is Scolopacidae. Sandpipers? Sounds like a band for a beach party, which became the theme for the story. Scolopacidae? Sounds like S-go-low-pass-idae. I imagined entering the party by dancing under a horizontal limbo pole. If you can't go low enough, you can't pass. For large families, such as the sandpiper family, I added little landscape journeys. Mixing memory technologies just seemed the natural thing to do.

The stories I created often had some kind of moral lesson for humans, although that was not my deliberate intention. I found that the characters in the stories, despite having bird names, were very human and quite un-avian until I was familiar with the bird in the wild. The characters started to morph into part bird, part human as is so often the case in indigenous characters. The marsh sandpiper is distinguished by distinctly long legs, so Marsha became a beautiful leggy girl. When I am at the beach, I know to look for the very long legged wader to help identify the species. The stories became more complex as I added more and more detail of identification, habitat and behaviour.

One little member of the sandpiper family is the sanderling. This tiny bird feeds at the water's edge, running in and out with the wave fronts collecting insects in the wet sand. One day, at the point in the landscape journey that is allocated to the sanderling, I danced up and down imitating, in my imagination at least, the movements of the bird. The dance of the sanderlings made the behaviour more memorable and I rarely pass that point without a little jiggle.

I found myself loving saying the Latin family names once I knew them. Dromaiidae, Anatidae, Megapodiidae, Phasianidae, Podicipedidae—I started to sing my lukasa. The bird calls entered some of the songs. My songs are not tuneful as much as rhythmic, but the barely musical phrases now feel like music to me. As I sing each family name, I can see the birds in the family. I don't need to enunciate them. They are not words but characters, active images which invoke emotional responses.

I tried sketching the lukasa without it present. As I did so, I was seeing the birds and the stories. I added little squiggles to my sketch, wing shapes and beaks, features that I now imagine on the lukasa. I soon understood why indigenous people will make sand paintings or draw in the earth, arrange leaves or paint on bark only to throw their creation away. The process is powerful and rewarding, intellectually and emotionally, and really enhances memorability of the knowledge.

I started playing with the stories just for the pleasure of engaging with the characters and no longer just for memorisation. The Pacific gull and the kelp gull are very alike. Both large gulls, the distinguishing feature in the field is the bit of red on the end of their beaks. The kelp gull has red on the underside of the tip, while the Pacific gull has it on the 'nose' as well. My gull story tells of the Pacific gull, said with the slur as if I am drunk. His excessive drinking is why he has a red nose. The kelp gull is a health fiend. The two brothers (my subtext for members of the same genus) vigorously debate their contrasting lifestyles. It amuses me to imagine conversations. In my imagination, they are men. On the beach, they are birds. I never mix up the two species.

It surprised me how naturally the different memory methods all worked together to create ever more effective recall of my field guide for the birds. My lukasa, the landscape spaces for the larger families, songs, stories and movement all intermeshed into an extremely effective whole, which greatly exceeded the sum of the parts. My stories became ever more mythological with time but the information I need in the field is always readily available. I like to meditate on a story when I am gardening or going to sleep. Sometimes they will permeate my dreams. This happened naturally. I did not plan it. My stories naturally became reminiscent of so many of the indigenous stories I had read.

A myriad memory spaces

I have carved one piece of wood to replicate genealogy staves like the rākau whakapapa of the New Zealand Māori. The critical role of genealogies in structuring knowledge systems in Pacific cultures will be explored in Chapter 12 because that understanding underpins the reason for erecting the famous statues of Easter Island. I have chosen to memorise the European royal families and Chinese dynasties to explore different genealogical structures.

One of my small, incised memory boards is designed to encode the native plants in the Victorian bush and is based in size and incisions on what I have read of Australian tjuringa. I have incised a small wooden board with decorations deliberately designed to represent the ever-growing corpus of songs and help me ensure that I repeat them regularly. It is loosely based on the Native American Winnebago song board of the previous chapter.

I am encoding a history of the world's art to knots, colours, twists, plaits and cords on my version of the Inca khipu described in the previous chapter. I am astounded by how easily I can adapt the design to suit the information I want to encode. I am not surprised that this device was so instrumental in the success of the Inca.

I use an inscribed leather scroll, based on the Native American winter counts. This reinforces the Journey Through Time, giving me every year since 1900. Many cultures, including the Inuit and Pacific Islanders, use string games to tell stories. I am using my loop of string to tell Aesop's fables. Posts and poles, carved and painted, are used across the world, so I have used the shaped post on the verandah outside my studio to encode the 139 species of Victorian mammals, in taxonomic order with identification and behaviour, and all those pesky scientific names. I am encoding the pantheon of Greek and Roman gods to six wooden blocks carved as hearts, each with a distinctive grain. These mimic the way I imagine the Poverty Point culture used the clay balls I will talk about in Chapter 11. I imitate the sixteen-cowrie 'divining' method of the African Yoruba described in the previous chapter to encode the plants in my garden—decorative, edible and weeds. The first toss will give me one of the sixteen plant groups while the second enables each of these to be matched with sixteen attributes, including the history of the species, planting time, flowering/harvesting time, propagation, cultivation needs, pests, diseases and all the varieties.

All these experiments convince me that these memory devices are incredibly effective. In all cases, information is attached to specific locations within the memory space. The knowledge is encoded in vivid stories, which are secured to that location using imaginative links.

My most meaningful experiment is creating a songline as close as I can to my understanding of Australian Aboriginal singing tracks. I am using a walking track in the bush near my home. I have named many locations along the track. I find that by singing the names I have given these 'sacred places' I can imagine every step of the walk in a way I would never have thought possible. I am gaining an intimate knowledge of the bush to a depth that has never happened in the years I have walked this park before. I am incorporating songs and stories from some of the memory devices described above, especially birds, mammals and plants, and anchoring each song in a particular place on my songline. I am using the seasonal flowering of the plants, arrival of migratory birds and as many other features as I can to create a calendar linked entirely to terrestrial events, as many mobile cultures do.

The more I used my smorgasbord of memory spaces, the more relaxed I became about creating songs, stories and dances. My knowledge system has become an integrated aggregation of information from which I have no trouble selecting what I need whenever I need it. It has now become so complicated and so interwoven that I am unable to explain what is going on in my mind. It is such a vivid, lively and reliable way of knowing, so different from anything I have used before. I understand why it is almost impossible for indigenous cultures to explain their

PLATE 1.1 Uluru, in Central Australia, from the air. Every notch and crevice around the perimeter of the rock is used as a location by Indigenous Australians to memorise information. (IAN ROWLAND)

PLATE 2.1 A Mbudye 'man of memory' points to features of a lukasa memory board as he narrates Luba histories or other stories. (MARY NOOTER ROBERTS)

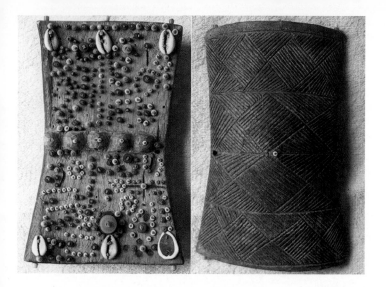

PLATE 2.2 A lukasa created by the Luba people, Zaire, now the Democratic Republic of the Congo. The memory boards were used by the secretive *Bumbudye* society until well into the twentieth century. (THOMAS Q. REEFE)

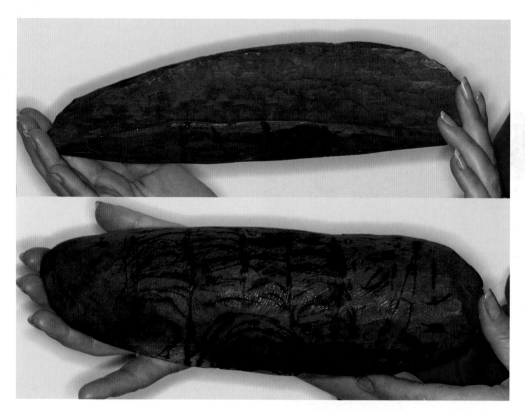

PLATE 2.3 An Australian Aboriginal coolamon. The underside has abstract carvings used as a memory aid. (DAMIAN KELLY)

PLATE 2.4 Lone Dog's winter count records 70 years of memorable events for the Nakota Sioux. (MUSEUM OF NATIVE AMERICAN HISTORY, BENTONVILLE, ARKANSAS)

PLATE 2.5 Kachina dolls as displayed at the Peabody Museum of Archaeology and Ethnography. *Left:* Saliko mana (Salako Maiden, Hopi) stands at over 50 cm. *Right:* Kwewu (Wolf, Hopi) is just over 20 cm tall. (LYNNE KELLY)

PLATE 3.1 The author's memory board in the style of the Luba lukasa, made from wood, beads and shells. (LYNNE KELLY)

PLATE 5.1 An artist's depiction of the Whitehawk Neolithic Causewayed Enclosure, Brighton. (IAN DENNIS, CARDIFF UNIVERSITY, WALES)

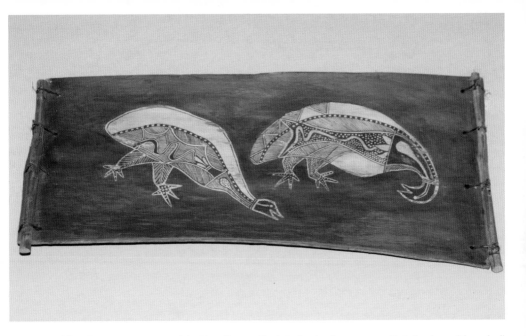

PLATE 4.1 *The Doves*, an artwork in the Oenpelli style by Indigenous artist Andrew Munakali (1940–1988). This artwork is representative of the longest continual art tradition in the world. Aboriginal art serves as a memory aid to the knowledge system. (DAMIAN KELLY)

PLATE 5.2 The stone circle at Boscawen-Un in Cornwall. (DAMIAN KELLY)

PLATE 5.3 Stonehenge. One of the smaller bluestones can be seen in the centre. In the foreground are the remains of the ditch. (DAMIAN KELLY)

PLATE 5.4 Carved chalk plaques from near Stonehenge. (COURTESY OF SALISBURY MUSEUM)

PLATE 5.5 A Grooved Ware pot from Durrington Walls, reconstructed by Dr Rosamund Cleal at the Alexander Keiller Museum, Avebury. (DAMIAN KELLY)

PLATE 6.1 The arrangement of timber posts at Stanton Drew in Somerset was revealed by English Heritage's 1997 magnetometer survey. (REPRODUCED FROM *STANDING WITH STONES* BY RUPERT SOSKIN, THAMES & HUDSON LTD, LONDON, 2009)

PLATE 6.2 The West Kennet Long Barrow. *Left:* The forecourt facade. *Right:* The passage. (DAMIAN KELLY)

PLATE 6.3 *Left:* Part of the circle and ditch at Avebury. (DAMIAN KELLY)
Right: An artist's impression of the Avebury ditch as it may have looked in the Neolithic. (PETER ROBERTS, WWW.AVEBURY-WEB.CO.UK)

PLATE 6.4 Silbury Hill today; the truck and car give an idea of the size of this Neolithic construction. (DAMIAN KELLY)

knowledge systems, which are based on hundreds, if not thousands, of years of experience.

Had I not actually tried these memory methods, I doubt I ever could have understood. I can only hope that some of my readers will do exactly the same.

CHAPTER 4

A journey through time

▌▌▌▌▌▌▌▌▌▌▌▌▌▌▌▌▌▌▌▌▌▌▌▌▌▌▌▌▌▌▌▌▌▌▌▌

I can journey through time. Through all of prehistory and all of history. My little dog and I leave home through the front gate as the very first life is appearing on earth. We walk about a kilometre past numerous memory locations to finish back home in the present.

The critical part of establishing memory journeys is to get the structure in place first. You can use a suburban block, a bush track or any landscape that you can walk in a reliable order. My Journey Through Time starts from home and wanders around a few blocks of houses in my country town. The first stage was to establish the dates for each section of the journey. After much experimenting, I found the need to rush time until the first hominids arrived, and allocate more distance when there is more detail to record, especially once modern humans have appeared.

I don't have to remember the chronological order of the world's history, the landscape does that for me. I can add more information to any location along the journey whenever I like. Once I assign significance to a location, be it a gate, rock, window or letterbox, then that feature will always leap out at me leaving all the unassigned features as background noise waiting to become significant if I need them. I make the stories memorable, grotesque, funny, vulgar and outrageous, and fill them with colourful characters from history, real or imagined, as the ancient Greek text book, the *Rhetorica ad Herennium*, recommended. Anywhere, at any time, I can walk the streets of my country town in my imagination and recall everything I have encoded there.

It was in a mathematical mood that I named my little dog Epsilon-Pi, epsilon being the mathematical sign for a very small amount and Epsi is a very small amount of dog. Pi is my favourite number. In this chapter, Epsi and I shall walk our Journey Through Time passing all the cultures we will meet throughout this book.

The earth was formed, so the experts tell us, around 4600 million years ago. As Epsi and I walk down the drive from home, the first life—the first photosynthesis—is happening. Multicellular animals emerge in the garden of the house opposite, with the first land plants and the Cambrian explosion behind the stone wall towards the corner. We walk through geological eras and eons, one per house: Hadean, Archean, Proterozoic, Paleozoic and into the Mesozoic. The last house on the block has a very messy garden, which makes remembering that this is the Mesozoic very easy.

For a reason I have never been able to discern, Epsi doesn't like the Mesozoic and tries to head back home when we get there. I pick her up and nod to the dinosaurs as I carry her through the Triassic, Jurassic and Cretaceous. From the Pliocene on, she is perfectly happy to walk, even though the big noisy dogs are at the house with Lucy, the famous australopithecine from the Pliocene who has no idea the stir her skeletal remains will one day cause when they are found over three million years later.

I turn the first corner in the Jurassic, 200 million years ago. By the time we reach the next corner, now well into the Cenozoic, we have encountered many long-extinct hominid species. *Homo erectus* stands upright just as I get to the last house on this block. The corner is one million years ago, which I decided was the best place to change from geologic time to archaeological time and enter the Paleolithic.

Time slows down a bit for the next side of the block, with each division, be it house or fence, representing 100,000 years. Peking man, Neanderthals, they're all there. Eventually we meet the first modern human, *Homo sapiens*, coming out of the gate halfway up the block. As we pass the next house, the very first art has appeared, the first memory spaces.

The first modern humans

Still in the Paleolithic, we pass a letterbox with a cavernous opening for the mail. This is the Blombos Cave in South Africa. Even if the owners are so inconsiderate as to change or even remove their letterbox, I will just update the link on the next passing. It is too important a location to lose. The earliest known prehistoric art in Africa was found here, dated to around 70,000 BCE. Two pieces of ochre rock have been incised with geometric abstract signs and left lying alongside some shell beads. Abstract signs are used to encode multiple layers of knowledge, but more evidence will be needed before I can declare that Blombos Cave was a memory space.

The next corner is 40,000 years ago. Humans have made it to Australia. On the ground is a round drain cover, which represents Lake Mungo, nearly 800 kilometres inland from Sydney. Human remains at Lake Mungo have been dated to at least 40,000 years ago but some academics consider that they arrived even earlier. Australian Aboriginals, from whom I have learnt so much, have joined my journey and will be with me right up to the present day. Indigenous Australians tell us that images painted or carved onto a vast range of media are key to their knowledge system. All over the world for tens of thousands of years, images were being painted onto rock or carved into it.

As Epsi and I continue our walk, I note a gap in the rock wall and my mind fills with some of the most magnificent images of rock art in the world. Around 30,000 years ago, artists adorned the Chauvet Cave in France with horses, bison, mammoths, panthers, rhinoceroses, lions, bears, hyenas and other animals with a skill that astounds everyone who sees them. Archaeologists think that the cave was abandoned after about 2000 years of painting but that around 26,000 years ago it was used again. There are the remains of hearths and smoke stains from torches dating from this time. A child walked across the clay floor leaving footprints preserved by a landslide that sealed the entrance until the cave was rediscovered in 1994.

A painted cave would make a perfect memory space. There were often many deep recesses beyond the cave entrance, so both public and restricted spaces were readily available. By 20,000 years ago, a small fence on the journey acts as the reminder for the Cave of Lascaux in France with its animals, humans and abstract images numbering in the thousands. The Spanish Cave of Altamira is also adorned with extraordinary Upper Paleolithic cave drawings. Although signs of human occupation have only been found at the mouth of the cave, paintings are found throughout its 300 metres of twisting passages and chambers.

Epsi and I climb the slight hill at 26,000 years ago to reach the Late Glacial Maximum, and towards its end we marvel at one of the most inspirational sites in the world, the Australian Burrup Peninsula. Also known as Murujuga, this site in the Pilbara region of Western Australia is often likened to the British and European Neolithic sites. The Burrup site is much older and includes megalithic standing stones, circles and lines, cairns, numerous small conical mounds and, most exciting of all, the world's largest collection of petroglyphs. Numbering over a million, it is thought that the petroglyphs represent a continuous tradition spanning tens of thousands of years. Many represent animals that are no longer found in the area, including the extinct Tasmanian tiger or thylacine. The extraordinary level of preservation is due to a combination of very hard rock and low rainfall.

Around 12,000 years ago in our journey, Epsi and I move to a different art site, that of West Arnhem Land around Oenpelli (now Gunbalanya). The earliest rock engravings involve geometric shapes that not only occur repeatedly but are found continuously up to the most recent examples. Anthropologist Howard Morphy considers this to be the most complete record of continuous rock art tradition in the world. He described a sequence of styles over at least 12,000 years as 'almost unrivalled anywhere in the world for its complexity and the information it seems capable of yielding. The paintings themselves record a time of enormous change, during which the landscape of the Alligator rivers region was transformed and new groups were constantly moving into the area.'[1]

Interpreting any traditional art without the oral component of the knowledge system is highly speculative. Because of its permanence, rock art plays a more significant role in the archaeological record than other forms of art such as the bark painting in the same style as shown in Plate 4.1.

The production of permanent marks does not prevent change in the knowledge associated with them. Any performance can reinterpret the image, especially in the case of abstract designs, updating the associated knowledge to contemporary understanding. This flexibility is critical to the adaptive ability of modern humans. Hunter-gatherer cultures may be less complex socially but should not be assumed to be less complex intellectually. We need to acknowledge indigenous intellect when interpreting ancient monuments. Technical, historical, religious intellect—yes. But also rational intellect—a scientific understanding resulting from continued observation of the known landscape.

As Epsi and I walk on from the famous rock art sites, the grassy bank reminds us that wheat was first domesticated in the Levant around 12,000 years ago. The Chinese and Japanese are starting their Neolithic transition. It is also around this time that evidence of domesticated dogs appears in the archaeological record. At the Natufian site of Ain Mallaha in modern-day Israel, an elderly woman was found buried with a puppy. I pat Epsi at this point, which ensures I never forget the location in time of this critical site.

We have reached the time when the first monuments were constructed as memory spaces.

Monumental memory spaces

Epsi and I pass a particularly lovely house at around 11,000 years ago. This house is one of the oldest in the neighbourhood, while the fascinating site of Göbekli Tepe in modern-day Turkey is considered to be the first example of monumental architecture in the world. I believe the Natufians, a group of hunter-gatherers, built this as the first monumental memory space.

Ever since German archaeologist Klaus Schmidt led a team to start excavating in 1996, the world has been fascinated by the extraordinary finds. The Natufians erected more than 200 limestone pillars in about twenty circles, each circle containing two taller pillars in the middle. The pillars are decorated with abstract designs and bas-relief images of gazelles, boars, snakes, foxes, spiders, scorpions, donkeys, insects and birds, particularly vultures. The pillars are up to six metres in height, weighing up to twenty tons. Some of the T-shaped pillars are adorned with what looks like arms and hands on the lower half, leading archaeologists to suggest that these are stylised human forms. The pillars are connected by low stone walls with benches in the walls, indicating that these are restricted performance spaces.

T-shaped pillars and animal images were also found at other settlements in the area. Throughout this book a pattern will appear repeatedly. Major monuments are surrounded with smaller versions of the same architecture. Knowledge keepers would need to meet at the larger ceremonial spaces but also replicate the memory system in their own villages.

Unfortunately, Göbekli Tepe was labelled a temple by Schmidt and everyone discussing it since has used the term, leading to the assumption that it was primarily a religious building.[2] With no sign of habitation, it was not domestic. Situated on what was a forested plateau, but is now desert, there was no nearby water. There are no burials and no sign of a wealthy hierarchy. However, there are signs of feasting, public and restricted performance spaces, and stone pillars in clear sequences. Göbekli Tepe has all the indicators of a memory space.

Göbekli Tepe was built by non-farming people. It has long been assumed that to build monuments, people needed to be farming to free the time for such labour-intensive activities. I believe that in order to settle, it was essential that indigenous peoples found some way to create a local memory space. This would gradually replace the knowledge system embedded in the broader landscape. Any strongly sequenced set of objects, such as standing stones or posts, could be used to replicate the locations along the songline or pilgrimage trail. The fact that many of these monuments are circular is indicative of the way time is cyclic for indigenous cultures when they talk of resource management and agriculture. The monuments need to represent the landscape locations while also providing both public and restricted performance spaces.

As Epsi and I reluctantly turn the corner at 10,000 years ago, we lose sight of Göbekli Tepe but I cannot lose its position in the chronology without picking up my neighbours' houses and changing their positions. I can never lose sight of the fact that the rock art on the Burrup Peninsula is older than Göbekli Tepe and that I have yet to arrive at Stonehenge. It is five houses away, another 5000 years.

At this corner, I convert from quoting the number of years ago to using BCE. So the corner is both 10,000 years ago and 8000 BCE and every house from now on represents a thousand years. Turning the corner, Epsi sees home and speeds up past the elaborately decorated Neolithic site of Çatalhöyük in Turkey. She ignores Cheddar Man, Britain's oldest complete human skeleton, who peers over the hedge just before 7000 BCE. At the next house, around 6000 BCE, I want her to slow down. It is here that I get the first glimpse of stone circles and passage cairns, two of my favourite forms of memory space.

In the garden of the house at 6000 BCE are the Iberian megalithic cairns. Just like the passage cairns in Brittany, Britain and Ireland, some of the Iberian cairns have astronomical alignments. At the house where I have encoded the Iberian Neolithic sites is a letterbox which represents the passage cairns. I imagine myself posting stone plaques in the letterbox, plaques with abstract designs carved onto them. The Iberian plaques have been interpreted as representing genealogies, by one of the few archaeologists who constantly refers to knowledge systems, Katina Lillios.[3] The circular newspaper holder beneath the letterbox reminds me of the Iberian stone circles. The largest Iberian megalithic complex, Almendres Cromlech in Portugal, for example, consists of nearly a hundred stones that were placed in oval configurations and constantly moved over the thousands of years it was used as a ceremonial site.

Around 4500 BCE, stone circles were being built in Egypt. The megalithic stone circles at Nabta Playa were built with alignments to the summer solstice. Archaeologists claim this is the earliest known stone circle that demonstrates an astronomical alignment. For a millennium, the builders continued to construct ever more complex megalithic structures.

Fortunately the next house has lots of buildings and a very fancy garden because there is so much that I need to encode into it. Starting around 3600 BCE, the early farmers on Malta constructed at least 30 ceremonial buildings. These were not built as burial sites. Collective tombs were elsewhere. With no sign of habitation or burials, these buildings have been labelled as temples, which implies that they were purely religious monuments. A more complex narrative is indicated by the archaeology, such as that of sociologist David Turnbull who refers to the buildings as 'theatres of knowledge'.[4]

The layout of the chambers usually took the form of a cloverleaf. As ruins today, they appear relatively spacious, but when roofed and complete, the inner chambers would have been dark, small, confined spaces. The builders added semicircular forecourts with carved stone facades and decorations in red ochre as public performance spaces. Openings referred to as 'oracle holes' provided a way for the small group deep inside the chambers to transmit information to those outside.

The earliest were the two Ġgantija temples on the Maltese island of Gozo which were enclosed within a single stone wall with a sixteen-metre-high facade. The larger and older of the two had five semicircular recesses surrounding a central passage. Of a similar age is the Mnajdra, a megalithic complex on Malta consisting of three temples built over hundreds of years. Some stone pillars were decorated with horizontal rows of pitmarks, while others were dressed with spiral carvings. The elders would have been able to maintain a calendar using a number of different features that are illuminated by sunlight on the solstices and equinoxes.

A few hundred years later, work started on the Hypogeum of Ħal-Saflieni about 500 metres from Mnajdra. Natural caves were enhanced to produce a subterranean structure of fantastic proportions and properties. The Hypogeum was built over burial grounds. It is estimated that 7000 individuals have been found in the lower level in a mass grave. There was no sign of individual wealth or elite burial. All were equal in death there.

However, the needs of the elders maintaining the knowledge system were also incorporated in the Hypogeum. The circular main chamber was carved out of rock with real and false entrances. One of the smallest side chambers is known as the Oracle Room because of particularly impressive acoustic resonance and the heavily decorated ceiling. Another room is also elaborately decorated with spirals, while others appear to have been for storage.

Over the next 2000 years of our walk, Epsi and I pass a vast array of Neolithic structures added to the ever-changing landscapes of Ireland, Britain and Western Europe, the focus of the next few chapters. Many of these structures are reminiscent of the megalithic chambers in the Maltese temples and the Iberian monuments. The Irish built passage cairns in the Boyne Valley of County Meath from around 3300 BCE. Almost universally referred to as tombs, the archaeology of Neolithic passage cairns tells a much more complex story. I am convinced that they were primarily restricted memory spaces, some of which also served as burial sites for the most revered of the elders.

Archaeologists estimate that the Neolithic began in western France around the same time. The region of Brittany is home to richly decorated passage cairns and over 3000 standing stones, known as menhirs. Some menhirs once stood alone, one being three times the size of the largest stone at Stonehenge. Others formed stone circles, while most of the standing stones were raised in parallel rows stretching for kilometres. The monuments of Orkney and Avebury were also started in the fourth millennium BCE when cairns, stone circles and henges all appeared in the ever-changing landscapes.

I can't help but anticipate the next house, which represents 3000 BCE. It is here that I am always reminded of the extraordinary day on Salisbury Plain when I first visited Stonehenge. It was around 3000 BCE that the first stage of Stonehenge was built and it continued to change over 1500 years in a way that exactly matched the needs of elders in the transition to farming.

But we are not at Stonehenge yet. As Epsi and I pause to look at the rather gorgeous garden of the house of the Maltese temples, with the different parts of the garden taking my thoughts to the British, Irish and Breton passage cairns, I notice some small mounds which remind me that monumental constructions were starting to happen in the Americas as well. Chapters 9, 10 and 11 tell the story of the widely differing cultures that built mounds, platform pyramids and plazas throughout the North and South American continents. The very first monument of mounds was built by a hunter-gatherer culture at Watson Brake in Louisiana around 3500 BCE. Hunter-gathers would build mound structures for thousands of years before agriculture took hold. Dating from 2600 BCE, the first traces of the Mayan culture appear in the archaeological record. They will eventually erect enormous mounds and pyramids in their spectacular cities. Looking down the street, I can see the Maya going right around the next block and to the present. Like the Australian

Aboriginal cultures, they are still going today. I can just see the location that I associate with the first Mayan script and the peak in their city-building. It is still over 2000 years away. Meanwhile, the earliest city in the Americas was emerging in the Peruvian desert at a place now called Caral.

Around the same time, the Pyramid of Djoser was built, the first of the Egyptian pyramids. Every discovery about these extraordinary monuments has enthralled Egyptologists and the general public alike for centuries. Through central and southern Egypt, step pyramids were built with no internal chambers and no burials, and take the form of the memory spaces in the Americas. However, the majority of Egyptian pyramids were built by a literate civilisation that had used hieroglyphs since around 3300 BCE. Although I have placed the Great Pyramid of Giza and the Sphinx and many more of the incredible Egyptian monuments in my journey, they are sadly not part of the story being told in this book.

When we reach 2000 BCE, Epsi and I have walked right round what I think of as our prehistory block and reached our own front wall. Sometimes we stop here but often we keep walking and continue our journey around a different block. From home, we walk half a block to the next corner, which I have declared as zero CE. The four corners of the block are 500, 1000, 1500 and 1800, with home being 1900 CE. I have markers every 25 years. Major events are then associated with trees or rocks, fences and gates, guttering, road markings and odd-shaped bricks in the wall. A significant location, once chosen, will from then on stand out from the surroundings, and I can estimate to within a decade of the actual event just from picturing the location. From 1900 on, I have every year allocated to a journey around the garden and house.

Looking down the street from home, I can see that the story of the Americas is moving at a rapid pace. At 1800 BCE, I am reminded of the dense cloud of huge mosquitoes I encountered at the huge mound-builder site of Poverty Point in Louisiana. By 1400 BCE the hugely influential Olmec culture has emerged in Mesoamerica, while the pre-Inca Chavín culture will soon build their city at Chavín de Huántar. But it is not all about the Americas.

East of Malta in the Mediterranean Sea is the island of Crete and the home of the Minoan culture. Although there is ample evidence of Neolithic occupation dating well before the Minoans, Crete is far better known for the real and mythological city of Knossos, often referred to as Europe's oldest city. The first palace dates to around 1900 BCE. Homer tells of Minos, the king of Knossos, in the *Iliad* and *Odyssey*. From where I am standing at 1700 BCE I can look down the street to 800 BCE and see Homer waiting there. There is a maze of well over a thousand rooms of Knossos decorated with images of land and sea animals, plants and mythological creatures. I am intrigued by the two scripts found there known as Linear A and Linear B. But the palace at Knossos is not primarily a memory space, so I must move on.

As Epsi and I pass 1000 BCE, stone 'circles' are being created in the shapes of ships in Scandinavia, fitting perfectly with the purpose that will be granted to Neolithic stone circles in the coming chapters. In Jordan giant stone wheels have been found, which resonate with the medicine wheels of the Great Plains tribes of the United States. Over 900 ancient carved megaliths have been found in central Asia and southern Siberia. Some are over five metres tall. They are known as deer or reindeer stones named for the flying deer thought to have been carved into the surfaces by Bronze Age hunter-gatherers around 1000 BCE. The megaliths are also adorned with an array of abstract symbols and mythological images alongside realistic pigs, cows, horses, birds, tigers and frogs. No burials have been found associated with the megaliths and I feel certain that they formed memory spaces.

We start to encounter the 'ancestors' I have assigned to playing cards as described in the previous chapter. First is Homer at around 800 BCE. Each appears enmeshed in all the events going on around them and shares the stage with their contemporaries. Pythagoras, Buddha, Confucius, Socrates, Plato, Aristotle and Alexander the Great. I can see who came before influencing their lives, and who is ahead and will be shaped by them. I can't get the order wrong. They are grounded in the landscape, the details of their lives encoded within the narratives of the cards.

The short walk from 1000 BCE to the corner at the year zero covers the Zhou Dynasty in China, the first Olympics, the rise and fall of the Babylonian Empire, the foundation of the Roman Republic and the Warring States Period in China. I watch the Great Wall of China being built as I admire Euclid with his geometry and Archimedes in his bath. I glance down the Silk Road while the Maya develop their first writing with symbols for sounds. I notice that humans have made it to the Marquesas Islands as I nod to Cicero, Julius Caesar and Jesus Christ.

As written history starts to dominate my journey, I realise the difference writing makes to the permanence of knowledge. Yet, I can still see plenty of signs of non-literate cultures creating memory spaces. On the plains of Peru between 200 BCE and 600 CE, the Nasca people moved millions of stones to create huge animal glyphs, geometric shapes and very long lines. As will be explained in Chapter 10, the Nasca Lines formed a memory space on the flat infertile desert between the coast and the Andes.

As Epsi and I walk past 400 CE, the huge church hall shades the path so it never sees the sun. It amuses me greatly that it is at this moment in my journey I have entered the Dark Ages. The Roman Empire has split into East and West, the West following my path and the East taking off through the church grounds. As I reach the church, Alfred is burning the cakes for the church stall around 878 CE. He may have never actually done this in history, but he amuses me by doing it every time I pass.

On the other side of the footpath Epsi and I walk, the Ancestral Pueblo have started building their 'great houses' in the most inspiring place I have ever visited, Chaco Canyon in New Mexico. There is a lovely natural stone gutter that I associate with the stonework of Chaco Canyon, the subject of Chapter 9. As I turn the corner around the church at 1000 CE, with Chaco at its height, I imagine I can hear the hymn-singing, which reminds me that I am now in the Song Dynasty in China. The gutter ends around 1150 CE (if I rig it a little bit) when Chaco is abandoned.

Have people reached Easter Island yet? Archaeologists debate when the Rapanui people first landed there. Dates vary between 600 and 1200 CE. I have put them in the journey at 600 CE but the narrative there includes this controversy. Taking the non-literate use of landscape and the Pacific tradition of ordering knowledge by genealogy, Easter Island becomes a statuesque memory space, the topic of the final chapter of the book.

Many events, and people, images and ideas later, Epsi and I arrive at the year 1200. I have just walked past King Richard I, with a lion in his tree. All Richards are located in trees. I imagine a lion in Richard I's tree, which gives me Lionheart. But he's a quarter of a house behind me, so about ten years ago. Right on the corner is King John, so he has just ascended the British throne. Robin Hood is there, too, hiding in the rose bushes. Up the lane, the African civilisation at Great Zimbabwe is at its peak. The Ancestral Puebloans have started building their cliff houses at Mesa Verde in Colorado. Oh, and Genghis Khan is on the rampage. He's the tall rusty garden ornament with evil-looking claws.

As I walk the next 30 metres or so, I see the Magna Carta being written, greet Thomas Aquinas and watch the Mongols invade Russia. Looking ahead I note that the next few decades will see the start of the Ottoman Empire. We're into the Yuan Dynasty over in China, and Marco Polo is heading out there. Over in South America, the Inca have appeared in the landscape, while the Aztecs have started their dominance of Mesoamerica. I had always thought they were much older than this. Glancing up to the corner at 1500 CE, I can see a lot of wars ahead, but also the Renaissance coming, Vasco da Gama reaching India and Christopher Columbus heading out to the New World. Oh dear, around the corner the Spanish are going to destroy all that I have written about in Chapter 11; the short-lived Aztecs and the Inca culture will be lost, but the long-established Maya will continue on.

Can you imagine the questions arising in my mind? Why did little Spain and England head off and take over so much? Why did the Puebloans stay in their own domain and not try to dominate the world? Thousands of questions arise which compel me to find out more, which then gets added. I just have to hook the data onto the trees, doors, gates, walls, ornaments, cracks in the pavement, marks on the road—there's plenty for everything.

Is it really worth all the effort to prepare a physical landscape journey? Consider a much more common mnemonic method, the poem to memorise British monarchs in order. It starts from William the Conquerer and continues to the present.

> Willie, Willie, Harry, Stee,
> Harry, Dick, John, Harry three;
> One, two, three Neds, Richard two
> Harrys four, five, six . . . then who?
> Edwards four, five, Dick the bad,
> Harrys VII and VIII, then Ned the Lad . . .

If I know this poem I know the kings and queens in order. However, I have no sense of their dates and, more importantly, the structure cannot be expanded. For example, I now learn that the body of Dick the Bad, better known as Richard III, has been found in a city council car park in Leicester. The news is full of lots of lovely facts about him and the debate surrounding his reburial. How do I add all that into the poem? I can't. But on my landscape journey, Richard III is a tree, placed at around 1483, the time of his coronation. A tree has so many branches and knots, patterns in the bark, roots and canopy, that I can find bits and pieces to link to everything about him. A bowed branch to remind me of Richard III's curved backbone, concrete at the base to remind me of the car park. My tree becomes a cultural object, it has life, spirits, a story. Just as with indigenous cultures and their landscape journeys, more and more knowledge can be added as I am initiated higher and higher in my journey.

With trees and journeys, stories and decks of cards, it seems that I am remembering far more than the information I want to memorise, which is true. But I am memorising in a way that is extremely efficient and in effect takes much less effort than more conventional study techniques. I could not have imagined this emotional attachment and the pure joy of walking my vivid landscape, had I not experienced it myself. I may only be glimpsing a non-literate mindset, but it is an essential glimpse for understanding.

What's happening in my head is not a verbal narrative. I've walked my Journey Through Time with others, trying to point out everything that's going on. It's not possible. It would take far too long and that's not the way my brain is seeing it. When Socrates dies in 399 BCE, I see him dead in front of the garage of a neighbour. No words happen in my head other than his name. I see an image.

I see actions. I respond emotionally. And if I want to recall the information and verbalise it, then I always can. But to verbalise every image and story that is triggered throughout the journey would simply be impossible.

And all this while walking the dog.

CHAPTER 5

The ever-changing memory spaces at Stonehenge

▐▐

Stonehenge was built and then continually changed by peoples undergoing the slow transition from a hunter-gathering lifestyle to one of settled farming. Archaeologists work entirely with material remains to reconstruct past societies. I needed to explore the physical impact of both mobile indigenous groups and sedentary farming societies to understand what an archaeologist might see in the archaeological record as the builders stopped travelling the broad landscape to settle in villages. But humans don't only eat, sleep, breed and build shelters when they gradually remain in one location for most of their time. They also think and know. I needed to identify the signs of the memory devices that could be detected in the archaeological record. I then needed to show that these were all present in the archaeology reports about the Stonehenge landscape.

Until I was standing on Salisbury Plain in 2008, it had not occurred to me that my research on the way indigenous cultures memorised vast amounts of information could be applied in the archaeological context.

As I listened to the tourist commentary, I learnt that the iconic stones, the massive sarsens in the centre, had not arrived until 500 years into the story of the monument. Stonehenge had originally been a larger circle, about a hundred metres across, formed by 56 posts or standing stones around the perimeter.

At that moment I asked myself, what would a mobile culture do about maintaining their songlines, their memory trails, their set of sacred memory locations across the landscape when they settled down? They could not afford to lose the knowledge but they were no longer travelling the wider landscape. It seemed immediately obvious that a circle of stones, each individual, each well separated from the next, was the perfect way to localise the sacred places visited over the annual cycle. They had created a memory space.

As I listened intently to the commentary, none of the theories about the purpose of Stonehenge even mentioned memory or knowledge systems. It was about burials and gatherings at the solstices, which made sense. There was talk of an astronomical observatory and of a healing place, both of which also fitted with the embryonic theory forming in my mind. There was mention of nebulous rituals, which didn't seem based on any evidence. But nothing suggested anything that might resemble a memory space.

What are the material remains that an archaeologist would see to indicate that Stonehenge was used as a memory space? I knew that unless my ideas were consistent with the archaeology above and below ground, then I could not expect anyone to take them seriously.

A mind game of transition to settlement

Let's play a mind game, imagining a narrative that would have played out over many, many generations, over thousands of years.

Imagine you can remember not only your immediate past, but that of all your forebears back to when you were part of a hunter-gatherer group, no longer nomadic but still mobile, still moving between known food sources over the year. At some locations you adapted the environment to improve the prime resource, maybe creating fish traps in a good fishing area or clearing land where yams naturally grew well. Each time you returned, generation after generation, there was more food available and you stayed longer, becoming better acquainted with other resources there. You gradually produced more food locally, fenced in your herds and reduced your dependence on wild resources. You traded for seeds and animals, and the knowledge about them, with tribes from far away. You started to favour one home over all others. But there was a problem.

As a mobile hunter-gatherer, your tribe had performed the rituals, the ceremonies, the knowledge, at sacred sites located right around the path you moved over during the year while travelling from seasonal resource to resource. You painted or engraved rocks and trees, caves and shelters, and embedded knowledge in the landscape, your vast memory space.

As you started to stay in one place for longer periods, a system of pilgrimages enabled elders to return to sacred sites, to perform the now ancient ceremonies and ensure that knowledge was retained. To settle permanently, though, a solution was found: your elders replicated the sacred places from right around the landscape at a site close to your village. They used stones or posts to represent the sacred sites and the knowledge encoded there: animal and plant properties, navigation, genealogies, agreements about resource rights, cultural expectations and, of course, religion and history.

Monuments, used as memory spaces, required a huge investment of labour, but this was willingly given because everyone recognised the importance of these stories for the survival, both physically and culturally, of the group. Stones were not erected randomly; timbers were not just put up anywhere. Circles and rows, circles within circles, rows in parallel, mounds and plazas all met the need for an ordered structure. Performance spaces, both public and restricted, were incorporated in the design of ceremonial plazas. Over the centuries, changes kept being made, enabling better enhancement of the sounds and making it possible for the growing population to participate. Movement while chanting was also used to recall the stories, so avenues and other forms of walking paths were built, maintained and revered.

When you were still in small bands, your group was almost completely egalitarian, with the level of initiation being the only path to power and to the restricted knowledge of the elders. As the population grew, knowledge specialists formed powerful groups to protect their particular part of the information system and to ensure it was maintained accurately. The groups resembled the secret or medicine societies of the Native American and African agricultural tribes.

Maintaining a calendar for both the agricultural and ceremonial events was essential, so timekeepers were powerful members of your society. It often required a trip of days or even weeks to travel to the ceremonies at the major villages, so someone had to know when you needed to leave, and how to navigate there. From long ago, way back in the hunter-gatherer times, your elders used the blooming of plants, movement of stars and migration of birds to maintain a calendar. With settlement, it had become much easier to observe, record and predict the solstices, the lunar standstills and other astronomical events that depend on repeated observations from one place to record them accurately. Monuments were aligned with the solstices and other astronomical events.

In a small proportion of ceremonial sites, such as Stonehenge, the knowledge elite were so highly regarded that these had become famous centres for knowledge to be celebrated and taught. People travelled great distances to meet there and join in the ceremonies. The major knowledge centres became more and more elaborate, while smaller versions were made across the landscape performing a similar, but simpler, role in the local communities. There were no individually wealthy chiefs and no one was buried in graves with valuable grave goods. Knowledge really was power.

Your community, now a farming village, was becoming far less dependent on your elders. They still used the old memory spaces, which had been adapted over the millennia to the changes around, but the egalitarian ideals were being broken down as the desire for wealth and individual power had spurred some to enforce their rule. Farmers knew about growing their crops or breeding their stock. Bakers were experts on baking, metalworkers on forging, warriors on killing. The elders now claimed a special link to the mythological beings who were once, many many generations ago, available to all. They called them gods and worshipped them in shrines within the bounds of defended sites. No longer were the practicalities of daily life intricately intertwined with the spirits. Religion was its own realm with its own specialists.

The ancient memory spaces still stand but the songs have long ago gone silent. It is left to archaeologists to try to reconstruct your world.

Every part of this sequence could be many times its current length and the multitude of variations expounded. However, any culture that made the transition from hunter-gathering to farming must have moved through some kind of scenario like this over the hundreds or thousands of years that the transition took. As long as the people were still dependent on wild resources for a significant portion of their food and materials, travelled for trade, needed a legal and ethical system, wanted to retain genealogies, history and a reasonably consistent set of beliefs, then they needed a complex knowledge system and memory spaces to help them retain it. Having spent our entire lives in a book-filled environment, it is difficult, if not impossible, to understand people who derived all their knowledge from memory. But it is essential that we try, because any reconstruction of an oral culture without consideration of their orality must surely be deficient. However, every society is unique and every archaeological site needs to be examined in its own right.

We'll start in the British context, where this transition to a farming way of life is referred to as the Neolithic. Salisbury Plain in Wiltshire, home to the famous Stonehenge, exhibits all the signs of the transition I've described.

Stonehenge and the British Neolithic

So what does the archaeology of Stonehenge actually tell us and how does that relate to the scenario presented above? Archaeological reports indicate that the communities that lived on Salisbury Plain for thousands of years right up to the Early Neolithic appeared to be egalitarian. There were no individual burials with valuable grave goods until later in the 1500-year story of Stonehenge and no sign that the populace was coerced into building monuments.

About 4000 years before the first stone circle was constructed at Stonehenge, a line of massive posts was erected less than a hundred metres from the current site by mobile hunter-gatherer tribes. People were starting to visit particular areas regularly, maybe even staying for weeks or months. The Stonehenge landscape was significant long before the first stone circles.[1]

The Neolithic Era, or New Stone Age, is the time during which hunter-gatherers started the transition to a settled agricultural lifestyle. Permanent memory spaces would be essential to maintain the information system which for so long was embedded in the travelled landscape. Early in the Neolithic, they built various styles of monuments which predated the henges.

Causewayed enclosures were tracts of land enclosed by banks and ditches, so named for the entrances or causeways across the ditches. They were not defended enclosures because any enemy could easily enter. Nor were they settlement sites. It has been estimated that causewayed enclosures took in the order of 100,000 work hours to construct. That is, the equivalent of one person working for 100,000 hours, or 100 people working for 1000 hours. The huge labour required to create the permanent ceremonial sites would be seen as justified by the hunter-gatherer tribes as these would enable the maintenance and exchange of information as well as finding marriage partners and trading material goods.

There is huge variation in the structures built by the Neolithic Britons. An archaeologists' reconstruction of the Whitehawk Neolithic Causewayed Enclosure near Brighton (see Plate 5.1) shows areas that were separated by banks and ditches, granting increasingly limited access. Circles of posts and internal post settings would have provided a memory space. It is hard to imagine a more perfect structure for teaching the knowledge system at increasingly restricted levels of initiation. It is also hard to imagine what else would justify this exact design, which would have required an extraordinary amount of work.

The Early Neolithic Britons also created monuments by using large parallel ditches with internal banks to enclose long stretches of land. Early British archaeologists thought such elongated monuments might have been courses for Roman athletic competitions and gave them the Latin name 'cursus'. The Stonehenge Cursus is about three kilometres long and varies between 100 and 150 metres in width, the closest point being less than a kilometre north of Stonehenge. It predates the first stone circle at Stonehenge by hundreds of years. Archaeologists now consider that the cursus was a processional site. The concept of walking along processional routes while chanting songs is one which will recur throughout this book because there is no better way to create a memory space. Even when the chanter is away from the site, they will be able to imagine their procession and recall the songs and associated knowledge.

Around 3000 BCE henges started appearing across the British Neolithic landscape. A henge is defined as an area of ground enclosed by a ditch with an external bank. Many henges, but certainly not all, have stone or timber circles within them. On average, henge monuments are believed to have taken about one million work hours to build. Stonehenge was one of the first henges, just a simple ditch, a bank and circle of stones or posts.[2] It was constantly reworked to become the most elaborate of all henges, and the last to stay in use. It is estimated that Stonehenge took in the order of 30 million work hours by the time the final phase was completed. Although these estimates are clearly broad approximations, it is obvious that henge constructions were not trivial work for the small populations of the time. They were constructed for a purpose that the entire population must have considered very important.

There is still debate among Neolithic archaeologists about the dating of the various stages during the long life of active use at Stonehenge, but there is general agreement on the main stages. The following sequence of events is based on the reports of The Stonehenge Riverside Project, a major excavation that took place from 2003 to 2009, as described by one of the directors and an acknowledged expert on Stonehenge, Professor Mike Parker Pearson.[3]

First stage: 3000–2920 BCE (Middle Neolithic)

A few hundred years after the cursus was constructed, the first phase of Stonehenge was built around 3000 BCE during the period known as the Middle Neolithic. It was a simple henge monument: a ditch and bank about 110 metres in diameter. There was a main bank on the inside of the ditch, and a smaller bank outside it, built from the excavated chalk. Technically, Stonehenge was not a true henge because the definition dictates that the bank be outside the ditch, while the larger portion of Stonehenge's bank is inside. The position of the bank makes no difference to the argument that Stonehenge was a memory space.

Enclosed by the ditch and bank was a circle of 56 pits known as the Aubrey holes (see Figure 5.1). There is debate among archaeologists about whether it was Welsh bluestones that originally stood in the Aubrey holes or whether it was posts, with the bluestones arriving later in the history of the monument. Recent reports are

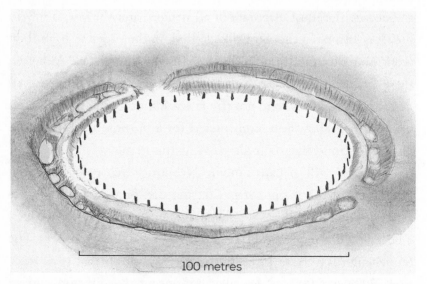

100 metres

FIGURE 5.1 Impression of Stonehenge, first stage, approximately to scale and with the bluestones forming the circle in the Aubrey holes. (LYNNE KELLY)

compelling that it was bluestones, so I shall assume that is the case. Either scenario fits well with the need for an ordered set of locations implemented as a memory space.

Stonehenge's initial circle is the perfect design for a memory space. The elders would have used the space to repeat and teach the songs to initiates as well as for public and restricted performances in ceremonies, as is the practice for oral cultures the world over. Each bluestone could be easily distinguished from its neighbour as they were left in their natural rough state. (The term 'bluestone' is used as a general term to represent a variety of geologically similar rocks, mostly igneous, including the most common of the bluestones at Stonehenge, spotted dolerite.) The 56 stones in the circle are separated by about six metres, a distance which would ensure that each stone is encountered on an individual basis by anyone walking the circle.

According to the Greek practitioners of the method of loci, the set of locations should each be easily distinguished from its neighbour. They should be well spaced, in good light and away from passing distractions. As I walked around stone arrangements in the United Kingdom, Ireland and France, it was obvious that each stone was significantly different from the one next to it, well spaced and with ample lighting because they were in the open air. I was dubious about the idea of encoding information to a stone until I tried it. I used a sequence of 35 large edging stones in my garden, linking them to books that have had a major influence on my thinking and my personal philosophy. One stone represents Charles Darwin and evolution, another is about chaos theory and the impact James Gleick's words had on me when first I read his famous book on the subject. A few stones represent great novelists. Looking back as an elder wanting to explain to the next generation, I realised that I could talk about the impact but had forgotten most of the content of these influential writings. Using the natural stones as memory spaces, I soon found that the huge variety of indentations and crevices, bumps and lichen on the surface formed patterns, much like the shapes that emerge when watching clouds. All I needed was human imagination and I could link whatever I wanted. I have no doubt that the Neolithic Britons possessed ample imagination. Post circles would be even easier to link to stories as the posts could be carved or painted. I've only used one post in my memory experiments: the verandah post encoded with the native mammals of my state. It works well.

The origin of the bluestones is one of the most intriguing aspects of Stonehenge archaeology. Recent reports suggest that the Stonehenge builders dragged the stones from a megalithic bluestone quarry at Craig Rhos-y-felin in the county of Pembrokeshire in southwest Wales. In fact, Parker Pearson and his team think that some of the bluestones may have originally been part of a monument in Wales and then moved to be re-erected at Stonehenge. If so, the Neolithic Britons moved their entire memory space over 200 kilometres to Salisbury Plain.[4]

Although most archaeologists agree that the bluestones were deliberately hauled all the way from Wales by the builders of the monument, there are some who believe that they were transported there by glaciers long before. The glaciation theory suggests that builders simply used the stones lying around. Archaeologist Aubrey Burl described the bluestones as 'a mongrel collection of dolerites, rhyolites and tuffs, from various parts of south-west Wales'. He went on to argue that if 'men really did transport the stones hundreds of miles they would not casually collect an indiscriminate mixture of stones'.[5]

One group of the glaciation-theory proponents wrote that 'this great variety does not speak of careful human selection'.[6]

However, if we are to accept the idea that the stones were chosen for a circle to replicate the landscape and act as a set of memory locations, then the more contrast, the more variety, the more spots and blobs and shapes and colours within the natural rock, the easier it would be to create the variety of memory images needed. The bluestones were perfect. The builders of Stonehenge chose exactly what they needed.

Henge ditches

Despite the Stonehenge ditch being deliberately backfilled and significantly eroded over 5000 years, it is still visible quite clearly today. The ditch was not evenly cut right around the perimeter. It was cut in segments with each segment having a flat base.

In archaeological reports, henge ditches are usually described in passing, mostly considered to be the source of the material for the banks, which may have served as viewing areas, or merely to mark the area. If Stonehenge is to be considered primarily as a cemetery, observatory or healing centre, as the current theories suggest, then why was so much effort put into cutting the ditch segments with flat bottoms? Given the diggers only had picks made from deer antlers as tools, the effort they put into digging the ditch was enormous. To carefully flatten the base seems to be an unnecessary added effort.

I struggled to see why the ditches were cut with steep sides and a flat bottom if they were purely to provide soil for the bank. Even more confusing was the ditch at the massive henge site of Durrington Walls, which was spectacularly deep and wide when compared with that at Stonehenge. Durrington Walls, built near Stonehenge and a few hundred years later, is considered to be part of the Stonehenge complex of monuments. Over hundreds of years, henge builders had continued to go to a great deal of effort to ensure the bases of the ditch segments were flat. Why dig such deep ditches and flatten the floor if they merely needed chalk for banks or wanted to mark out the sacred grounds?

I was sitting in a stepped lecture theatre trying to visualise the size and shape of the Durrington Walls ditch when I realised that the dimensions were similar to the very room I was sitting in. There in front of me, at the bottom, performing on a flat base, was the lecturer. It struck me that if the elders were performing at the base of the ditch, not among the stones, then the shape of the ditch would work as a theatre. The larger segments may have been for public performances, while the smaller segments could have easily been protected from the prying eyes of the uninitiated. I could readily imagine the elders chanting, their songs resonating from the steep stone walls, their torchlight reflecting from the pure white sides. It must have been spectacular.

In reading hundreds of archaeological reports of henges and other monuments with ditches, I found it difficult to find information about the ditch profile for many of the sites. Most important was whether the base was flat, V-shaped or rough. A V-shaped ditch tends to indicate a defensive ditch as was commonly the case long after Stonehenge's active life, in the Iron Age. Rough-cut ditches tend to imply that they are markers or sources of bank material. The ditches along the Stonehenge avenue were roughly cut without flat bases. It is only flat-bottomed ditches that would suit as performance sites. In fact, after further research I discovered that flat-bottomed henge ditches seem to be the norm, although many henge ditches have not yet been excavated.

The bank was six metres wide at the base and estimated to have been about two metres high, with the bank segments matching the irregularity of the ditch. Constructed from dazzling white chalk, the bank would have been highly visible from a distance. The ditch was cut into about 60 segments rather than dug as a continuous trench. Why? The answer is simple if you imagine that the performers were in the ditch with the observers on the bank above. The entire ditch circuit, just over 340 metres in length, would not have been used at a single ceremony. The width of the segments varied from two to almost five metres. The depths also varied, some segments being over two metres deep. The ditch would have been cut to suit the various ceremonies moving around the circle over the year. Segment 18, for example, is described as being particularly flat and wide, which would suit a ceremony requiring a large number of performers and dancing, such as the major gatherings in midwinter. Smaller segments would have accommodated the more restricted events. There are some quite small ditch segments, which would relate to ceremonies only involving a few participants, such as initiation rites.

It is only by envisaging Stonehenge as a memory space that the reason the ditch was cut with a flat-bottomed profile and in segments becomes obvious. The imperative is to perform the ceremonies. If the songs are not sung, the stories not told, the knowledge not repeated, then valuable information may be lost. In all documented oral cultures, there are threats of punishments such as poor hunts, failed crops and even illness and death if the ceremonies are not performed. The ritual cycle dominates cultural life. Neolithic Britons would have expected cold winds and rain in winter, when the archaeology indicates the largest gatherings were held. Any assumption that the performances were in the centre of the circle with the observers on the banks around the perimeter is hard to justify. It is unlikely that the audience, 50 metres away, would be able to hear the words of songs or oratory from an unaided human voice. Any wind would obliterate coherent sound at that distance.

Of course, there is no reason to assume that some ceremonies were not held within the circle as well, particularly in summer, nor that an audience was always seated on the banks. The banks may be more a result of digging the essential ditches than anything to do with the need to provide for an audience. The ditch would have been perfect for covering with skins suspended from stakes in the banks in the case of bad weather. In midwinter, with short days and early darkness, the light of the torches reflected by the clean white chalk of the ditch walls would increase the visibility of elders and dancers. It is possible that symbols were carved into the ditch walls or that they were even painted, but that these motifs have been lost in the thousands of years since it was used.

The builders deliberately deposited significant objects in the Stonehenge ditch. Most notable are the animal bones. Some of these were already between 70 and 420 years old when they were purposefully buried at the base of the newly cut ditch, and included an ox skull, a deer tibia and two cattle mandibles without teeth yet kept smooth. Archaeologists argue that this means the bones had been cared for over a long period and not buried soon after death.

In other segments of the ditch, more animal bones had been deposited. Archaeologists found fox, wolf and raven bones, which are not food species or commonly found in Neolithic remains. One segment contained multiple fox bones, while a piglet skeleton and complete dog paw were found in another segment. A similar combination of bones was deposited centuries later in the same segment. The archaeologists concluded that the assemblage did not reflect daily life but seemed to be demonstrating a much broader context. This is exactly what you would expect if the bones were related to the knowledge being performed at the ceremony associated with the ditch segment. The ancient bone relics buried at Stonehenge were likely to have made reference to part of the memorised repertoire from the previous hunter-gatherer life.

There were also human bones buried at Stonehenge. During the Neolithic, human bones were circulated widely and treated as relics. Only a very small proportion of the remains of the entire population were preserved. The use of human and animal bones as memory aids in ceremonies is known from indigenous cultures across the world. The Akan from Ghana and Ivory Coast, for example, used skulls and jawbones of past rulers in rituals, a perfectly logical thing to do when recalling the events of the ruler's time and knowledge associated with them. Similarly, the highly secretive cult master of the Baktaman of New Guinea used bones of human ancestors and brush turkeys among a range of sacred objects as memory aids. The human bones circulated as relics and those buried at Stonehenge would have been those of the most revered elders.

The archaeology indicates that some of the ditch segments were deliberately backfilled soon after digging, others were allowed to silt naturally over time, and still others were repeatedly recut and maintained in useful form. With settlement, some ceremonies would retain their significance, while others would become irrelevant. New ceremonies would be introduced. The ditch was almost certainly adjusted to suit the changing needs of the elders and their ceremonies.

The stone circle could be entered from a wide entrance to the northeast. Participants could also enter the circle through a causeway, or possibly two, left uncut to enable participants to cross the ditch from the south. The constant changing of the central area over the 1500 years of use means that archaeologists can't really be sure what the arrangements were and when they were placed there. Various arrangements of posts and possibly standing stones are thought to date to this early stage, perhaps aligned with the northern major moonrise, the culmination of the 18.6-year cycle of the moon, and maybe aligned with the sunrise at midsummer solstice.

Stonehenge was part of a broad cultural phenomenon. There were a thousand or so open circles of stones in the British, Irish and Western European Neolithic landscape. The proposed purpose of these sites needs to justify the variation from very small stone and timber circles to the huge henge at Avebury in Wiltshire, which is 420 metres in diameter.

I visited stone circles, large and small, to try to understand their relationship to Stonehenge. The three large circles of The Hurlers on Bodmin Moor in Cornwall are spectacular. The moor ponies rub their hinds on the ancient stones, quite oblivious to the tourists, and have probably been doing so for thousands of years. It was just as profound an experience standing in the small circle of Boscawen-Un in Cornwall with no other visitors present. Boscawen-Un is more of an oval than a circle, averaging about 24 metres in diameter (see Plate 5.2). There are nineteen stones fairly evenly spaced, with a wider gap to the west. The stones vary in size, mostly just over a metre high with the smoother sides always facing the interior of the ring. As I walked slowly around the ring, it was evident that every stone was individual and could be easily identified from any other. The stones were separated by about three metres, so that at any moment only one stone was in focus. In the middle is a leaning monolith, which excavations indicate was deliberately placed at that angle by the builders.

Just as we have large knowledge centres in major cities and smaller versions of them in towns and villages, so would the Neolithic people have needed smaller sites for local elders to use to retain the critical knowledge for daily survival, physically and culturally, in the smaller settlements. It is likely that these local elders travelled to larger sites such as Stonehenge for inter-tribal gatherings, for trading of both knowledge and material goods.

Stonehenge: the theories

Five hundred years after the henge was first built, Neolithic Britons dragged the huge sarsens to the Stonehenge site and raised them to form the inner circle and trilithon formations that are so famous today. Any explanation for the purpose of Stonehenge needs to explain why it was initially a circle of stones with a very similar structure to a thousand other circles across the British Isles. It was only later constantly altered into a much more restricted site. The archaeology, to me, tells the story of a prominent knowledge centre for a hunter-gatherer society that was slowly settling and adapting to farming.

There are an extraordinary range of theories as to why Stonehenge was built, many of which pay scant attention to the actual archaeology and the way it constantly changed over the 1500 years or so that it was in use. No credit will be given here to theories relating to wizards, aliens, ley lines and other phenomena that have no basis in science. I have spent many decades evaluating claims of the paranormal and these ideas about Stonehenge are very easy to dismiss due to the lack of any archaeological evidence to support their validity. As the Druids came much later in prehistory, they play no part in Stonehenge's story.

The most widely accepted theory at the time of writing is that Stonehenge was primarily a place for the dead—a cemetery. Human remains were interred at Stonehenge from the very start. These were not bodies laid out in individual graves along with their most precious possessions, as the word 'burials' implied to me before I became used to archaeology-speak. When they talk about Stonehenge burials, archaeologists are talking about collections of cremated bones. The original location of these bones at the site, and the way they were grouped, has been lost due to poor excavation and recording methods by early antiquarians, but the total number of individuals buried at Stonehenge has been estimated at around 240. Given the life of the monument is in the order of 1500 years, this is clearly the site of some kind of selective burial. Almost everyone who died in Neolithic Britain left no trace. It is logical to think that the most revered of the elders would be honoured by having their cremated bones interred at their most sacred site.

At the time the initial circle of stones was constructed, and for most of the history of Stonehenge, individual burials were unknown. Bodies buried with grave goods do not appear in the archaeological record until a thousand years after the first circle. In the Bronze Age, when farming was the established way of life, individuals began to be buried in circular mounds known as round barrows, many of which can be found in the Stonehenge landscape.

The most prominent advocate of the cemetery theory is leading Neolithic archaeologist, Mike Parker Pearson. After discussions with his colleague, Madagascan indigenous archaeologist Ramilisonina, about megalithic stone monuments erected for the dead in Madagascar, Parker Pearson proposed the idea that Stonehenge was essentially a monument belonging to the ancestors, to the dead. As will be described later, a massive henge was built nearby, about 500 years into the life of Stonehenge. There the huge circles were built of timber, leading Parker Pearson to argue that this site, Durrington Walls, was built for the living just three kilometres northeast of Stonehenge. The distance between is easily walked in less than an hour. Parker Pearson sees the two sites as linked by the River Avon, which served as a ceremonial pathway associated with death. In September 2015 archaeologists announced that they had found over 50 megaliths in a row stretching over 300 metres, which appear to have been buried by the bank at Durrington Walls. There is insufficient archaeology yet to be certain of the chronology, but a stone row would be perfectly consistent with my ideas of Durrington Walls serving as a public knowledge space.

I find Parker Pearson's argument that the two sites are part of one complex of monuments compelling, but I believe that the two sites represent public and restricted ceremonial areas rather than spaces for the living or dead. However, there is a great deal of overlap in these ideas, as the knowledge taught and performed at Stonehenge would have almost certainly been attributed to the ancestors—be they mythological or forebears, or some combination of the two.

If human bones are found, does that mean that we are excavating a burial site? Possibly, but also possibly not. In many indigenous cultures curated bones of forebears and animals acted as memory devices linking knowledge to the stories of the human ancestor or the animal totem. The bones used would not be an entire body but selected bones such as the skull or the larger limbs.

The trend to individual burials during the Neolithic is exactly as would be predicted by the imagined scenario given above. As a more restricted and powerful elite emerged with settlement, and the size of the community grew, the most powerful elders would have been buried with signs of wealth. So Stonehenge was a cemetery of sorts, but I believe that is only part of the story.

Another prevalent theory is that Stonehenge was primarily an astronomical observatory. Henges, stone circles and timber rings built throughout the British and Irish Neolithic demon- strate low-precision astronomical alignments. Observations of the skies were certainly part of the role of Stonehenge and the associated monuments. It must be remembered, however, that all that is required to track the movement of the sun and identify the solstices is two sticks, or one stick and a horizon. The original stone circle, ditch and bank offers little to the astronomer. The solstice alignments, which are so much a part of the later stages, and the indicators that there were probably solstice and lunar alignments in the early arrangements, offer a convincing case that Stonehenge was built, at least in part, as an astronomical observatory.

Some of the claims for advanced ancient mathematics and complex astronomy, however, are very hard to justify. The stones that stand alone, as well as those in the various arrangements of circles, ovals and horseshoes, it is argued, were part of a complex array forming a mathematically designed observatory. Draw lines through all of these stones and timbers and you will find a pointer to any heavenly body, because there are just so many lines and so many objects in the night sky. It is particularly intriguing that those who claim such advanced knowledge about astronomy do not also argue for a depth of knowledge about all the other domains that are indicated by the anthropology of oral cultures the world over. I am much more strongly inclined to the purpose being linked to knowledge that would have been essential to the users of the monument than to abstract skills that would pose no practical gain. It is much more logical to think that the Neolithic Britons maintained a knowledge bank across the disciplines, as is the case with all known indigenous cultures.

One of the contemporary proponents of the complex observatory theory, British archaeologist Euan MacKie, argues that Neolithic Britain was controlled by a class of 'astronomer-priests' who performed sophisticated astronomical observations, created a sixteen-month calendar and utilised complex geometry. I have no doubt that the elders ran a calendar using solar, stellar and lunar observations while telling stories of characters visible in the night skies. Although the elders will have almost certainly guided the spiritual aspect of the culture, ethnographic evidence does not support the concept of the religious speciality that the word 'priest' implies. So, much as I agree with MacKie's proposed knowledgeable elite, I cannot accept his term of 'astronomer-priests' nor the depth of mathematical and astronomical knowledge he attributes to them. There is little doubt that Stonehenge served as a low-precision astronomical observatory, but again, this forms only part of the story.

Archaeologists Timothy Darvill and Geoffrey Wainwright proposed that Stonehenge operated as a sort of Stone Age health spa, a theory widely reported in 2008. The Neolithic Britons would have had no shortage of health issues to deal with, including abscesses and inflamed gums, malnutrition, polio, sinusitis, tetanus, tuberculosis, osteoarthritis, plague and malaria. They would have been poisoned by foxgloves, crocus and the black cherries of the nightshade, as well as suffering from broken bones, cuts, abrasions and all the risks associated with hunting. Meanwhile, there would have been attacks from vipers, hornets, wolves, aurochs, brown bears and wild boar. Like all human communities, individuals would have suffered from headaches and backaches and aching joints as well as mental illness. And like all human communities, there would have been a knowledgeable elite who would have treated the ailments to the best of the knowledge available. They would have known how to bind wounds and use a pharmacopeia of drugs and poultices derived from indigenous plants. With Stonehenge as a knowledge centre, I have no doubt that the elite there would have maintained and taught the healing knowledge, but again, that would have been only part of their repertoire.

All these theories are consistent with the concept that Stonehenge was primarily a knowledge space, and that death rites, astronomical observations, timekeeping and healing were all part of the complexity that is seen in historical indigenous knowledge systems.

Second stage: 2620–2480 BCE (Late Neolithic)

About 500 years after the first circle was built at Stonehenge, with its surrounding ditch and banks, the next major phase of work was undertaken. The massive sarsens, the huge stones so familiar today, were brought from 30 kilometres away at Marlborough to construct the five huge trilithons (two stones surmounted by a third lintel stone) which stand at the centre of the circle, towering over all other stones at the site. The bluestones from the original Aubrey holes were moved into the centre of the circle, possibly into various other arrangements before attaining their final placement. The original ditch and banks were left to erode, their stone circle now gone.

Thirty upright sarsens were then placed in a tight circle enclosing the central area and the trilithons (see Figures 5.2 and 5.3). The most unique feature of Stonehenge is the way the sarsen circle is topped with a carefully worked interlocking ring of lintels along with the five lintel-topped trilithons. These features are

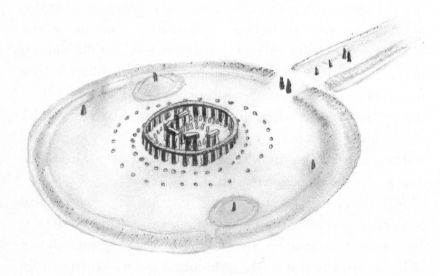

FIGURE 5.2 Stonehenge as it appeared in the final stages of use. (LYNNE KELLY)

FIGURE 5.3 An impression of the space enclosed by the sarsen ring and trilithons. Drawn approximately to scale, the human figures have been added to show how restricted the space would have been. (LYNNE KELLY)

constructed of notoriously hard, silicified sandstone, or sarsen, which is incredibly heavy to move and difficult to work. Depressions, or mortises, were painstakingly carved into the lintels creating a perfect fit with tenons, or bumps, on top of the upright sarsens. The builders must have spent endless hours shaping the sarsens by striking with hammer stones. Tongue-and-groove joints between the lintels secured the sarsen circle, helping to maintain the flatness of the lintel circle. Mortis, tenon and tongue-and-groove constructions are associated with timber construction, not usually with stone. The freshly worked sarsens would have been bright white. As people approached the new setting of massive stones, the sight must have been awe-inspiring.

If Stonehenge was a memory space, then each stone was significant in its own right. Archaeologists have noted that there was a deliberate use of different sources of stone for the trilithons and very marked deliberate dressing distinguishing each of them. From an open ceremonial space 500 years before, Stonehenge had become a much more secretive and restrictive space. The exotic bluestones were now hidden deep within the monument and almost impossible to see from outside (see Plate 5.3).

Restricting the access to the most sacred elements more and more over long time spans is exactly the pattern that I expected as the mobile hunter-gatherer culture settled into farming life, but there must still be a public performance space. Stonehenge had lost its open space when it was reduced to a tiny controlled area within the imposing sarsens. Soon after I returned from England the first time, I also discovered that the ditch at Stonehenge had been deliberately backfilled in parts, and then allowed to silt up to the stage that it was useless for performances. The theory I had begun to formulate was buzzing in my brain, but the scenario I had imagined so vividly seemed to be falling apart. Without a public performance space to complement the sarsen-enclosed elite domain, I was struggling to match the pattern so familiar from historic indigenous cultures. Until that moment, I had no need to come up with creative explanations, the evidence so clearly matched the script in my head. I was bitterly disappointed.

It took very little further research to discover my error. Like so many writers on Stonehenge, I was focusing on one set of very impressive stones and ignoring the context. It was then I started following the academic reports, especially those of The Stonehenge Riverside Project. The project placed Stonehenge firmly in a much broader landscape of human activity. Critically, it linked Stonehenge to one of the largest henges in England, Durrington Walls.[7]

Around 2500 BCE, Stonehenge had become a restricted site, the bluestones enclosed by the newly erected sarsens. At the same time, two new henges were constructed within walking distance: Durrington Walls and Coneybury Hill. Although there is little sign of feasting in the archaeology at Stonehenge, there is a great deal of ceramics, stone tools and animal remains at both the new henges. People partied there on a grand scale. Britons were herding cattle and pigs to Durrington Walls from as far away as Wales.

Durrington Walls was constructed close to the River Avon, an essential water supply for the large village that archaeologists now believe thrived there. The immense ditch at Durrington Walls, over a kilometre in length, encloses a circular area over 400 metres in diameter and about twelve hectares in area. Surrounded by a heaped bank, the ditch was divided into about 22 segments.

Mike Parker Pearson was one of the lead archaeologists working on the site. He described the ditch at Durrington Walls as having 'the appearance in plan of a partially merged string of sausages, with each . . . being on average 40 m long, up to 10 m wide and over 5 m deep'.[8]

A five-metre-deep ditch is simply massive. Anyone at the base of the ditch would have been dwarfed by the walls towering above them. The builders cut into solid chalk for well over a kilometre to excavate this ditch, a monumental undertaking today, let alone when every basketful of chalk was chipped away with the antler of a deer and then hauled by hand to the bank.

Why did the builders dig such an incredibly deep ditch around Durrington Walls when a two-metre depth would enable protection from the wind and rain? I believe that the answer lies with another well-known memory aid, that of music. In fact, some anthropologists argue that hearing is a more important sense than sight for indigenous cultures. There is no doubt that songs are much easier to remember than prose and that any acoustic enhancement will make the performances more memorable and more entertaining, the two being closely entwined.

Archaeologists specialising in acoustics have shown that rhythms resonated from standing stones and in Neolithic chambers, reflecting the sound in ways that created strange acoustic patterns. The more entertaining and the more varied and special the sound, the more the songs would have resonated in memory. Not only did the strange sounds create a sense of awe but they made the knowledge encoded in the chants and songs easier to recall.

Acoustical analysis of Stonehenge's sarsens demonstrates that they would have caused reverberation, and intensified sound and echoes within the sarsen circle, while restricting transmission beyond it. There have been no acoustic studies of ditches as no one has before suggested that the performances were held on the ditch floors. My analysis of some elementary ray diagrams indicate that the effects would have been detected within the smaller Stonehenge ditch. How much more pronounced would the effects have been in Durrington Walls's ditch, which is more than twice as deep? (see Figure 5.4).

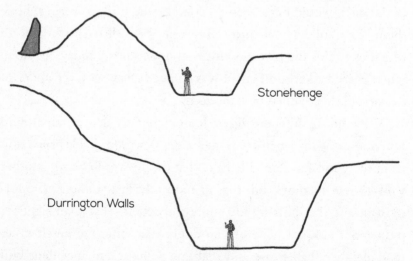

FIGURE 5.4 A comparison of the ditch profiles of Stonehenge and Durrington Walls. People have been added to indicate the way these ditches would have worked as performance spaces. (LYNNE KELLY)

My analysis suggests that those on the surface and bank would hear distorted sounds, which would appear to emerge from the ground as well as from the ditch. Similar effects have been recorded in experiments with drums played within the Neolithic passage cairn of Camster Round in the Scottish Highlands, where the resulting sound outside was not only distorted but also perceived to be coming up from the ground rather than from the cairn itself. For anyone standing above the Durrington Walls ditch, it must have been an awe-inspiring experience. They would have heard the enriched sounds due to the resonance and interference of the sound waves, while watching the performers in the reflection of light from the white chalk. For those performing in the ditch, the effect would have been mesmerising.

The henge ditch at Durrington Walls also enclosed two huge, uncovered timber circles, the southern of which has been excavated. The Southern Circle, as it is known, was 40 metres in diameter and contained more than 200 posts. Excavations of the post holes reveal that they were dug and re-used over at least 300 years. Even though there were six concentric circles, archaeologists have observed that people entering the circle always seem to move around it in a particular direction. If it was created as a sequence for a knowledge system, you would expect this to occur. The Southern Circle provided a fairly restricted area within the huge public henge site.

A circle of timber posts would work well as a memory space, even if the timber was left in its natural state. The posts would clearly be even more effective if carved and painted like totem poles. No satisfactory theory has been proposed for the purpose of these post circles to date, but as a memory space, they would have been perfect.

Only 70 metres from Durrington Walls is the more isolated and restricted site of Woodhenge. Estimations from the size of the 168 post holes suggest that the timbers they held would have been over seven metres high. With a diameter of just over a hundred metres, a ditch with an outer bank enclosed the huge posts in six concentric circles. The tremendous posts would overwhelm anyone within the henge. The ditch was flat-bottomed, over two metres deep and up to twelve metres wide.

Although the concrete markers are only low, I found walking the site gave me a very good idea of what it must have been like when each of those little markers was a towering post. As I walked around the circles, it was clear that there was little room for anything other than to engage with post after post. The closely packed site had a clearly defined sequence with which to progress through the circles to the centre hearth. There were also about five standing stones forming a small enclosure or 'cove'.

At Stonehenge, around the same time as the sarsens arrived and Durrington Walls was being built, two D-shaped buildings were constructed near the now empty Aubrey holes. These were later covered by low earthen mounds known as the North and South Barrows against the inner bank and two of the four Station Stones were erected within them. Other stones, named with no relevance to current understandings, such as the Heel Stone and Slaughter Stone, were probably erected around this stage as well.

Well into the second phase of Stonehenge's life, when the sarsens had been erected, formal burials of wealthy individuals had started to appear in the landscape, buried with personal ornaments and weapons. Nine such burials have been identified in the wider Stonehenge area. One of these individuals, nicknamed the 'Amesbury Archer', had come from Europe and was buried with high-status grave goods.

Third stage: 2480–2280 BCE (Copper Age)

During Stonehenge's third stage, in what is known as the Copper Age, the builders created an avenue, running to Stonehenge's northeast entrance from the direction of Durrington Walls. It ran along ancient periglacial ridges that were approximately aligned with the solstices. It is possible that these natural landforms were one of the reasons that the site was significant to people of the area from long before the building of the henge. The avenue was constructed by digging out two parallel ditches with inner and outer banks enclosing the ridges. Eventually, the avenue stretched from the River Avon, turning a few bends, until it reached the final processional route into Stonehenge. Tellingly, the ditches that line the avenue do not have flat bases. Avenues were processional routes, not performance sites. The ditches were important, though. Archaeologists have shown that these ditches were filled and cleaned out again. At the same time, the ditch around the original circle at Stonehenge, by this time an ancient relic, was also cleaned out and new deposits were placed into the trench as it silted up again over time.

Of course, a critical aspect of the design of the sarsen trilithons at Stonehenge was the perfect alignment with the solstices. A significant proportion of monuments built during the Neolithic demonstrate astronomical alignments. The builders shifted Stonehenge's axis by several degrees when they erected the sarsens. This brought it into line with the midsummer sunrise and midwinter sunset. With settlement, solstice observations can be made reliably.

Timekeeping is an essential activity in agricultural communities. For farming, yields are optimised by adhering to a calendar of planting and harvesting. The farmers would still have collected wild animals and plants when they were in season. The primary purpose of astronomical observations would have almost certainly been to maintain the agricultural and ceremonial calendar. At Stonehenge, archaeologists have not found astronomical alignments in the circle of Aubrey holes holding the original bluestones. The rectangular plan of the Station Stones provided approximate alignments for the solstices and, on its southeast–northwest axis, to the southern major moonrise and the northern major moonset. It was with the sarsens and the realigned avenue, along with the building of Durrington Walls, that the connection with the solstices became profound.

The alignments at Stonehenge, Durrington Walls and Woodhenge together would have enabled multiple observations of the solstices over a number of days. Stonehenge and Woodhenge both provided observations of the midwinter sunset and midsummer sunrise. The entrance to Durrington Walls was aligned on the midsummer sunrise, while the Durrington Southern Circle was aligned to the midwinter sunrise. Complementary observations of all four critical times, midwinter and midsummer, sunrise and sunset, can be made from within the two linked sites. The redundancy would have allowed for inclement weather and enabled timekeepers to check on their observations.

Current opinion is that the settlement at Durrington Walls was for the labourers building Stonehenge. There is no evidence of anything being made or grown there, nor have any goods been identified as having been produced there. So what was being exchanged for the labour, foodstuffs and building materials needed for the monumental complex of Stonehenge, Durrington Walls and Woodhenge?

As is the case in both non-literate and literate societies, material goods and labour are exchanged for knowledge. Education always comes at a cost. The gatherings would have served a multiplicity of purposes, as they have in non-literate societies documented from around the world. I believe that people came to the public site at Durrington Walls, the more restricted site at Woodhenge and the very restricted site at Stonehenge to partake in the ceremonies, learn the songs and gain the knowledge encoded in them. On returning home, the elders from the distant communities would have been able to encode the knowledge essential to their local role onto their own stone and timber circles. The elders could ensure they maintained the information needed by every community, all enmeshed in the mythology and beliefs of the time.

Fourth stage: 2280–2020 BCE (Early Bronze Age)

By the fourth stage of Stonehenge's story, Britain had entered the Early Bronze Age. The transition to a farming lifestyle was complete. The bluestones had been rearranged for the final time into an oval between the outer sarsen circle and the trilithons. The oval consisted of bluestones of various materials still in their natural state and probably those that, a thousand years before, had been in the Aubrey holes. A few decades later, an inner bluestone circle was built inside the trilithons, until recently thought to be a horseshoe. Whatever its configuration, the circle contained only spotted dolerite and the stones had been worked. Despite all the moving of stones around the site, the two types of Welsh rock were kept separate. This indicates strongly that the material and individual stones were significant throughout.

During the Bronze Age elite burials with costly grave goods appear in the archaeological record in circular mounds known as round barrows. An adult male was buried in the most famous of these, the Bush Barrow, about a kilometre southwest of Stonehenge. He was buried between 1900 and 1700 BCE with a range of objects that would have been immensely valuable at the time. The most famous of the objects is the gold sheet known as the Bush Barrow Lozenge. The lozenge is a diamond-shaped sheet of gold decorated with triangles in a delicate and very precise pattern. The skeleton was also found with a gold belt plate, daggers and an axe made of bronze, a stone macehead and other valuable goods.

Fifth stage: 1680–1520 BCE (Middle Bronze Age)

During the Middle Bronze Age, between 1680 and 1520 BCE, the stones were no longer moved. The only activity that can be detected in the archaeology is the cutting of two concentric rings of rectangular holes around the outside of the sarsen circle. Known as the Y and Z Holes, each hole was about four metres in perimeter, tapering about one metre deep to a flat base. They contained some antler picks, which could have been used to dig them, but tellingly, some of the holes also contained antlers that were already possibly hundreds of years old when they were deposited in the pits. To have been kept so long, these must have been valuable items. By the Middle Bronze Age, no new monuments were being built in the British landscape.

It seems as if the elders had lost their power and were no longer able to command large labour forces. Pits, containing memory aids for the songs and ceremonies, would work just as well as massive stones, if rather less spectacularly. Pit rings were also dug in other areas during the Neolithic and Early Bronze Age. Excavators have discovered deposits such as carved chalk objects, Grooved Ware pottery, animal bones, antlers and flints, all of which can be associated with the knowledge system. Human remains were found in some of the pits, but were secondary deposits, having been added later in the life of the pits.

Most telling of these pit deposits are the carved chalk objects and Grooved Ware. Both would serve the purpose of portable memory aids, much like the tjuringa of the Indigenous Australians and the lukasa of the African Luba described in Chapter 2.

Portable objects

If Stonehenge was a memory space, then we would expect to find objects akin to the portable memory devices used by non-literate cultures across the world. I think of these as miniature memory spaces because when I use them, my brain is working the same way as when I use the landscape memory spaces. I am assigning portions of the knowledge to locations on the device. The designs, shells or beads on the objects give an order to the information, fixed in sequence on the device.

I had to avoid my tendency to assume all portable decorated objects were once formal memory devices. Sometimes objects are just props to be used during performance or storytelling. Phalluses are found in many Neolithic sites, including Durrington Walls and Stonehenge. Ribald humour has been documented, not surprisingly, from a huge range of non-literate cultures. Sexual innuendo is a human trait, but there are also narratives that provide lessons about sexual expectations and taboos, a common aspect of oral tradition. The line between items that add a visual sweetening in performance and those that are memory technologies is a blurred one.

Some portable artefacts were decorated in a way that indicates they could have been used by the Neolithic elders as formal memory devices. These include the Stonehenge chalk plaques, inscribed chalk cylinders known as the Folkton Drums and, most important of all, Grooved Ware (see Plates 5.4 and 5.5).

The designs on many of these objects are very similar to those found in rock art and the chambered monuments, including those that will be discussed in the following chapters for sites in Scotland, Ireland and the Brittany region of France. These communities would have all been in contact with each other. Archaeologists often comment on the fact that British Neolithic motifs tend to be almost entirely abstract rather than representational. This is to be expected if we are looking at the memory aids for the knowledge system. As in Australian Aboriginal art, it is the abstract designs that enable elders to ascribe multiple levels of meaning to a single object.

It was a surprisingly emotional moment when I was shown carved chalk plaques at the Salisbury Museum. It was overwhelming to see these extraordinarily rare objects only a few centimetres away and realise how perfect they would be as memory aids. Chalk is a soft stone, but still heavy. The plaques were about two centimetres thick and close to ten centimetres across. The etchings were clearly deliberate, but didn't represent anything recognisable. No purpose has been suggested for the plaques other than the nebulous 'ritual items'. Very few inscribed chalk plaques have been found, although a number have been excavated in the Stonehenge area. If they were the restricted items I suspect, then they would not have been common at the time. It is highly unlikely that these objects, hidden in a landscape built on a massive chalk plain, would even be noticed by anyone other than an archaeologist.

Similar to the chalk plaques, but much more refined, are a unique set of incised chalk objects known as the Folkton Drums. On display in the British Museum, it was easy to see that these three cylindrical objects were also a suitable size for handheld memory devices. Ranging in diameter from 104 millimetres to 146 millimetres, the Folkton Drums are covered in designs similar to those on Grooved Ware.

Grooved Ware pottery was formally deposited at the henges and other ceremonial sites, including Durrington Walls. The close relationship of this style of pottery and the henges was demonstrated in an analysis of the ceramics recovered at the massive Mount Pleasant henge in Dorset. Archaeologists have determined that the proportion of Grooved Ware in the pottery assemblage rose from 0.5 per cent to 98.6 per cent when the henge was constructed.

The designs on Grooved Ware are far more complex than any of the pottery found that predates it. The same designs are also found in the megalithic passage cairns, which will be discussed in the following two chapters. Archaeologists believe that Grooved Ware was deliberately broken before it was deposited. This is entirely consistent with a restricted knowledge technology, as many cultures will destroy sacred memory objects if there is no suitable initiate to take them over. These objects cannot be allowed to fall into the hands of the uninitiated.

I was intrigued when Grooved Ware expert Dr Rosamund Cleal showed me a large pot from Durrington Walls that she was painstakingly reassembling at the Alexander Keiller Museum at Avebury. The patterning included triangular sections of striations or dots. It would seem that such regular patterning would be difficult to use as a memory aid, but the pattern is very similar to the patterning of the back of the lukasa that I discussed in Chapter 2. In that case, the design representing a stylised tortoise shell is found on the reverse side of every lukasa. We know that each striated triangle or square on the lukasa acted as a memory prompt to critical narrations because the Luba elders have demonstrated exactly how they did it. Having used my own version of a lukasa to encode information on bird families and species, I now know that these abstract designs can be very effective as a memory aid.

Dr Cleal showed me the Grooved Ware after our meeting in 2010. We had talked about Stonehenge and Durrington Walls, the similar purpose for the various stone circles across the British Isles and Ireland and my ideas on the ditches. But it was when we talked about Grooved Ware that I knew I could not let my ideas about British Neolithic memory spaces go.

Dr Cleal's own research was particularly enlightening. She explained that Grooved Ware pots were four times more likely to be repaired than other ceramics of the time, indicating that they were more significant than simple decorated storage vessels. In fact, broken pots were often repaired to the stage when they would no longer be useful for storage. It seems that the symbolic information was more important than their utilitarian function.

I talked about my visit to Chaco Canyon in New Mexico where certain decorated ceremonial vessels, known as cylinder jars, displayed the same feature. They too had been repaired far more than could be justified in a utilitarian drinking beaker. Cylinder jars once held cocoa, a very rare drink of the time, and were only found in a few rooms of the great houses that I will describe in Chapter 9. The more I could see the same patterns in memory spaces around the world, the more logical my theory seemed.

A few years before, I could not have imagined getting so excited about a discussion comparing ancient pottery sherds. That day, I was enthralled by it. As Damian and I left Dr Cleal's office, my decision was made. Ancient memory spaces would be my PhD topic and the focus of my writing for many years to come. I couldn't have been happier.

Memory spaces, mines and moving on

One question I often get asked is whether I can make all archaeological sites fit the pattern I see in the Stonehenge landscape, and claim that they are all memory spaces. The answer is no. When in the United Kingdom in 2013, Damian and I visited the Neolithic flint mines in Norfolk known as Grimes Graves. The mines were worked from about 3000 BCE right through the time that Stonehenge was an active site. The Grimes Graves landscape is still pitted with the mine shafts, but they form no pattern. There is no sense of order, no performance sites and no artefacts that resemble memory devices. There is clear utilitarian purpose in the archaeology. As I descended the nine-metre ladder into the pit open to the public, it was clear that the descent served a single function: to take flint miners down to the floor where the horizontal flint-mine shafts took off in every direction. Nothing at this site resembled a memory space.

Stonehenge was a memory space, as were stone and timber circles all over the British Isles and Ireland. Unfortunately, Stonehenge does not store the content of that memory space. The knowledge only existed in the memories of those who used it. The songs, narratives, dances and mythology are all long gone and can never be recovered.

During the early second millennium BCE most of the monuments in use during the previous 500 years, including Durrington Walls, were abandoned. By the start of the first millennium BCE, a thousand megalithic stone and timber circles as well as the henges and chambered cairns, and even Stonehenge, had all been deserted after 3000 years of use. Stonehenge was one of the first monuments constructed and one of the last to be abandoned.

As specialists emerged in the increasingly large and complex communities, no single group could control the knowledge system. Powerful individuals gained wealth. Egalitarianism was a thing of the past as a high status warrior class emerged. When knowledge had been the prevailing source of power, the memory spaces were the predominant sign of the culture. Once wealth and violence replaced knowledge as the determining factor for control, the massive labour required to build megalithic monuments could no longer be justified by the community. Hillforts started appearing in the landscape, fortified settlements on the top of hills surrounded by ditches with internal banks. With a V-shaped ditch profile and bank inside from which to defend the site, it would have been extremely difficult for anyone to penetrate the barrier. There are even examples of hillforts being built on the location of former henges, with the ditches recut from flat-bottomed to a sharp V-shape.

Knowledgeable elders would still have been needed to maintain genealogies, religion, history, astronomy and the stories that dictated the ethical expectations of the culture, even though they could no longer command the power they once had. The solar alignment of the round houses during the later Bronze Age and Iron Age will have replaced some of the role of the timekeepers. Within the archaeology of the hillforts, there is evidence of shrines and performance spaces, seasonal gatherings and sensitivity to the agricultural cycle. In fact, some archaeologists consider that viewing the hillforts purely as defensive sites may be simplistic, as they contain all indications of ceremonial centres as well. Knowledge specialists were still needed, and probably still powerful, just no longer at the top of the hierarchy.

We have some indication of the knowledge-keeping role from the first documented contact with British oral tradition over a thousand years after Stonehenge was last in use. Julius Caesar and other classical writers described the customs of the Gauls and Britons, including the maintenance of calendars by an elite class referred to as the Druids. Caesar wrote about the presence of these oral specialists who were exempted from military service, taxes and civil duties. 'These pupils are said to learn by heart a vast number of verses. Some, in consequence, remain under teaching for as many as twenty years.'[9] Many of the verses noted by Caesar dealt with celestial phenomena.

When knowledge was power, the Neolithic peoples built a memory space still unparalleled today. When wealth and violence became power, Stonehenge was abandoned. It had simply lost its purpose.

CHAPTER 6

The megalithic complexes of Avebury and Orkney

||||||||||||||||||||||||||||||||||||||||||||

The day I saw an artist's impression of Stanton Drew, I became totally convinced that Neolithic Britain was awash with memory spaces.

The design of the henge, found near the village of Stanton Drew in Somerset, was perfect for performing; the flat-bottomed ditch that encircled the space was over 100 metres in diameter (see Plate 6.1). A circle of stones stood just inside the ditch, just as they did at Stonehenge. Inside the stone circle were nine rings of posts, effectively hiding anything that might be going on at the centre of the circle. The initiates and elders could use these sets of posts, decorated by carving or paint, as a sequence of memory locations. The nine circles suggest nine levels of initiation. Archaeologists have estimated that there are over 400 post holes, each about a metre in diameter. The posts that once stood in them must have been massive. It would have been overwhelming standing inside that orderly forest of trunks.

Although the artist's impression is certainly idealised and the details less well known than the image indicates, I found it impossible to escape from the conclusion that Stanton Drew was perfectly designed as a memory space and useless for almost anything else.

I have walked only a few of the thousand or so stone circles in Britain and Ireland, some large and some tiny, but the stone circles did not stand alone in the prehistoric landscape. Many were part of more complex structures, with timber and stone circles, multiple stone circles or concentric timber circles. Some have ditches with banks, some just ditches, some with no earthworks at all. Some are associated with tombs, some of which are decorated. Sometimes there are stone rows and avenues. Most are associated with decorated pottery and other portable engraved objects. Some stone circles were over 400 metres in diameter and some were less than ten. In even the smallest stone circles, each stone differs significantly from the one that precedes it. All of them were built during the transition from hunter-gathering to farming ways of life.

Although all these monuments exist side-by-side in the archaeological record, they were not all in use at the same time during the Neolithic. I needed to understand the sequence of the monuments to see if the scenario I had proposed for Stonehenge would also work for other ceremonial landscapes.

I decided to focus on two of the most famous British Neolithic landscapes, but stay conscious of as many others as I could. Avebury is only 30 kilometres from Stonehenge, in Wiltshire, while the complex of Neolithic monuments on Orkney is over 1000 kilometres north. Sites within the Avebury and Orkney

landscapes have been excavated by some of Britain's best archaeologists and their reports offer sufficient detail to explore whether
the scenario suggested in the previous chapter works for major
ceremonial sites beyond Stonehenge.

I visited both sites in 2010 and again in 2013, and talked to
the archaeologists working at them. I even did my volunteer-
archaeologist training at the Ness of Brodgar dig on Orkney and
entered the trench with my trowel in hand. I soon learnt how
long and hard the archaeologists must work to discover even the
commonest of artefacts. All I discovered was how much my knees
and back hurt after a few hours scraping at the soil.

Avebury

Six thousand years ago, the first traces of agriculture appeared in the
landscape around Avebury.[1] The extent to which these people were
still hunting and gathering, to which they were still moving around
the landscape and to which they were gaining their nutrition from
herded animals and cultivated crops is still very much a matter of
debate. What is not debated is the fact that this was a transitional
phase, the time when people were staying in one area for much
longer periods than their hunting and gathering forebears. They
had started to farm. The memory spaces embedded in the travelled
landscape needed to be localised. Monument building commenced.

On a glorious summer's day in 2010, Damian and I spent many
hours walking the Avebury landscape. From the township of Avebury,
set in the middle of the largest-diameter stone circle in Britain, we
walked past the stones and through the causeway that crossed the
massive ditch. We walked along the tiny River Kennet past Europe's
largest prehistoric mound, Silbury Hill, and up to the seriously
impressive megalithic passage cairn, the West Kennet Long Barrow.
Heading east, we followed the pathway up to concentric circles of

markers that indicate where massive timbers and stones once stood to form the Sanctuary. Turning back towards Avebury, we could survey the expansive Avebury landscape, West Kennet Long Barrow to our left, Silbury and then the trees surrounding the henge. We descended to a series of round barrows on Overton Hill. A bit of backtracking, and we returned walking through the formal approach to the henge between the imposing pairs of megaliths known as West Kennet Avenue. That afternoon, we drove a short way from the village then tramped up to the causewayed enclosure on Windmill Hill. There was little to see, but it was great to be standing on such an important site. Figure 6.1 shows the extent of this complex of sites.

 Windmill Hill

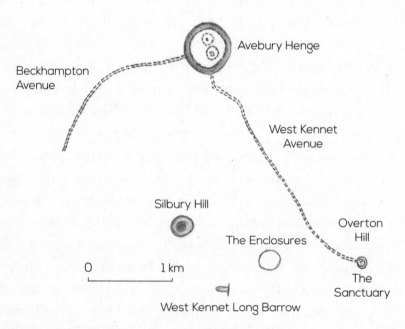

FIGURE 6.1 Map of the Avebury sites. (LYNNE KELLY)

Windmill Hill

On top of Windmill Hill, only two kilometres northwest of Avebury, three concentric ditches were carved into the hillside chalk. The Early Neolithic people invested about 63,000 work hours enclosing over eight hectares within three ditches. The outer oval-shaped ditch was much deeper than the inner two, with segments between two and three metres deep. This is just a little deeper than the initial Stonehenge ditch and would have provided a public performance space on the flat ditch floor. The ditch segment could have been covered in inclement weather. The innermost ditch enclosed only half a hectare with signs of a hearth at the centre. As was typical of 'causewayed enclosures' all over Britain, the ditches were not continuous but consisted of segments with entrance to the centre being provided by 'causeways', that is, gaps in the ditch.

Alexander Keiller, the archaeologist who excavated Windmill Hill, noted that the 'ditch segments are extremely irregular in almost all respects. Consistency is to be found only in the general similarity in shape, the invariably flat or flattish bottoms.'[2] As with the henge ditches discussed in the previous chapter, the flat bases were essential if performances were to be held within the protected depths of the ditch. These segments varied from four to seventeen metres long, reflecting various sizes needed for different ceremonies throughout the year. The deposits within each of the ditches were deliberate and significantly different, probably reflecting the different ceremonies performed there.

Born in 1889 in Scotland, Alexander Keiller was heir to the hugely successful family business, Dundee Marmalade, based on his great-great-great grandmother's recipe. He inherited ample money to invest in his passions for archaeology, fast cars, flying and women (four of whom he married). Keiller wanted to excavate at Windmill Hill, so he bought it and started excavating in 1925.

The bones of hundreds, if not thousands of animals, mostly from domesticated stock, were found at Windmill Hill. Archaeologists have dated the skeletons of a dog, a pig and a goat to between 3600 and 3300 BCE. Analysis of over 20,000 sherds of pottery of varying styles indicates that the gatherings attracted a large number of people from far afield. Around 100,000 pieces of worked flint have been collected. There is no evidence that people settled there on a permanent basis, although they possibly occupied the site for weeks or months at a time. There must have been huge feasts at the gatherings.

The huge quantities of animal bones were accompanied by smaller quantities of human bones, so this was not primarily a cemetery although it appears that some of the visitors brought human bones to be placed in the ditches. Children were also buried there; one small skeleton is still on display in the museum Keiller initiated in Avebury and which is now named after him.

While at Avebury in 2013, we spent time with Dr Ros Cleal at the museum. When we'd met in 2010, we talked about henges and avenues, standing stones and passage graves. This time, we focused on details of the small, decorated objects, a key component of non-literate memory systems. I was particularly keen to examine the chalk balls often mentioned in passing in the archaeological record of Windmill Hill. In the cabinets at the museum were spherical chalk balls mostly between five and six centimetres in diameter for which Keiller found no utilitarian purpose. Dr Cleal took the objects from the cabinet and we were able to see incised marks, only just visible, indicating that they could well have been used as memory devices. Given the softer nature of chalk, they are less likely to be as resilient as the harder carved stone balls of Scotland, which will be discussed later in this chapter. It was very exciting to talk about the concept of Windmill Hill

PLATE 6.5   An aerial view of the 2015 excavations on the Ness of Brodgar, Orkney; the Stones of Stenness are visible in the far background. (HUGO ANDERSON-WHYMARK)

PLATE 6.6   Rock art from the Ness of Brodgar excavations. (LYNNE KELLY)

PLATE 6.7   One of the houses in Skara Brae after excavation. (DAMIAN KELLY)

PLATE 6.9   Inside Unstan Chambered Cairn. *Left:* The chamber photographed from one end. *Right:* The passage which enters in the middle of one side of the chamber. (LYNNE KELLY)

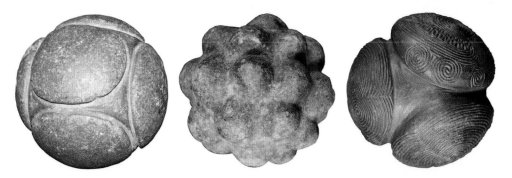

PLATE 6.8 A six-knobbed carved stone ball, a many-knobbed carved stone ball, and the elaborate Towie carved stone ball (all photographed at the Museum of Scotland). (DAMIAN KELLY)

PLATE 6.10 The Dwarfie Stane on the island of Hoy, Orkney, with the inset showing the recess carved into the middle of the hard stone. (DAMIAN KELLY)

PLATE 6.11 Part of the Ring of Brodgar with the Ness of Brodgar in the background and the Loch of Harray to the left. The Loch of Stenness is to the right. (DAMIAN KELLY)

PLATE 7.1   Approaching Newgrange in County Meath, Ireland. (DAMIAN KELLY)

PLATE 7.2   One of the 97 kerbstones surrounding Newgrange. (DAMIAN KELLY)

PLATE 7.3
Entrance stone to
Newgrange, with
the roof-box above.
(DAMIAN KELLY)

PLATE 7.4 At Cairn-T, the rising sun on the mornings around the equinox
illuminates the passage, chamber and highly decorated stone at the back.
This photograph was taken on the 22 September 2011 equinox.
(COURTESY MICHAEL FOX, BOYNEVALLEYTOURS.COM)

PLATE 8.1 The stone rows at Carnac, France. (DAMIAN KELLY)

PLATE 8.3 The passage cairn of Gavrinis from the boat on the Gulf of Morbihan, France. (DAMIAN KELLY)

PLATE 8.2 The Tumulus de Saint-Michel, France, dates from around 4700 BCE. The chapel was first built on top in 1663.
(DAMIAN KELLY)

PLATE 8.4 A cast of the stone showing the 'breasts' from Les Pierres Plates.
(LYNNE KELLY)

PLATE 9.1 The lower rooms in the great house, Pueblo Bonito, Chaco Canyon, New Mexico. (LYNNE KELLY)

as a memory space and examine the excavated objects from a new perspective.

Keiller finished excavations at Windmill Hill in 1929 after he drove his Bugatti, with a Miss Duncan as his passenger, at 135 kilometres per hour into a railway bridge on a country road near Marlborough. They were lucky to survive. Keiller wrote that he was driving 'at a reasonable speed, but not by any manner of means, I consider, an excessive one'.[3]

But he hadn't finished with the area. Keiller was aware there was a great deal more archaeology around the village of Avebury so he bought nearly four square kilometres in 1934. There he excavated, cleared rubble and undergrowth and erected some of the stones in their original post holes. He realised that the gatherings at Windmill Hill had been much earlier than those at the henge at Avebury.

When societies move from a predominantly hunter-gatherer lifestyle to a more agrarian society, increasing levels of secrecy become part of the power structures. Consequently, the need for restricted performance spaces increases. The response to this need is exactly what appeared in the Avebury landscape before the henge was constructed.

West Kennet Long Barrow

A few kilometres from Windmill Hill, the Early Neolithic Britons built one of the most impressive chambered cairns in the country. Despite the lack of firm dating, it is usually considered that West Kennet Long Barrow was constructed within a few hundred years of Windmill Hill, during the fourth millennium BCE (see Plate 6.2). Across Neolithic Britain, Ireland and Western Europe, large elongated mounds of earth were built by the first farmers. These 'long barrows' sometimes have chambers created with megaliths, however the passage and chambers usually only extend for a short portion of the entire length. Other barrows, referred to as 'earthen barrows', contain no passages or chambers and, in the area around Avebury, no burials either. The forecourts and top of the barrows, whether chambered or earthen, would have provided public performance sites, while the chambers in the megalithic long barrows would have provided ideal restricted meeting places.

The long barrows often have human remains, sometimes full skeletons and sometimes only a few bones, hence the common use of the term 'passage graves'. Although I do not question that most, although not all, long barrows were used to house human bones, that does not mean that their primary purpose was as a tomb. It is to be expected that fully initiated individuals, male and female, would be represented within the barrow chambers. Initiation can start at quite a young age, but it may be that the children of the most elite of the elders are also represented. Among the excavated bones, there is a skew to adult males, with adults of both genders much more common than children. West Kennet Long Barrow contained far more human bones than is often the case for these monuments. About 40 to 50 people were represented, of all ages. Even with a relatively large number of individuals, this represents only a tiny proportion of the entire population.

Significantly, the bones were all found in the side chambers, none in the passage or main chamber at the rear. Archaeologists have noted that particular decorating schemes on Peterborough Ware pottery sherds found in the barrow were limited to particular chambers. If decorated pottery is used as a mnemonic aid, as described in the previous chapter, this is exactly what would be expected. Archaeologists have noted that some of the pottery appears to have been deliberately broken, which again fits with the pattern across the world of restricted memory technologies being destroyed if there is no suitable initiate to take them over.

Archaeologists are unable to date each of the stages but using the various decorated pottery types as a guide, they estimate that activities continued in West Kennet Long Barrow for 1000 years after the last burial. The forecourt was partially blocked, a sign of increasing restrictiveness. Eventually, three large sarsens were erected across the forecourt closing the chamber completely. Meanwhile, a construction phase in the Avebury region commenced on a scale unparalleled in the Neolithic world.

Avebury henge

Around the same time as the first ditch, bank and stone circle at Stonehenge was constructed, the Avebury people, just 30 kilometres away, constructed a henge over four times the diameter, 420 metres across (see Figure 6.2).

FIGURE 6.2 Avebury henge reconstruction by artist Alan Sorrell.

First, they dug a ditch; the most impressive ditch ever known. When walking the henge at Avebury today, you can't help but be overwhelmed by the massive stones that once formed part of a huge circle, so large that an entire village has grown within it. But in the Neolithic, the stones would have been dwarfed by the ditch dropping ten metres below them, and the bank rising to at least five metres above (see Plate 6.3). The monument was built on an inconceivable scale.

Avebury's ditch is over a thousand metres long. That's one kilometre of excavation, ten to fourteen metres deep, up to 21 metres wide with steep sides cut from white chalk using only stone, bone and antler tools. Archaeologists estimate that it took them around three million hours. It was surrounded by a bank that is still four metres high after 5000 years of erosion. There had to be a very good reason for putting in so much effort.

Tellingly, the bottom of the ditch was flat. Different segments were cut to different depths, but all appear to have been provided with a flat base. Harold St George Gray, who excavated the site early last century (see Figure 6.3), remarked that the floor was so smooth and flat that he expected that it had been levelled using a water-trough, but he made no attempt to explain why this was so. If this is to be seen as a performance space, as described at Stonehenge, then a flat bottom would be essential.

As chalk is a soft, white, porous sedimentary rock, archaeologists have argued that the ditch would not have held water. Had it done so, it would not have been suited for performances. The acoustics, as analysed for the similar Durrington Walls ditch in the last chapter, must have been incredible.

As at Stonehenge, Avebury archaeologists consider that some of the deposits that were formally placed within the ditch were very old and had been well cared for at the time of their deposition.

FIGURE 6.3 Harold St George Gray's team excavating the ditch at Avebury in 1922. (ALEXANDER KEILLER MUSEUM)

As such objects are used as memory aids across a wide range of contemporary non-literate cultures, it is logical that they served exactly the same purpose in the Neolithic. Between 95 and 100 huge sarsens, all in their natural state, were erected just inside the ditch, creating the largest stone circle in Europe. The stones varied greatly in size and shape, a feature that would have suited the knowledge elite when using these stones as a formal memory space.

Two smaller inner circles were created inside the massive outer circle, providing more restricted spaces. Both circles are about 100 metres in diameter, with between 25 and 30 stones in each. These wide stones vary greatly from each other, have notably uneven surfaces and are known to create echoes and other sound effects, all traits that would enhance the inner circles as memory spaces.

The elders had also created small, highly restricted spaces. Within the southern inner circle stood a single stone known as the Obelisk, standing close to six metres high with a facade of nine smaller stones set close together. Within the northern inner circle, a box-like setting of three massive sarsens is known as the Cove. The Cove appears to be aligned with the solstices, giving the elders a means of running a calendar. A great deal of the area is not yet excavated, as much of it is covered by the village. There is evidence of freestanding posts and possibly timber circles but any number of settings could have once existed within the massive henge.

Although the henge has an enormous stone circle, even more standing stones were used to construct the two avenues that lead to the henge. The avenues were both around fifteen metres wide with pairs of stones of natural sarsen opposite each other every 20 to 30 metres. Approximately 100 pairs of stones, up to three metres tall, lined each of the avenues. Beckhampton Avenue approaches the western entrance of the henge and incorporated another cove monument.

The more obvious avenue in the contemporary landscape is West Kennet Avenue, which approaches the southern entrance of the henge for over two kilometres. Of course, we have no idea of which direction people moved along the avenues in the Neolithic. Quite a few of the original stones of the West Kennet Avenue still stand or have been re-erected. Walking it, I was reminded of descriptions by my Warlpiri colleague Nungarrayi about the appreciation Aboriginal people had for using the rhythm of walking and chanting while experiencing each sacred place in the landscape, enabling them to recall the knowledge associated with those places. The pairs of stones along the avenue are spaced perfectly so that only one pair of stones was within my immediate vision at any given time. As one pair faded behind me, the next pair started to gain shape, form and detail. It would have been an inspiring approach to the henge—chanting, walking and being drawn into the ceremonies.

The Sanctuary

At the other end of the West Kennet Avenue, the Neolithic Britons erected six concentric circles of timber and two of stone on top of Overton Hill. Now known as the Sanctuary, it must have looked like a smaller version of Stanton Drew as shown in Plate 6.1. As with most of the Avebury landscape, exact dating is difficult at the Sanctuary, other than to say it is thought to have been constructed around the middle of the third millennium BCE, at the same general time as the other major features.

The outer stone circle was approximately 40 metres in diameter and the inner circle about half that. Six concentric rings of posts were within the inner circle, although the stone and post settings may not have been standing at the same time. A single post stood in the middle. This setting is remarkably similar to Woodhenge, discussed in the previous chapter. I think that it is highly likely that the posts were carved or painted like totem poles, poles that record stories and other culturally significant information. Some archaeologists consider that the posts may have been connected by lintels, forming a timber version of the later Stonehenge sarsen circle and trilithons. Whether connected at the top or not, the suitability of these circles as a memory space is clear to see.

The outer and inner circles of the henge, the avenues and the circles at the Sanctuary all appear to have been designed to dictate the sequence in which the stones or posts were encountered, the primary requirement of a memory space. The structures would not have been viewed from the air as the maps imply, but as individual stones or posts as each was passed during the journey. The monuments would have served to localise the hunter-gatherer journeys through the landscape. The songs performed at each of the sacred locations along the 'songline' would have ensured that the cultural knowledge built up over thousands of years was repeated, reinforced and updated. For the elders of Avebury, the stones must have not only re-created the ancient landscape sequences but also enabled them to add new information associated with farming. The archaeology indicates that they adjusted their stone and timber settings to suit their changing needs over time. The Avebury monumental landscape, in its totality, was a dynamic memory space.

Silbury Hill

Silbury Hill is often referred to as the most enigmatic of the monuments in the Avebury landscape. Just over one kilometre to the south of Avebury, Silbury Hill is a circular mound with a diameter of 165 metres, covering over two hectares (see Plate 6.4). It rises 40 metres high, forming a truncated cone with a flat top 30 metres across. This hill is entirely man-made. The only way that

Silbury Hill could have been constructed was by digging out the chalk using deer antlers and cattle scapula and gradually building the hill, basket load by basket load. It has been estimated that a basket would have had to be loaded with chalk and carried onto the mound 35 million times to create this monument.

There is no evidence of burials or original tunnels within Silbury Hill. It is exactly what it appears to be—an incredibly huge mound of chalk. Dating is confusing; it is not clear whether Silbury Hill took a hundred or a thousand years to build, but it is known that it was built in three stages. The final form would be considered staggering even in modern times. Silbury Hill was surrounded by a six-metre-deep ditch, varying in width from about 20 to 150 metres. The top of the hill would have been much like the rooftop of a seven-storey-high cone-shaped building. There were two small causeways across the ditch and it is thought that there was a spiral rising around the mound to the summit. Although today the ditch is often filled with water in winter, archaeologists question whether that would have been the case in the Neolithic. With a public performance space in the wide flat ditch, it would have been difficult for the uninitiated on the ground to see or hear what the elders were doing way above their heads. Silbury Hill created an elevated, restricted performance space to contrast with the public performance space below. There are very few artefacts associated with the site although there are animal bones, giving the impression that there was probably feasting on the summit.

Evidence of two huge enclosures has been found recently between Silbury Hill and the Sanctuary. They were enclosed by what archaeologists describe as 'palisades', fences constructed from very closely spaced wooden posts, each post as much as a metre in diameter and six metres high. These highly restricted spaces have been dated to around 2300 BCE, after the avenues and the henge itself. There is evidence of pig breeding and feasting, as well as Grooved Ware. The sheer scale of the fencing, way beyond that which is needed to constrain pigs, indicates that the enclosures could well have been constructed as further restricted performance spaces.

With a number of restrictive spaces in place, it is only then, in about 2200 BCE, that the West Kennet Long Barrow was sealed. It had been in use for about 1500 years. This is the start of the British Bronze Age. Individual burials with grave goods in round barrows started appearing in the landscape. The now ancient egalitarian nature of their small-scale non-literate culture was giving way to a larger settled community with a much more defined hierarchy. Elders could no longer maintain absolute power based purely on control of knowledge. Weapons for battle are found in the archaeological record from this time. The tools for individual power, wealth and violence, had arrived. The dependence on understanding the wild species slowly reduced and the elders could no longer maintain the entire knowledge system. Information was dispersed among the various specialists, the farmers, bakers, warriors and tradesmen. As elsewhere, the monuments lost their purpose and were gradually abandoned.

Orkney

It is likely that much of what defines the Neolithic in Britain did not start in Wiltshire, despite the most famous of the monuments being found there. Archaeologists now believe that the first farmers and the first henges may have started at the very top of the country on the islands north of Scotland. The archaeology of Orkney is some of the most amazing on the planet and is only just being uncovered.

Orkney is special. Of all the monumental landscapes I have visited, Orkney stands out for its sheer beauty and the way in which so many aspects of Neolithic life have been preserved. The Orkney archipelago consists of over 70 islands clustered together off the north coast of Scotland. The current population of just over 20,000 is spread over less than a third of them, the rest being too small to live on. Remote and fertile, this archipelago has supported humans for over 6000 years. Best of all, the signs of those first settlers are well preserved (see Figure 6.4).

FIGURE 6.4 Map of Orkney indicating the islands and sites referred to in this chapter, along with the two major contemporary towns, Kirkwall and Stromness. (LYNNE KELLY)

For centuries, Orcadians have been walking and driving across a narrow land bridge in the middle of the main island, which separates the lochs of Harray and Stenness. They assumed that it was a natural feature. A geophysics survey in 2002 changed all that: The Ness of Brodgar was full of archaeology. Archaeologists had tramped in their droves from the Stones of Stenness via the Ness of Brodgar to the Ring of Brodgar. They had no idea that on their way, beneath their feet, lay spectacular Neolithic buildings, the likes of which have been found nowhere else on the planet (see Plate 6.5).

I joined the dig briefly in 2013, and the excitement was palpable as slabs of stone, covered in abstract incised decorations, were being carefully lifted (see Plate 6.6). During lunchtime on the dig, I stood on the hill and, at the invitation of site director Nick Card, addressed the assembled archaeologists. I was incredibly nervous and I'm sure when I started, many there had no idea why the woman with the strange accent was trying to say this was all about memory and knowledge when so much of the interpretation to date had been firmly fixed on religion and death. I emphasised the integrated nature of oral tradition in small communities. As my explanation went on, the audience was more intrigued. When I had finished, I was surrounded by archaeologists wanting to explain why they also thought there was another dimension to this site and many others they had worked on. I felt like I had passed a very important test.

Around the Ness of Brodgar, the massive ceremonial area contains three henge sites, various standing stones, a huge chambered cairn, Maeshowe, and a set of buildings of a complexity never seen before from the Neolithic. They are currently referred to as 'temples'. Although I don't like the way this label implies a purely religious function, they are clearly not residences. The Ness was constantly rebuilt during the Neolithic, culminating in all previous buildings being thoroughly decommissioned and the construction of the massive building currently being excavated, referred to as Structure 10. At 25 metres long and 20 metres wide, it was a huge building for the time. The five-metre-thick walls are even more astounding.

All over the islands, smaller cairns reflect the structure of Maeshowe, although there appear to be no other henges. Wonderfully preserved Neolithic villages, including the famous Skara Brae, enrich the picture of Neolithic life. The overall impression is of a central knowledge space based on the Ness, with smaller knowledge centres dotted across the islands. It is necessary to tell the story of these sites in the order in which they were built.

By 3500 BCE, crops were being cultivated and animals raised in Orkney. Substantial stone-built houses appeared in small settlements. It was a rich environment. Populations of fish, shellfish, sea mammals, waterbirds and aquatic plant life were enhanced by warm ocean currents, supplementing the farming produce.

Visitors to Orkney can freely walk around the remains of one of the small settlements dating from this early stage. A group of at least thirteen freestanding stone structures are adjacent to the Stones of Stenness, and were in use about the same time. Known as Barnhouse, there are domestic houses with central hearths, drains and bed recesses. There are also larger buildings that appear to have a ceremonial use. The settlement was inhabited for about 600 years. Whether Barnhouse was created for the elders who officiated at the various Ness monuments is a matter of debate among archaeologists. The same argument has been held over the role of the inhabitants on the much more famous site of Skara Brae, about ten kilometres to the northwest, which was in use for hundreds of years longer than Barnhouse.

Skara Brae

For over 4000 years, sand covered the tiny village of Skara Brae, preserving it in near perfect condition. It was only exposed in 1850 during a severe winter storm. Walking around the village of Skara Brae, you can see the houses exactly as they would have been in the Neolithic, each a single large room with a hearth at the centre (see Plate 6.7). A single low entrance door could be bolted from the inside and a large stone dresser with heavy stone shelves sat against the wall. Thin stone slabs were set on their side to define the beds, with small shelves in the wall above. Each house had at least one cell set into the thick stone wall with drains leading away, suggesting that they were used as toilets. Interconnecting covered passageways allowed movement between different houses without going out into the notorious Orcadian winter wind and rain.

One building stood separate from the interconnected houses. It has been interpreted as a workshop or possibly some kind of communal house. Although it may well have served these purposes, every small settlement requires some location for the elders to perform the knowledge and for the formal oral tradition to be retained, or the risk of loss of information is just too high. One of the most revered genres of knowledge in all societies is that of medicine. At Skara Brae, archaeologists have found many small puffballs, a plant known as a blood-clotting agent and used in the past to dress wounds.

In a severe climate, such as the Orkney winters, preservation of food would have been essential. There is ample evidence of whaling, which would have provided essential fat in the diet but also whale oil for lighting. Techniques for cooperative hunting of such large animals are performed in the 'hunting magic' of contemporary indigenous cultures, ensuring that everyone going out on the hunt is reminded of the animal's behaviour and the group dynamics needed for the challenges ahead.

Because of the often extreme conditions, elders would have needed incised art to act as a memory aid. Using standing stones and other landscape structures would have been impossible at times and something smaller and internal would have been used instead. Neolithic art is found within the buildings at Skara Brae and the building at the Ness of Brodgar. It is likely that the art was coloured with haematite, ochre or other substances found in Orkney sites.

Carved stone balls

The most exciting event at the Ness of Brodgar dig in 2013 was when Nick Card, the site director, realised his dream of finding a carved stone ball (see Plate 6.8). The most clear-cut examples of Neolithic memory devices are the carved stone balls of the Scottish Neolithic. To date, no one has provided an adequate explanation for why such effort was put into the creation of these objects. I envisage that they were used much as the African lukasa, the Australian tjuringa, the Native American song boards and birchbark scrolls; that is to recall vast amounts of practical and cultural information.

Nick Card's newly found carved stone ball adds to the collections of about 400 of these objects found in Scottish Neolithic sites, including five at Skara Brae. The vast majority have diameters of about seven centimetres, although a few are larger. When I held these objects, it was clear that they were the perfect size to be held in the palm of one hand and manipulated as a memory device.

Nearly half of the balls have six knobs, some decorated, some not. If the carved stone balls were to be used as memory aids, then it would be necessary to be able to identify individual knobs and follow them in sequence. Of course, they could have been coloured, which would solve the problem. Those that were highly decorated, such as the famous Towie Ball found in Aberdeenshire, would also have been easy to sequence. The decoration on the Towie Ball and many others match the motifs on other objects I believe were used as memory aids, such as Grooved Ware pottery and passage-cairn art across Britain and Ireland.

To be certain that all the balls could act as a memory aid, I needed to convince myself that it would be possible to sequence an undecorated ball with a large number of knobs. I examined carved stone balls at The Hunterian at the University of Glasgow and from the collection held at the Museum of Scotland in Edinburgh. A specific orientation and sequence for the knobs could always be determined immediately once I could examine the stone balls at close range. I have no doubt that they were used as memory aids.

Stones of Stenness

It is the standing stones on the Ness of Brodgar that provide the most dramatic monuments, attracting thousands of visitors every year. Around 3100 BCE, the Orcadians constructed a megalithic stone circle, the Stones of Stenness, on the southern end of the Ness. Of the twelve original stones, four are still standing on a circular platform. The largest is nearly six metres high. The stones, just like those at the later Ring of Brodgar henge, were brought from distant locations, despite suitable stone being available nearby. These foreign stones would have served as direct references to landscape locations. The Stones of Stenness have all the characteristics of a memory space; they are each different from their neighbours, well spaced, in the open and thus well lit, with a sequence naturally built into the structure. The Stones of Stenness were in use for several centuries, possibly much longer.

The circular platform on which the stones stand was surrounded by a bank around a ditch, seven metres wide and over two metres deep cut into bedrock. As with Stonehenge, a ditch of this depth is exactly what would be needed to ensure that the elders could perform the ceremonies no matter what the weather.

Chambered cairns

Around the same time that the Stones of Stenness were erected in the Late Neolithic, over 80 chambered cairns were constructed around Orkney, usually referred to as passage 'tombs' or 'graves'. A typical cairn, readily accessible to the visitor, is Unstan Chambered Cairn (see Plate 6.9). For the same reasons as given when discussing the 'passage graves' of Avebury, I believe the primary purpose of these structures was to be used as restricted performance sites for the initiated elders. A few of the cairns were even built on tiny uninhabited islets. As well as human remains, large numbers of a wide range of domesticated and wild animal bones were also interred. External performance areas were part of the design of most chambered tombs and all of the cairns seem to have been designed to be entered repeatedly.

As Orkney archaeologist Caroline Wickham-Jones wrote:

> The presence of human bone inside the chambers has coloured
> our interpretations of these sites. It is important to remember that
> in most cases only a very small proportion of the people who were
> in a community has ever been found in them (if indeed anything
> has survived at all). Furthermore, the human bone is nearly always
> only part of an assemblage from a tomb. Other material goods, and
> the bones of other species, are often just as abundant.[4]

Having visited a number of passage cairns, I have no doubt that they would have served wonderfully well as a dry, warm, highly restricted memory space. Featuring dry-stone walls and roofs, most are entered through a low passage lined with massive stones, taking you into a chamber which would comfortably hold a dozen or so adults. In those days, most were covered by a mound. Although the number of chambers and side cells varied they all had a similar structure. Individual communities will have built a cairn to suit their local needs.

One of the cairns, Isbister, did have a large number of human bones, although not complete skeletons. The remains of at least 342 people were found in the cells built at each end of the central chamber. The bones had been cleaned before interment, probably by leaving them out for scavengers. Isbister is well known for the 30 human skulls found within. It felt surreal when, having crawled through the low entry passage and escaped the driving winds buffeting the South Ronaldsay cliffs, I was suddenly alone in the silent chamber. Lit by modern skylights, I found myself staring at human skulls rather tastelessly displayed behind a plastic sheet and chicken wire. Human bones are used as part of ceremonies recalling oral tradition in some contemporary cultures. It may be for this reason that skulls from incomplete skeletons are found in chambered cairns.

But it was not just human bones. Huge quantities of animal bones, including fish and lamb, were also found in the 'tomb' with calf bones outside. Then there are the eagles. Isbister is better known as the 'Tomb of the Eagles' due to the bones of fourteen sea-eagles found there. However, there's a salutary lesson in the many theories about eagles being the totem of the builders. In 2006, the publication of radiocarbon dating proved that the eagles died between 2450 and 2050 BCE—the cairn was built around 3000 BCE.

In some cases, the animal bones do seem to have been a significant part of the ceremonies held within the cairns. At the Cuween Hill Chambered Cairn, I was able to experience a chamber reconstructed in its original form. Cut into the side of a hill, the roof was intact. Having climbed the hill in blustery Orkney wind, I crawled into a silent, still, warm, totally dark space. As a restricted meeting place, it was superb. On excavation, 24 dog skulls were found in Cuween Hill Cairn along with bones from about eight people, including five skulls. The dogs have been carbon dated showing they were buried at the same time as the cairn was in active use.

The 'tomb' that had the greatest impact on me was on the spectacular island of Hoy. The Dwarfie Stane is an 8.5-metre-long red sandstone block considered to be Britain's only rock-cut tomb, but there have been no human remains found (see Plate 6.10). It was empty long before archaeologists examined it. It is thought that the Stane was hollowed out about 3000 BCE. The two cells on either side of the main chamber are too small for humans yet look like beds, hence the name. After a twenty-minute walk from the road in a steep-sided valley, I was stunned, as all visitors are, by the incredible effort which must have been involved in hollowing out this hard rock with only Neolithic tools. What surprised me more was that nothing I had read about the Dwarfie Stane referred to the best way to experience it. Crawling in, I sat cross-legged and found it remarkably comfortable, with a good few centimetres between my head and the roof and a smooth, curved floor and back wall. Chanting at a low pitch for my female voice, the resonance was striking. As a restricted location for three or four people to sit and sing the knowledge, it would have been divine.

Over on the island of Westray, a superb example of prehistoric spiral carving is on display. The Westray Stone was once part of a chambered cairn found at what is now the town of Pierowall. The designs are typical of the abstract motifs of non-literate cultures and remarkably like the stones that form the facade of the famous chambered cairn Newgrange in Ireland, which will be discussed in the next chapter. Similar designs appear on a range of Neolithic objects, small and large, fixed and portable, across Britain, Ireland and parts of Western Europe. The most rational explanation is that these designs were particularly easy to make and use for memory aids, just as similar designs are used by oral cultures today.

Maeshowe

The Orcadians became more ambitious in their passage-cairn designs. Built in the middle of the second millennium BCE, Maeshowe is the most spectacular of all. One of the largest passage cairns in Europe, the labour to construct it has been estimated at over 100,000 work hours. Maeshowe was surrounded by a ditch and bank and covered by a mound 35 metres across and over seven metres high. Archaeological evidence suggests that this broad flat space acted as an external ceremonial site, contrasting with the restricted space within. Tellingly, the passage to the chamber was fitted with a blocking stone that could only be closed from the inside. Even when the blocking stone was in place, a horizontal slit above the stone allowed the sun to light up the inner chamber. This is an inexplicable design feature for a building if the primary purpose was to house the dead.

Entering Maeshowe, I had to stoop to pass through the eleven-metre-long passage, emerging into a two-metre by two-metre chamber, originally five metres high. Spectacular dry-stone walls curve into a large capstone ceiling. The corbelled roof, as it is called, is held in place by gravity and clever stonework. There is no mortar. There are three side cells built into the walls of the chamber, each with their own blocking stones. Four huge standing stones, one at each corner, are not part of the supporting structure. It is thought that these were probably standing on a pre-existing ceremonial site before Maeshowe was constructed around them in such a way as to leave them as the dominant feature of the chamber.

Maeshowe was used for timekeeping. The long passage is carefully aligned to allow the setting sun to penetrate for a few days either side of the winter solstice. This stretch of time ensures that the elders will be able to observe the effect even if the weather is poor on the actual midwinter date. It is likely that the elders at Maeshowe dictated the calendar for the whole of the Orkney Islands.

The Ring of Brodgar

Towards the end of the Neolithic, around 2500 BCE, the most prominent feature of all was constructed. Unfortunately there has been very little excavation at the Ring of Brodgar, so little is known about any features in the middle of the stone circle. What is known is that the Ring of Brodgar is very similar to the first stage of Stonehenge in its size, the shape and design of its ditch, and in the number of stones in the monument (see Plate 6.11).

The Ring of Brodgar was initially a ditch just over a hundred metres in diameter, about six metres wide and cut to a flat bottom at a depth of about three metres. It did not have a bank, but it was the ditch that mattered. Like Stonehenge, the ditch is exactly the depth needed to ensure the ceremonies could be performed in a covered environment, protected from the notorious Orkney winds and rain. Even after five millennia of erosion and fill, standing in the ditch enabled me to experience the awe of the massive stones towering above me.

However, a number of leading archaeologists had surmised that the ditch was waterlogged—the Ring of Brodgar reflecting the landscape of islands surrounded by water. If the Brodgar ditch was not used for performances, then my theory was greatly weakened.

When I discussed the topic with Dr Alison Sheridan, Principal Curator of Early Prehistory in the National Museum of Scotland, in 2010, she said that the waterlogged ditch theory is now debated. Returning to Orkney three years later, I was delighted to find that archaeologist Caroline Wickham-Jones had shown that the sea levels were in fact much lower 5000 years ago. Standing on Brodgar's rise, it is clear that the ditch would have been well above the water level. The waterlogged ditches are no longer a given.

A circle of about 60 stones was erected inside the ditch. It is estimated that about 80,000 hours of work went into constructing the ditch and then the stone circle. Twenty-seven tall, flat stones still stand or have been re-erected. Walking from stone to stone around the circle, it was clear that the spacing is such that each stone would be in focus alone, and each was distinctive in shape, size and texture. Obviously, being a circle, the stones are in a fixed sequence, and they are in a well-lit location on a rise, away from the village. It has all the features of the memory space. There is no other purpose that so beautifully justifies the work involved in erecting the Ring of Brodgar. Many archaeologists believe that much of what defines the British Neolithic such as agriculture and herding, stone axes, pottery and monuments, originated in Orkney and spread south to many locations including Stonehenge. As the dimensions of the Ring of Brodgar are very similar to those of the first stage of Stonehenge, I was reassured that the open stone circle at Stonehenge surrounded by its ditch would have also served the elders perfectly as a memory space. Archaeologists have reported significant acoustic effects for the Ring of Brodgar, suggestive of those they have proposed for Stonehenge. Similarly, the acoustic effects in the ditch must have been just as effective as those at Stonehenge.

The Ring of Brodgar is surrounded by burial mounds, but they played no part in the purpose of the original ditch and circle. They were built in the Bronze Age. By 2000 BCE, the first copper and bronze objects had been imported into Orkney from the south. New technologies mean new social structures. The Bronze Age saw the introduction of individual burials in round barrows, grave goods and signs of individual wealth. Weapons appear in the archaeological record from this time. A new style of pottery known as 'beakers' had been introduced. Farming and metalworking skills were becoming specialised. The knowledge elite were losing their power, and the resources to build knowledge sites were diminished.

No new monumental sites were built and the stone circles and passage cairns were gradually abandoned. The transition to a hierarchical farming society was over in Orkney, as in the south.

CHAPTER 7

Newgrange and the passage cairns of Ireland

▌▌▌▌▌▌▌▌▌▌▌▌▌▌▌▌▌▌▌▌▌▌▌▌▌▌▌▌▌▌▌▌▌▌▌▌▌▌

N ewgrange is extraordinary. It is also hideous. Unfortunately, it is the hideous that provides the first impression
for a visitor to Ireland's most spectacular Neolithic monument. As
you approach the massive cairn, you are confronted by a vertical,
three-metre-high, glaring quartz facade, the white stones inset
with oval granite boulders (see Plate 7.1). It is reminiscent of a
badly designed 1970s auditorium, reflecting the architectural
fashions of the decade during which the restoration took place.
Prominent Irish Neolithic archaeologists Geraldine and Matthew
Stout have described it as a 'monumental mistake'[1] and it is
considered by many archaeologists to be one of the worst recon-
structions in the world.

Newgrange is only one of the many passage cairns in County Meath; passage cairns, both massive and modest, as well as stone and timber circles and a density of Neolithic art make County Meath the obvious choice when venturing beyond Neolithic Britain. Newgrange stands in the valley of the River Boyne along with two other huge passage cairns, Knowth and Dowth. All three are thought to have been built between 3370 and 2920 BCE.[2]

Unlike the grating stone walls of Newgrange, the quartzite stones at Knowth have been laid out in front of the entrance to the mound, which fits the context in which they were found and is consistent with terraces on passage cairns elsewhere. Today, Knowth gives a faithful impression of what it may have looked like 5000 years ago.

Newgrange is a massive cairn with a megalithic passage leading to a magnificent chamber. Internally, it is very like Maeshowe, well over 600 kilometres to the north, on Orkney. Also like Maeshowe, Newgrange is aligned on the winter solstice. Extraordinarily, the cairn at Newgrange was found to be almost intact and perfectly dry, 5000 years after it was built.

The Boyne Valley passage cairns did not stand alone. Within the valley were post circles, standing stones, cursuses and henges in a constantly changing landscape. A comprehensive chronology is still evading archaeologists. Smaller cairns can be found across Ireland, the best known being the group at Loughcrew in County Meath. I was captivated by the artwork in the most spectacular of these, Cairn-T, but it is Newgrange, Knowth and Dowth that dominate any discussion of Irish Neolithic monuments.

The monumental sites were not domestic settlements. They were gathering sites, set apart in isolated positions on the margins of the settled landscape. The outer public spaces were balanced by the highly restricted chambers within the cairns. The entrances lead to low, narrow passages, the chambers only accessible to the few allowed to pass. The cairns themselves were surrounded by elaborately decorated kerbstones, with stone circles and timber circles nearby. These complexes were perfectly designed memory spaces.

County Meath passage cairns

The mound at Newgrange contains about 200,000 tonnes of loose stones, each a few centimetres across. It is nearly 80 metres in diameter, covering half a hectare in area. The front is flattened for a forecourt, so it is not completely circular. Currently over thirteen metres high, the mound would have been much higher in Neolithic times. The large level area on the top of Newgrange is 45 metres in diameter and may well have acted as a performance platform, as I suggested was the case for Silbury Hill near Avebury.

Entering Newgrange was both an exciting and worrying experience. I am not very keen on enclosed spaces but it was overwhelming to finally be in such a revered place. The inner passage and chamber are exactly as they would have been 5000 years ago. The passage is nineteen metres long and only reaches about a third of the way into the cairn. It seemed a very long way, as it is only a metre wide and half that again in height, so most visitors need to bend to pass through. The complexity of decoration on the stones increased as I approached the enclosed chamber. The largest of the capstones is four metres long, nearly two metres wide and estimated to weigh 10,000 kilograms.

The central chamber rises to a corbelled roof six metres above the floor. A dozen people could stand in it quite comfortably and would have room to sit with ease. Five-centimetre-wide grooves were cut into the stones, which were slatted on a downward slope to guide rainwater away. Even on a rainy day the floor is bone dry.

There are three smaller recesses leading off the main chamber. Some stones are completely covered in geometric motifs that form a chaotic appearance. It is hard to imagine a human designing them for aesthetic values, but such compositions would be superb as mnemonic devices. Experiments at Newgrange have indicated that the acoustics within the cairn create unusual sound effects, especially at the tone of male voices.[3] Corbelled chambers are particularly suited for reflecting and reverberating sound, enabling singers to produce dramatic sound effects which would make the experience far more memorable.

The enormous mound is surrounded by 97 kerbstones each of which has been carefully buried to give a uniform height of one metre above the ground. They are estimated to weigh between two and five tonnes each. The kerbstones are a material known as greywacke and were brought from Clogherhead, 30 kilometres to the north. This may simply have been a preferred choice of stone, but more likely makes reference to a significant landscape site from earlier times, as alternative stones were available closer to the site.

The decorations on the stones vary. Some are highly decorated while others have been left natural. Many are not yet excavated. Archaeologists are not sure if they were originally freestanding or were always fitted into the wall of the mound as they are today. In either case, elders would find the sequence of stones provided a highly effective memory space. Walking the perimeter at Newgrange, I found each stone was of such a size that they came into focus one at a time, forming a perfect memory journey of nearly 300 metres (see Plate 7.2).

At Newgrange, there is also a freestanding stone and pit circle. No purpose has been ascribed to this circle, but like all other stone and timber circles, it would have worked extremely well as a memory space. A level area extends about 25 metres in front of the cairn.

Archaeologists have estimated that thousands of people could have gathered and all been able to witness any activities at the entrance of the cairn due to the gentle slope of the forecourt. Megalithic cairns all over Ireland had public forecourts that contrasted strongly with their restricted inner passages and chambers.

The other two cairns near Newgrange show similar properties. Knowth consists of a central mound, 67 metres in diameter and 12 metres high encircled by 127 kerbstones. It contains two separate passages, the eastern passage extending into three chambers. There are eighteen smaller mounds at Knowth surrounding the primary cairn, and the whole site covers around a hectare. Nearby Dowth is about 85 metres in diameter and 15 metres high, also surrounded by kerbstones, some of which are decorated. Three stone-lined passages lead into the mound from the west and include some decorated stones. There is a small post circle at Knowth.

All three cairns are set on high points, each with a broad view of the surrounding landscape. Newgrange, in particular, is positioned high enough to see the Wicklow Mountains around a hundred kilometres to the south. Significantly, this mountain range is the source of the quartz brought to the site by Neolithic visitors and used by the twentieth-century archaeologist Michael J. O'Kelly to construct the white wall. The use of significant landscape features as memory aids for ceremonies linked to the locations is well established. Travellers were almost certainly bringing a token representation of the Wicklow Mountains to Newgrange, making reference to the knowledge base embedded in the landscape there.

Not only were many significant landscape locations visible from the cairns, the Neolithic builders incorporated unworked stone from a wide variety of locations up to 80 kilometres away in each of them. In this way, the cairns serve as a model of the wider landscape through identifiable pieces of geology; different colours and textures telling different stories. This is exactly what would be expected if the purpose of the monument was to localise the memory locations originally associated with the broader landscape. In this way, they would retain the knowledge encoded in the rituals associated with the source of the stones.

The location of Newgrange also provides an unobstructed view to the southeast, enabling observation of a ridge over which the sun rises on the winter solstice. The elders must have planned the construction carefully to ensure the huge rocks lining the passage were positioned perfectly for the solstice illumination of the back stone in the main chamber.

Like about ten per cent of the passage cairns in Ireland, Newgrange is aligned on the winter solstice. The recess at the furthest end of the chamber is illuminated by the sunrise in midwinter, the entire light show only lasting seventeen minutes from the moment the light first enters the passage and crawls towards the chamber until it has withdrawn and left the participants once again in darkness. Only on the actual day of the winter solstice does the light reach the far end of the furthest recess, although the effect is visible for a few days on either side of midwinter.

Newgrange builders added a roof-box above the entrance, a metre-wide stone box with a 60-centimetre-high aperture (see Plate 7.3). The light entering this box is then filtered through a twenty-centimetre-high gap between the first and second lintels of the passage. The ground level in the passage rises to be two metres higher than at the entrance. The roof of the passage entrance is therefore at the same height as the floor of the chamber so the light coming through the roof-box hits the floor of the furthest recess. The passage veers slightly to the right, reducing the entering light to a narrow beam. The preciseness of this feature can only be due to deliberate design. Wear marks indicate that the aperture was opened and closed often over the long time it was in use. Various stones in the roof-box were decorated, with some hidden from view.

At nearby Dowth, the passage is aligned on the midwinter sunset. With the observations at Newgrange being midwinter sunrise, the two chambers enable multiple observations to be taken within the immediate vicinity for corroboration. Over the five or six days when the effect is apparent, with observations possible at both sunrise and sunset, there is a good chance that the timekeepers for the Boyne Valley could be sure of at least one clear event whatever the weather. With Dowth and Newgrange covering the sunrise and sunset, there was no need for Knowth to be aligned with the winter solstice, and it isn't.

Neolithic art

The vast majority of the passage cairns in Ireland are in the Boyne Valley. They contain over 60 per cent of the megalithic art of Europe. There are over 600 decorated stones. All of the Boyne Valley art is abstract, none representational. All of the associated knowledge would have required training, as none would have been obvious from the design. Although Knowth contains more examples of megalithic art, it is the entrance stone to Newgrange that is the most famous. At about three metres long and over a metre high, it weighs about five tonnes. Carved large on it is the triple spiral so often used as a symbol of the Irish Neolithic.

Some of the art inside the Boyne Valley cairns was found on the back of stones, on surfaces that were hidden. It may be that these stones were just hard to see in the early stages of the monument and eventually became inaccessible. It is also possible that the stones were put in place when the knowledge encoded in their symbols was no longer current. They had ceased to serve a practical purpose so the stones had been recycled. Some of the stones were clearly decorated before being placed in the chamber as portions were covered by other stones when they were engineered into place. Others exhibit signs of reworking, designs partly obliterating earlier motifs. This is entirely consistent with the way Australian Aboriginal artists will rework the designs in rock shelters as the story is retold and adapted over time.

The elders at the passage cairns were overseeing dynamic memory spaces; historic non-literate cultures are not static, but adapt their art and knowledge to the needs of the time. The elders of the Boyne Valley would also have been constantly adapting their memory spaces over the many centuries that they were in use to reflect the changing needs of their culture.

Monuments of the dimensions of these three cairns were not achieved in a short time. At Newgrange there is evidence of layers of earth forming on the mound as various levels lay exposed for a prolonged length of time. There must have been leadership and forward planning. There must have been a serious purpose for investing so many millions of work hours into building these monuments. As there is no evidence of individual wealth or coercion during this time, it can be assumed the mounds were not for the aggrandisement of any individual. There is no sign of domestic settlement in the immediate surrounds of the cairns. Power was almost certainly earned by control of knowledge, as has been the case in small-scale non-literate cultures across the world.

The purpose of the passage cairns

Theories about the purpose of the passage monuments vary. They are almost always referred to as 'passage tombs', but sometimes as observatories or religious monuments as well.

Archaeologist Michael J. O'Kelly led the 1962–75 excavations at Newgrange. He referred to Newgrange along with Knowth and Dowth as 'the cathedrals of the megalithic religion', describing this religion as a 'cult of the dead'.[4] O'Kelly's attempt to marry the actions of non-literate cultures to behaviours in contemporary Western religions acted as a barrier to understanding these complex sites. Buildings devoted specifically to religion are not found in small-scale indigenous cultures. Spiritual beliefs are integrated with all aspects of knowledge in historical oral cultures, so there is no reason to assume it would have been otherwise in the Neolithic.

O'Kelly, like many others, also believed that the solar alignments indicated that sun worship was an integral part of the religious practices held at the tombs. The solstice alignments certainly indicate that sun-watching was important at Newgrange. We have no way of knowing whether sun worship was involved, but we can be fairly certain that the Neolithic elders would have needed to run a calendar to schedule collection of seasonal resources, planting and harvesting of crops, animal husbandry and planning for the ceremonial cycle. By exploring only the religious domain of ancient Irish lives, the interpretation of the passage cairns is superficial at best. The Boyne Valley monuments almost certainly served a wide range of domains of practical and cultural life.

Archaeologists Geraldine and Matthew Stout, leading experts on Newgrange, write that:

Interpretations come in cycles, which often reflect the cultural background of the period: feminism, Freudianism, materialism, etc. Current interpretations, therefore, have more to do with the time we live in than with the Neolithic. It is also impossible to escape the legacy of the drug culture and its attendant interest in mysticism and shamanism. The inconvenient truth is, that in the absence of the original artists, we can never hope to have more than the very vaguest concept of what they were trying to convey.[5]

I agree that, unfortunately, we can never know what they were trying to convey, the meaning of the symbols, the actual content of the ceremonies or the knowledge they transmitted. We cannot know what they believed or the laws by which they lived. What we can know is that they must have memorised their laws and their beliefs alongside the practical information in the genres on which survival depended. What we can reasonably assume is that the elders would have memorised this information using memory spaces, given they had no writing. The archaeology supports this assumption superbly.

Because these monuments are almost universally referred to as tombs, the archaeology is then interpreted in terms of death rituals and religious functions. They are assumed to be places of funerary rituals, although the evidence for this being their primary purpose is sorely lacking. There is evidence of human remains, but only a very limited number of bones have been found. The scarcity of the remains is attributed to ransacking by early treasure hunters and antiquarians, which is possible, although tomb raiders usually took more commercial material than bone fragments. The antiquarian excavations were not, however, thorough in method nor documentation, so the archaeological reports are sparse.

A number of archaeologists now question whether burial was the primary purpose of passage monuments all over the British and Irish Neolithic landscape. Some suggest that they should be viewed as 'higher order ritual centres' or 'territorial markers'.[6] Both of these roles are consistent with my argument that they are gathering places, the internal chambers being for restricted performances while the forecourts were for public ceremonies.

Only a small number of human bones have been found at Newgrange. There were no full body burials uncovered. The bones that were collected represented only five adults.

> But there had to have been many more humans buried at Newgrange. This is evident in the unprecedented number of stone basins in the chamber, used to contain the bones of the deceased. There are four in Newgrange, more than any other tomb in Ireland … Even though no human bone was found in the north-west recess, the presence of a stone basin indicates that remains would also have been placed there. Both burnt and unburnt human remains were found within the south-west recess around and beneath the basin, but most human remains were found in the north-east recess. They were badly disturbed and had become mixed with non-prehistoric animal remains.[7]

I could find nothing in the archaeological reports to indicate that bones were once contained in the stone basins. No bones were actually found in the basins and there seems to be no definitive studies of the surfaces of these basins, which would indicate whether or not human bones had been present in them. The assumption that the basin stones were to hold the dead cannot be sustained. The archaeologists acknowledge that the 'basins are not far removed in size and appearance from saddle querns, which these communities used in their daily life for grinding corn'.[8]

'Corn' in Britain and Ireland refers to all grains, not specifically to maize. I am immediately reminded of the Pueblo traditions described in Chapter 2 whereby the complex rules of planting, harvesting and selecting corn seed was encoded in mythology and performed in rituals that were enacted within the restricted space of the sacred kivas. It was through these corn rituals that the Pueblo were able to keep multiple strains of corn pure for centuries, if not thousands of years. Surely the Neolithic Irish also required methods by which they optimised agricultural processes, including the selection of the best seed for planting. They needed rituals to memorise all knowledge relating to their various grains. It is logical that this knowledge was enacted in the restricted space of the chambers at Newgrange, Knowth and Dowth, among other spaces. The resemblance of the basin stones to saddle querns is exactly what is to be expected.

One thing is certain from the finds at Newgrange and other passage tombs: only a small proportion of the Neolithic population were buried in passage cairns. They must have been the most important members of their community. As this was before the time of individual burials and valuable grave goods, it is reasonable to assume that power was in the hands of the elders who controlled the restricted knowledge and it is those elders whose bones were deposited in the passage cairns.

Circles of timber and stone

As societies changed in the Neolithic, new knowledge and ways of knowing would have been added to the repertoire. The constantly changing landscape at Newgrange is reminiscent of the story at Stonehenge. Additions included seventeen hearths near the entrance, a sign of increased public feasting. Unfortunately, dating is still not available for most of the features so an accurate chronology cannot be constructed, although the way in which one feature digs into the remains of another can give some idea of the sequence. It is known that an enclosure of posts and pits was constructed some time after the mound. A circular ditch was also added with a diameter of nearly 70 metres. Inside the circle were six arcs of large posts, which were likely carved or painted. Pits, a metre in diameter and over a metre deep, were dug a metre apart, while rows of smaller holes contained animal remains. Many of these features included what archaeologists describe as 'ritual deposits', which in this context means deliberately placed there. Such ordered structures are perfectly suited to memory locations, with the deposits making reference to the knowledge encoded in the rituals associated with that specific location.

Grooved Ware pottery was found in the post holes at Newgrange as well as at a timber circle erected near to the eastern passage at Knowth. As was seen in the previous chapters, Grooved Ware is a decorated ceramic associated with stone and timber circles and rarely found in settlement sites. It is pottery associated with the elite members of the community with the potential to encode information in the grooved designs.

At some point after the large timber circle at Newgrange had gone out of use, Neolithic builders added what is now known as the Great Stone Circle. At just over 100 metres in diameter, it was about the same size as Stonehenge in its original form. The circle of standing stones was erected around the entire cairn, the distance from the kerbstones to the stone circle varying from six metres to eighteen metres, as shown in Figure 7.1. The large stones were separated by distances averaging about eight metres, perfect for a set of memory locations.

A wide variety of stone types was used in the Great Stone Circle, coming from many landscape locations. There is debate about whether the circle was erected at the same time as the monument. Many archaeologists believe that it was up to a thousand years later, in the Bronze Age. Whether contemporary or a later construction, the presence of a stone circle with elements relating to distant landscape locations is further evidence that the purpose of the Boyne Valley monuments was primarily as a gathering place where knowledge was formally communicated.

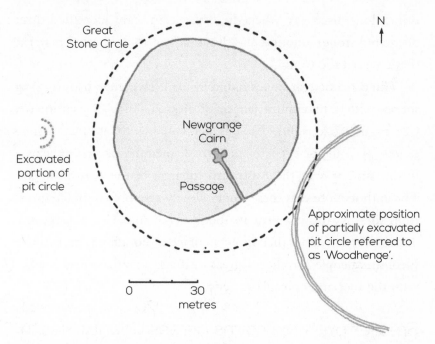

FIGURE 7.1 Diagram of Newgrange, including the Great Stone Circle. (LYNNE KELLY)

Newgrange was in use for more than a millennium. It is hard to understand the construction of circles of posts and pits and holes with deposits of animal bones, flints and artefacts, if the purpose of the monument was primarily a tomb. The archaeology makes far more sense if the passage cairns were primarily memory spaces with the bones of the elite knowledge specialists interred there.

Decorated stones

The portable decorated objects I consider so important as indicators of the presence of the knowledge specialists have also been found at Newgrange. It is likely that these objects were overlooked when excavations were less than thorough, as was so often the case until quite recently. Geraldine and Matthew Stout wrote that during the excavations at Newgrange it 'was an almost miraculous discovery when the excavation team identified three decorated stones amongst the thousands of tons of cairn material that covered the tomb'.[9]

The three flattish stones found inside Newgrange had irregular shapes with a maximum length of around 20 to 30 centimetres (see Figure 7.2, right). Each is decorated with abstract designs exactly as would be expected in portable memory devices to be used in the same way as the Australian tjuringa or the African lukasa. The authors note that these stones closely resemble portable stones from the megalithic cairns in Iberia. The similarity, I suggest, is due to purpose rather than direct contact, although it is known that Neolithic people travelled a great deal and may have had contact with the Iberian Peninsula societies.

Smaller passage cairns across County Meath

The passage cairns of Newgrange, Knowth and Dowth are all within a few kilometres of each other, in what would have been one of the richest agricultural areas in the Neolithic, with about 40 smaller passage cairns in the vicinity. There is a global pattern

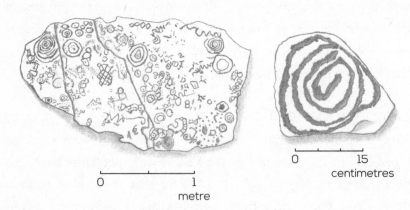

0   1
metre

0   15
centimetres

FIGURE 7.2 An impression of the decorations on one of the hidden sides of the large kerbstone 18 (left) and on one of the small stones found inside Newgrange (right). (ADAPTED FROM O'KELLY, PP. 157 AND 192, LYNNE KELLY)

of major monumental sites being surrounded by smaller versions in surrounding areas, as was seen with the stone and timber circles across the British Neolithic landscape. Societies would have needed the largest monuments for the most elite of the knowledgeable elders who served the entire region. Local elders would require smaller sites near their own villages, enabling them to teach the basics of the knowledge system and retain the information needed for daily life. Newgrange, Knowth and Dowth were the major sites serving the whole region. The smaller passage cairns would have served the local communities.

In the pouring rain, I climbed the hill up to a small cairn known simply as Cairn-T, one of many modest cairns forming the Loughcrew complex in County Meath. The rain stopped and the sun shone when I reached the peak. This tiny, wonderfully decorated megalithic passage cairn absolutely delighted me. I could imagine the way in which a small group of elders would have met in this highly restricted monument designed to permit only a few to enter at any given time.

With a diameter around 36 metres, the cairn is surrounded by kerbstones, each unique and easily distinguished from its neighbours. The narrow passage leads to a small chamber with elaborately decorated stones. Complementing the winter solstice alignments at Newgrange and Dowth, the passage at Cairn-T is aligned on the spring and autumn equinoxes, the morning sun lighting up the most heavily decorated stone at the rear of the chamber (see Plate 7.4). The combination of alignments would allow elders to maintain a more complex calendar than solstices alone. The autumn equinox would remind the smaller community of the need to prepare to travel to the major winter solstice gatherings. Elders would almost certainly have used the spring equinox to help organise planting and harvesting schedules.

Individual burials

As the Neolithic became the Iron Age, the importance of individual burial seems to have increased in Ireland as it did in Britain. The burial mounds of the later Bronze Age indicate that the power of the knowledge specialist in their apparently egalitarian society was diminishing. A hierarchical society emerged with wealthy leaders and a warrior class, but the transition was gradual. Although the massive passage cairns were no longer being built, the use of the henges and stone circles faded gradually as hillforts were built alongside them.

The picture drawn by the megalithic monuments of Ireland is one of public and restricted performance spaces associated with sequenced sets of memory locations and abstract art. It was a Neolithic complex of memory spaces writ large across the landscape.

The only other location that can even come close to the Boyne Valley in terms of quality and quantity of megalithic art is in the French region of Brittany. With around 250 decorated stones across 75 sites, most of the art can be found in passage cairns very like those of the Boyne Valley. Not surprisingly, all the other elements of memory spaces are also found there, as the next chapter will show.

CHAPTER 8

The tall stones and endless rows of Carnac

| | | | | | | | | | | | | | | | | | | | | | | | | | | | | | | | | | | | | | | | | | | | |

I was not prepared for the sheer scale of Neolithic Carnac in Brittany, a cultural region in the northwest of France. I had read the facts and figures and no photographs can do justice to an ancient landscape on such a grand scale. As Damian and I walked along the stone rows (see Plate 8.1), we had no concept of how far we would walk that day and how many thousands of standing stones we would see. We would still not see them all. We climbed the viewing tower and looked across the fields. The rows disappeared over the rises in both directions and veered out of sight. We had to remind ourselves that we were only looking at one of the sets of parallel rows of standing stones, which are the most famous aspect of this spectacular place.

After an hour of walking in the heat of the 2013 summer, we stopped at a small café to devour ice cream while we stared at standing stones by the hundred on either side of us. The rows were so close and there were relatively few people. One diversion took us to the remains of a rectangular enclosure. Nearby was a stone standing alone in the forest and towering over us. We were alone in this famous landscape, able to imagine what it might have been like 5000 years ago. The following day we sailed on the Gulf of Morbihan, in the south of Brittany, to see the most highly decorated passage cairn of all, with its small horseshoes of standing stones now submerged at full tide. Sailing on the shimmering gulf waters past the passage cairn of Gavrinis and the stones of Er Lannic was unforgettable. I loved Brittany. I loved the complexity of the monuments. I loved the way we could be almost alone with incredible megalithic structures, which are often almost totally ignored by the thousands of tourists who throng to the beaches and not to the archaeology.

The three days we stayed in nearby Vannes were not nearly enough. The medieval city on the Gulf of Morbihan provided a cacophony of impressions. The first day there we walked the narrow streets marvelling at the old buildings. We chanced upon magnificent town gardens full of people in medieval dress for a festival. They seemed unperturbed when American Western gunfighters appeared from nowhere and staged a brief shootout then disappeared again. The food surpassed anything else we had in France. And best of all, a local bus took us to Carnac and the largest array of standing stones in the world.

Brittany is on the westernmost peninsula of France with easy sea access to both Britain and Ireland. As Brittany contains such a wealth of Neolithic monuments, we could not hope to see them all in the brief time we had in France. We chose to visit the most unique and famous of the Breton sites, the stone rows at Carnac.

These rows did not stand in isolation. Like all other archaeological sites, they need to be understood in the context of other monuments that were in use at the same time and the changing landscape of the Neolithic as hunter-gatherers were slowly adapting to tending crops and raising livestock.

Brittany is considered particularly valuable to archaeologists because monuments representing the transition from hunter-gathering cultures through the Neolithic to permanent settlement can be seen in the same landscape, covering a time span of almost 3000 years. There were no individual burials with valuable grave goods in Neolithic Brittany. The leaders of the time maintained power through the control of knowledge. The monuments changed in tune with the elders' need for memory spaces.

By 4000 BCE, much of the forest was cleared and cultivation practices well established. The Breton transition to settlement and farming predated that in Britain and Ireland by hundreds of years. Many archaeologists argue that the agricultural lifestyle, including domesticated animals and cultivated plants, came to Britain and Ireland from Western Europe through Brittany. The hunter-gathering Bretons would have required information to manage the dramatic changes in food production and lifestyle. Localised memory spaces would have been essential, so they built monuments.

There is still much debate about the exact chronology of monumental forms in prehistoric Brittany but despite the varying dates given in the major references, the overall pattern is reasonably clear.[1] Current thinking places the earliest activity in Brittany around 5000 BCE. There is very little evidence of settlement, suggesting to archaeologists that the megalithic builders were still quite mobile in their lifestyle, moving from camp to camp rather than living in permanent villages. Small concave depressions, known as cup marks, are found on the rocks still in situ. These are considered one of the oldest forms of rock art and serve to mark sacred locations in the landscape. It is likely that the actual formation of the cup marks could be encoded with information in some way but there is insignificant evidence to justify this claim. What can be fairly certain is that they marked sacred locations that had knowledge associated with them, as is the pattern with non-literate cultures the world over.

Across Brittany, rocks that had been decorated with cup marks were later quarried and re-used in Neolithic monuments, such as in the capstone covering the central chamber at the Tumulus de Saint-Michel at Carnac. There is no doubt that the users of the monument would have been able to recognise the unique markings and the distinctive geology of the source.

Farming seems to have commenced around 4500 BCE. There had been no monuments. Within a few hundred years, the region was transformed into cultivated farmlands where monuments were prolific, so there can be no doubt that the purpose of the monuments was intrinsically linked with the lifestyle change. There is little doubt that Neolithic Bretons were travelling large distances to trade material goods, and so almost certainly traded agricultural knowledge and domesticated crops and stock, enabling them to establish their fields and herds rapidly. The knowledge technologies—represented by the megalithic monuments, art and performance spaces—were part of the Neolithic package. For example, there is evidence that the people of Brittany had established links with early farming communities from Central Europe, known as the Bandkeramik or Linear Pottery culture, before they started farming in Brittany.

The first standing stones are thought to have been erected in the middle of the fifth millennium BCE. The French term for standing stones, menhirs, is used by archaeologists when discussing megaliths in the French context. Many of the menhirs were decorated with representational motifs. The Bretons did not just find stones that were already free of the bedrock and stand them up, despite having plenty of such stones readily available. Significantly, they cut slabs from natural formations, including many that had already been marked with cup marks. They were clearly using stones that had a significance in their natural landscape setting and then re-using them to create their localised memory spaces.

The largest of all standing stones in Europe was the Grand Menhir Brisé erected at Locmariaquer, on the southwest coast of Brittany. When it was a single standing stone, the Grand Menhir measured 21 metres in length. It rose almost twenty metres above ground. The Grand Menhir would have towered over the tallest of the sarsens of Stonehenge, which stands a mere 6.7 metres above ground.

Archaeologist Chris Scarre wrote that:

The erection of the Grand Menhir Brisé could be considered the greatest project ever undertaken in West European prehistory. At 21 m and 300 tonnes it significantly surpasses every other megalithic block raised by these Neolithic societies. Cutting it from the bedrock and pounding it into shape would have been an enormous enterprise, but even that would have paled in significance alongside the superhuman task of dragging it the several kilometres to Locmariaquer and raising it upright.[2]

The whole enterprise is an astounding effort. It has been estimated that it would have required over 2000 people to move the Grand Menhir along level ground, using a wooden sledge and rollers. Having managed to get the monster rock in place, over 3000 people would have been needed to pull on ropes to erect the stone.[3]

When it fell, presumably some time later, the Grand Menhir broke into four pieces. It still lies as it landed, just beyond the western terminal of the Er Grah long mound. Archaeologists debate whether it fell or was pulled down. Although an earth tremor seems to be the most popular theory for the demise of the Grand Menhir at the time of writing, some menhirs seem to have been felled deliberately.

The Carnac Mounds and the Tumulus de Saint-Michel

Walking the Carnac landscape, we followed a sign to the Tumulus de Saint-Michel. Archaeologists use the term 'tumulus' for large mounds in France. We searched around for the mound while standing next to a small hill with a chapel taking up about half the summit. It took much longer than it should have done for us to realise that the hill we were walking around was the tumulus itself (see Plate 8.2). Around 4700 BCE the prehistoric people had moved around 40,000 cubic metres of material, basket load by basket load, with no metal tools and no mechanical aids to help them. The tumulus is 125 metres long, 60 metres wide and 10 metres high. It is a small hill.

Over several centuries, Neolithic monuments were built on all the prominent hilltops around the Carnac area. Seven Grand Tumulus monuments lie within a twenty-kilometre radius of Carnac, each containing small passages and chambers. At the Tumulus de Saint-Michel, the two megalithic chambers were very small. A stone circle six metres across and a range of small coffin-like stone boxes known as cists, most too small for burials, were clustered around the chambers. One, slightly larger, held animal remains, thought to be from a sheep or cow. The floor of the chambers was covered with a dust of charcoal, ash and small bone fragments, which all date from before the chambers were built. It is still debated whether the bone is human or animal. Within the chambers were bone and ivory artefacts and flint flakes. There were also pendants and beads made from a stone known as variscite, which had come from the Iberian Peninsula. The variscite, or the manufactured items, must have been carried for over 800 kilometres, although it may have passed through many hands to reach Brittany. There is no doubt that Neolithic Bretons were travelling long distances. They had to navigate. They had to survive. They needed knowledge.

The most telling finds at the Tumulus de Saint-Michel were nearly 40 polished stone axes. They had been embedded in the floor with their cutting edges facing upwards. As some of the axes were nearly 50 centimetres in length, archaeologists have concluded that they could only have been ceremonial objects. As monumental structures changed through the Neolithic, one thing remained a constant: axes were valued and exchanged as elite and restricted objects. The axe factories were situated on significant landscape features and rocky outcrops, even though there were more convenient locations to mine the necessary materials. The axes found at megalithic sites were often imported, yet the material used offered no functionality better than an axe made from local materials. However, the axes, which were widely traded, were made from stone that visibly identified the source, offering a reference to the distant landscape for those using the axe in ceremony. Axes were also a major item of the practical toolkit. Millions of axes were produced in specialist factories to be used in Brittany and the Channel Islands during the Neolithic.

Over time, the small passage cairns were covered completely, allowing no further access from the outside. However, the Bretons continued to add to the mounds. The Grand Tumulus monuments grew larger, their purpose being far more than just to cover the tiny passages.

Still in the Early Neolithic, a tradition of building low earthen mounds, known as *tertres*, became popular. Around a hundred are known, mostly from the Carnac region. Less than three metres high, they varied in length, the largest being nearly 80 metres. They were initially a rectangular or trapezoidal setting of stones, a ceremonial space, which has then been filled to become a cairn. Archaeologists are uncertain how long these spaces were in use before cairns were built over them. Cists, cairns and hearths are often found enclosed within mounds. Significantly, there is no evidence of a funerary function and no human remains have been found associated with the *tertres*.

Large mounds and small will all serve as performance spaces. The higher the mound, the more difficult it would be for those below to know what was happening on top. The Grand Tumulus monuments became more and more restricted. It was around this time that the Middle Neolithic Bretons started building passage cairns, which would have provided the most restricted performance spaces of all.

The Middle Neolithic passage cairns

The Carnac Mounds were reaching their full size as Brittany moved into what archaeologists refer to as the Middle Neolithic around 4250 to 3250 BCE. The first of what are generally called 'passage graves' or 'passage cairns' were starting to be built on hills, often replacing the earlier monuments. Archaeologists acknowledge that the purpose may have been broader than purely burial, but the constant use of the term passage graves is misleading. The number of individuals buried in the passage graves appears to have been relatively small and probably only some bones, not full bodies.

It is hard to make definitive claims as bones are not preserved well in the acid soils of Brittany, but human remains were found in similar monuments from the same era in the Paris Basin and Basin of Aquitaine. These cairns were used over many centuries, even after the building of new monuments had ceased.

The passage cairns indicate an increasingly secretive group of powerful elders was slowly emerging from a more egalitarian mobile hunter-gatherer culture. Only a small number of people could have passed through restricted passages to participate in ceremonies within the chambers. As there was no sign of individual wealth or of coercion of an underclass being forced to build the monuments, it is reasonable to assume that power was granted to the elders on the basis of their control of knowledge. They needed public and restricted memory spaces, which is exactly what they built. I am convinced that the passage cairns were primarily memory spaces.

Many of the passage monuments were built on the location of earlier monuments. Decorated portions of menhirs were re-used, while further decoration was added to stones within the passages and chambers. The motifs used were predominantly abstract when compared with the more representational form on the menhirs. They included concentric arcs, chevrons and circles, often carved before the stones were put in place. The evidence indicates that although the cairns may have been used for some burials, this was not their primary purpose. The monuments had changed to become more restricted spaces with settlement. This is a familiar pattern.

One of the most impressive passage cairns of all, Barnenez on the north coast of Brittany, incorporates eleven passages with simple chambers. It was built around a decorated menhir that had been left standing. A decorated capstone at the cairn was previously part of a much larger menhir, which would have measured about ten metres in length. The uppermost section of that stone has yet to be found. The third part of the capstone at Barnenez was used in the heavily decorated cairn known as Gavrinis, over a hundred kilometres to the south.

When Damian and I took that boat trip out on the Gulf of Morbihan, the richness of the environment was evident from the extensive oyster beds and the many vessels fishing the inlets and out to sea. Our tourist boat was surrounded by very expensive leisure craft, the sight of them skirting around the estuaries and oyster beds was delightful. A crew member pointed at a small island in the distance. At the water's edge was Er Linnac, two horseshoes of standing stones. Just above, on the rise, I could see the most famous passage cairn of all. Gavrinis is famous for its 25 elaborately carved stones. These line the passage and chamber of the cairn (see Plate 8.3). At Gavrinis, a dry-stone facade of granite blocks several metres high curves around the entrance to the passage. We could see the facade from the boat even though we were a hundred metres or so away.

The Gulf of Morbihan was an estuary system until around 6000 BCE when the sea started to rise and the gulf started to form. In 5000 BCE, the sea level was four metres below its present level. By the time Gavrinis was built, between 4200 and 3900 BCE, it would have been on a low-lying peninsula. Gavrinis and Er Lannic were not far across country from the other monuments in the area. I tried to imagine the gulf in Middle Neolithic times, before loud-speakers and the irritation of tourist boat commentaries. The sounds would have included songs, some repeated only in ceremony, but public songs sung in less formal settings as well. There would have been the sounds of daily life, of the fishermen on the gentle waters and others on shore. There would have been human chatter, birds and other natural elements.

Two stone circles were erected on what would have been a small island in Neolithic times, only a few hundred metres from Gavrinis. Two of the stones in the Er Lannic circles had images of axes, the implements so critical to daily life and to ceremony. It is likely that the southern circle was erected first, but the rapid rise in the sea level made it inaccessible at high tide, so the elders built the northern circle on higher ground. The southern circle can only be seen at low tide, while the northern circle is also partially submerged during high tide. We could see the stones easily during our boat trip, the tide being low. Cormorants were perched on many of the stones; it is likely that the Neolithic Bretons saw exactly the same sight.

The elders could not have designed and positioned monuments more perfectly to provide the public memory spaces they needed. Although there is limited access to the actual cairn at Gavrinis, a portion of the decorated passage is replicated at a museum at the megalithic necropolis of Bougon. The museums at Carnac and Vannes have casts of the carved stones from other passage cairns. Standing in front of those stones left me with no doubt that they were perfect as memory aids for telling stories. One cast in particular fascinated me. It was a stone from the allée-coudée known as Les Pierres Plates in Locmariaquer (see Plate 8.4). The term *allée-coudée* refers to a passage cairn with a bend in the passage.

I was strongly attracted to this stone because it seemed so familiar. The carvings were so very like many Australian Aboriginal designs in which the horseshoes represent seated people and the circles represent campfires or waterholes. To interpret a French Neolithic stone according to Australian designs would be highly speculative, if not ludicrous. Without the oral tradition that told the stories of the stones, we cannot have any real idea about the content of the associated knowledge and beliefs. Yet speculation is rife. This same stone is interpreted by archaeologists as representing breasts.[4]

They may well be right, but I can't see the reading as being other than guesswork. In fact, there seem to be an awful lot of breasts in Breton archaeology. There is a row of disembodied breasts on one rock in which the arcs enclosing the breasts are thought to be necklaces. I have never known necklaces to hang that way.[5]

The stone rows of Carnac

The most famous, most spectacular and most mysterious of the Morbihan monuments in Brittany are the incredible stone alignments at Carnac, shown in Plate 8.1. Walking those rows in 2013 was one of the most memorable days of my life. Although we had to travel for an hour by road from the Gulf of Morbihan to Carnac, the distance would have been a twelve-kilometre walk had we been able to go cross-country. For Neolithic people, Gavrinis, Er Lannic and the other monuments in the area around Morbihan would have all been part of the same ceremonial landscape.

A thousand or so stone row settings are known from Neolithic and Early Bronze Age Western Europe, including Britain. Only those at Carnac continue for such an extraordinary distance. The Carnac alignments extend over three kilometres. They originally included over 3000 individual standing stones in at least eleven alignments consisting of parallel rows. I walked the three main groups of alignments, Le Ménec, Kermario and Kerlescan. The rows were built of stones that ranged in height from small boulders less than a metre in height to huge stones that towered over me. The larger stones, often over four metres tall, are at the western end of the rows. Walking those rows on a beautiful summer's day was exhausting and exhilarating. Some archaeologists have suggested that other alignments may once have been part of the Carnac complex, suggesting that the rows may have originally covered over eight kilometres.

When I walked the avenue at Avebury, I was conscious of the discussion I had with my Indigenous Australian colleague Nungarrayi. I was very much aware that had I been chanting and moving in a rhythm with a song, each of the stones of the avenue would have come into my focus one at a time. I was also aware when walking the small circle at Boscawen-Un in Cornwall that each stone was clearly distinguished from its neighbour but that they were much closer together than the massive standing stones of the Avebury avenue. The interaction was different, the former involving a stationary contemplation while the latter favoured movement towards the henge. One action was studious, the other ceremonial.

It was not the shape of the arrangement, but the size and distance between stones that mattered. When I walked a single row at Carnac, stone after stone came into view too quickly to enable much to be chanted. Each stone was in its natural state and each quite distinctive in shape and texture from its neighbour. I see the Carnac rows much more as sequenced memory locations, to be used for learning rather than as processional ways.

What is critical, however, is that all settings show sequence. None of the settings consist of randomly erected stones. The natural stones vary greatly. Natural stones involve more variety, more pits and bumps and dips and crevices than dressed stones, which have been carefully smoothed. By varying the size and leaving the stones in their natural state, the Neolithic builders optimised the ability for the student to readily identify each stone as unique, to imagine links between the shapes and textures and the knowledge related to that particular stone. Straight lines of stones would suit the training of a large number of people using different parts of the many rows each. There is ample space between the rows for individual initiates to walk and stand without interfering with each other. The archaeology indicates that the rows were the result of centuries of additions rather than erected in a single event, as would be expected for a memory space evolving during the time when communities were settling and growing larger.

Archaeologist Mark Patton talks about the possibility that the erection of the stones may be part of an initiation ceremony, with the stones not used for further activity after they have been added. He draws the analogy from male initiation ceremonies on Melanesia.[6] This is an intriguing suggestion. Erecting series of stones and associating a given information set with each would be a highly memorable experience. The initiate would then be able to return to their local clan and erect stones locally along with the recitation of the knowledge acquired. This would explain why there are such long stone rows at Carnac and other major ceremonial centres, and shorter rows across Brittany and beyond. Initiates could keep coming to Carnac for higher levels of initiation, then add to their local rows on returning to their own villages. This suggestion is entirely in keeping with the ethnographic analogies on knowledge acquisition in oral cultures and with the archaeological record across Brittany, but there is insufficient evidence to do more than speculate on this process.

The rows are neither regular nor perfectly straight. It is almost impossible to find any astronomical connection in their direction. Much of the knowledge stored by indigenous cultures is not cyclic and does not depend on the seasons, especially navigation, genealogies, laws, resource rights and the properties of plants and animals that are not seasonal. Long rows of stones would work perfectly for memory training in these genres. However, the need for time-keeping for resource and ceremonial cycles would have been essential. Not surprisingly, the Carnac alignments are associated with stone circles ranging from 33 metres to 180 metres in diameter.

At the western end of Le Ménec alignment, the stone circle is still standing, while archaeologists have detected the previous existence of circles at either or both ends of all the alignments. There are also other circles standing nearby, ample for use by the elders in their timekeeping roles for their communities.

Archaeologists suggest that many different stone arrangements may have been in use concurrently, and they should be seen as complementary monument forms. Hence the very restricted passage monuments and mounds could have served the most restricted of the ceremonies. The stone rows could well have served initiate teaching, with the spaces associated with them providing public performance sites. At the upper end of several of the rows is a megalithic enclosure with stones placed close and end-to-end, providing a restricted space. All the requirements for various levels of secrecy are there in the archaeology.

Gallery and lateral entrance graves

The construction of passage cairns seems to have ceased by the end of the fourth millennium BCE. Some of the larger passage monuments were deliberately sealed. As communities had become increasingly dependent on agriculture and animal husbandry, the transition phase was coming to an end. The power associated with the elders was also coming to an end. Individual wealth was taking over from the control of knowledge as the new sign of power. The egalitarian ideals found in small-scale oral cultures would have been giving way to a more hierarchical society. In the Paris Basin, where human bones are better preserved than in Brittany's acid soils, it is at this stage that numerous individual burials appear in the archaeological record.

A new form of monument appeared in large numbers across the landscape. Known as 'gallery graves' and 'lateral entrance graves', these were less complex monuments than the passage cairns of the Middle Neolithic. The term 'graves' is appropriate given the evidence of mass burials. The gallery graves had long chambers without passages, while the lateral entrance graves had short passages from the edge into the long chamber. Art was rare and more representational than the previous period. If there were carved motifs, these were placed towards the light and not in restricted positions as in the earlier passage cairns, when the favoured location was in the dark recesses.

As the gallery graves became common, a small number of Late Neolithic cairns appeared without any chambers at all. Tending to be circular, the mounds varied from 17 to 40 metres in diameter, with heights varying from 2.5 to over 7 metres. There is no evidence of burials within the chamberless cairns. Pottery, flint, arrowheads and polished stone axes were found during excavations. Archaeologist Mark Patton wrote that 'perhaps the most remarkable feature is the presence of broken querns. The significance of these depositions is unclear, but it seems difficult to interpret them as anything other than ritual deposits.'[7]

This is an interesting comment, as the saddle querns in the Irish passage graves were used as an indication that the monuments were tombs, as discussed in the previous chapter. As rituals, the repeated performances in historic oral cultures so often encode the practical information for daily life, it is highly likely that querns were used at the monuments as part of the singing of the knowledge associated with grains and the preparation for storage and use.

These chamberless mounds could have served as performance sites. In contemporary indigenous farming cultures, the knowledge specialists are still present and perform the knowledge. They just no longer have the ultimate power and tend to serve the chiefs. Their memory spaces do not draw on the massive resources that would have been available in earlier times when power was invested in those who controlled information. I suspect the same pattern is evident in the changes in the Breton monuments over the millennia.

During the third millennium BCE, the megalithic monuments were abandoned, their entrances ritually closed. The transition was over. As with most larger indigenous farming societies, a hier-archical society would have been led by chiefs or 'Big Men' who acquired personal material wealth. The knowledge specialists would serve these new leaders, preserving key information such as geneal-ogies and land rights. The knowledge elders and their monumental performance spaces were now a thing of the past.

New exchange networks arose trading precious objects, the signatures of individual wealth and power, such as copper axes and daggers, gold jewellery and schist wrist guards. These items were ornamental rather than functional. As the power became associated with wealthy individuals, those few were buried in individual tumuli accompanied by valuable grave goods. Daggers in graves alongside these symbols of wealth only appear after the collapse of the Neolithic order.

Power invested in the elders who held the knowledge was superseded by power associated with wealth and coercion. That pattern is very familiar.

CHAPTER 9

The unparalleled architecture of Chaco Canyon

|||||||||||||||||||||||||||||||||||||||||||||||

M y logic went something like this: there is a clear pattern of memory spaces and decorated portable objects in the monuments of Western Europe and the British Isles. If all modern humans have essentially the same brain capacity and structure, if we are all the same species, then there should also be monumental memory spaces in small-scale non-literate cultures that had no contact at all with those around Britain.

On a different continent at a different time and in a totally different environment, the Ancestral Pueblo constructed some of the most remarkable architecture on the planet. When I travelled to Chaco Canyon in New Mexico, I arrived with calm intellectual interest intending to do my research and move on. I left profoundly affected by the time spent there and a sense of the presence of those now long dead. It is not something I have felt anywhere else. I was deeply moved by the incredible achievement enmeshed in the immense stone buildings. But much more than that, the ruins are set in a staggeringly beautiful desert environment, which is almost silent. At the end of fourteen kilometres of dirt road through a landscape of mesas and buttes, valleys and dramatic red cliffs, the tourists are few. My sense of awe was greatly enhanced because I could explore the ruins of these astounding buildings uninhibited by the bustle and noise that pervade most of the significant archaeological sites accessible to the general public.

Chaco Canyon is located in the New Mexican desert 240 kilometres northwest of present-day Albuquerque. There are remains of more than a dozen 'great houses', massive buildings up to four storeys high and with hundreds of rooms. Yet there is little evidence that these immense structures were residences. The question has to be asked: why would such vast buildings have been built in an isolated desert canyon?[1]

A thousand years ago, Chaco Canyon was the centre of influence of a culture spreading widely over what is now the Four Corners area, where the states of New Mexico, Arizona, Utah and Colorado meet. This culture is often referred to as the Anasazi, a Navajo word. It is now generally accepted that the people who once flourished in the canyon were the ancestors of the contemporary Pueblo people, not Navajo. Chaco is an Ancestral Puebloan site.

Hunter-gatherer tribes had populated the area from at least 5500 BCE. The first pottery appeared around 500 CE. At the same time, domesticated plants and animals were introduced into the region. The ancient culture grew corn, beans and squash, and also made elaborate coiled and twined basketry, so this time is referred to as the Basketmaker Period. From 750 CE on, large villages were built while some people continued to live in dispersed settlements. From around 900 to 1150 CE, large communities focused their attention on their ceremonial centre at Chaco Canyon. This period is known as Pueblo II, and is the focus of this chapter.

During the Pueblo II Period, wild plant and animal species were being exploited as dependence on domesticated animals and farmed crops was increasing. The old knowledge was still needed, while new information was being added constantly to enable the change in lifestyle.

After the Pueblo II era, large pueblos—the Spanish word for village or town—were built across the region and Chaco was abandoned, possibly due to severe drought. A huge population became based in the Mesa Verde region of southwestern Colorado with its spectacular cliff houses. By 1600, this area had also been abandoned and the Pueblo people migrated south, eventually to settle in the large villages identifiable as present-day Pueblo communities in New Mexico and Arizona.

Pueblo Bonito

Standing in the plaza of the largest of the ruined great houses in Chaco Canyon, Pueblo Bonito, was overwhelming. On a hot day in the perpetually dry atmosphere, the reds of the cliffs reached towards clear deep-blue sky. My guide, archaeologist Larry Baker, often left me alone to appreciate the soundless rooms and open spaces. At other times, he pointed out the various types of stonework or the wooden ceilings and structural elements, which looked as if they had only recently been placed there. The dry atmosphere means they have not decayed at all over the centuries. Using the tree rings from the wood on the ceilings and elsewhere, the building phases can be dated to the month the tree was felled a thousand years ago. As we moved from great house to great house, the canyon only proved to be more and more intriguing.

All the great houses had large central plazas, which provided open public spaces. Even with Pueblo Bonito in ruins around me, there were ample stone walls still standing for me to imagine the impact a performance must have had in this broad open space surrounded by so many storeys of superb stonework (see Plates 9.1 and 9.2). The audience would have been sitting on the surrounding roofs, much as they do in modern Pueblo villages. The circular ceremonial rooms, the kivas, are also still evident. They would have created restricted spaces with no viewing areas around them.

Archaeologists agree that there was little violence during the time of great house construction in Chaco Canyon. Despite the immense input of labour needed to build the great houses, ceremonial roads and other aspects of the Chacoan landscape, there is no sign that the labour was brought about through coercive force. There is no sign of a wealthy elite. Yet Chaco was not a village.

The rooms feature beautifully crafted sandstone masonry, however archaeologist Steve Lekson estimated that only about twenty per cent of the roofed space of the rooms in the great houses showed any sign of domestic use. These were not primarily residences. He considers the twenty or so great houses of Chaco Canyon to have been home to around a thousand members of the small and powerful elite, out of a total population in the San Juan Basin of tens of thousands.[2]

Around me, as I stood in the plaza that day, were the remains of the largest of the great houses. Pueblo Bonito was once an enormous D-shaped building, which stood at least three storeys high with over 650 rooms. Embedded within its structure were 47 kivas.

A dozen great houses were built in the broad canyon, all on a similar plan to Pueblo Bonito. Outside the canyon, smaller great houses served local communities. Archaeologists refer to them as Chacoan outliers, as it was clear the same social structure was operating there. Well over 200 great houses were built across a region of 100,000 square kilometres. Although they shared a similar design, they varied greatly, indicating a local implementation of a common theme. This is a familiar pattern. Like the British and European Neolithic monuments, the Chacoan world also consisted of major ceremonial centres with numerous small ritual centres in outlying areas.

The Ancestral Puebloan communities appear to have been egalitarian when it came to material wealth. I am convinced that power was invested in those who controlled information. That knowledge was maintained and conveyed to the elders from the many outliers by the knowledge specialists based in the great houses. In fact, one of the contemporary Pueblo language groups, the Hopi, talk about Chaco Canyon in their oral tradition. It is called 'Yupköyvi', which means 'a place where knowledge was to be shared'.[3]

There are relatively few infants in the burials when compared to domestic sites. It is only towards the end of Chaco Canyon's regional dominance that elite burials appear, and even then there are only a few. The two males found in Pueblo Bonito had been buried in rooms that were built nearly 200 years before their deaths. They were interred with thousands of pieces of turquoise.

Learning from contemporary Pueblo

The people who created the great houses at Chaco Canyon were the ancestors of today's Pueblo peoples. All cultures evolve, so we cannot simply transport contemporary Pueblo back in time and a short distance in space, and imagine Chacoan society to be the same. We can, however, gain some insight into cultural practices to act as a guide. The Pueblo moved to the Rio Grande in

New Mexico around 1600 where nineteen villages (also referred to as pueblos) were established.[4] There are twenty pueblos divided into seven language groups: Keres, Jemez, Taos, Tewa, Tiwa, Zuni and Hopi. It is the language that most strongly identifies a Pueblo affiliation. All but the Hopi are now resident in New Mexico. The Hopi Reservation in Arizona is entirely surrounded by Navajo Nation lands.

Traditionally, individual Native Americans did not accrue personal wealth. Status may be hereditary, but was also dependent on ceremonial knowledge, character, interest, skill in oratory, intelligence and the ability to memorise long, difficult chants. As with all small-scale oral cultures, access to knowledge was restricted and taught through various levels of initiation into secret societies. These secretive organisations are sometimes referred to as medicine societies, although the knowledge stored is far more complex than just that of healing. For example, timekeeping is dependent on careful recording of the movements of the sun. The Pueblo sun-watcher, consequently, is a very powerful member of each village and may be rewarded with labour for his fields and other advantages. Power is moderated by spreading the knowledge between the various societies, so no individual knows enough to be able to control the village.

Cultural and pragmatic knowledge, the sacred and profane, are interwoven in narrative form, chant, or in the visual or gestural symbols that permeate the culture. Initiates gain only a portion of the knowledge systems and then only after a long period of training, which includes formal memorisation of a large corpus of material. They learn through their involvement in performances and ceremonies in kivas, society houses and shrines. The language used is also a restricted, ritual language. If an uninitiated outsider asks for information, he or she may be deliberately given misleading responses. The laws of secrecy are maintained with the threat of severe supernatural or physical punishments to ensure there is no leakage of information.

Archaeologist William D. Lipe has worked extensively with Pueblo people. He explained to me that Pueblo society may be dependent on each of the groups using their specialised knowledge in ways that benefit the group, but there is no overall central power that can require them to share that knowledge. He sees no reason to assume that it would have been any different in Ancestral Puebloan times.

Although this process of secrecy grants power, it also stops the loss of accuracy through the so-called 'Chinese-whispers effect'. Survival depends on the accurate handling of resources, especially given there are frequent times of stress in such a harsh environment. Planting regimes, such as that of corn described in Chapter 2, cannot be chatted about casually around the campfire, or the knowledge based on centuries of experience can be rapidly corrupted to the stage of being useless.

In 2009 I went from the emptiness of Chaco to the vibrancy of contemporary Pueblo life around Albuquerque. I talked to one of the dance leaders from the Keres-speaking Acoma Pueblo. He assured me that restricted dances and chants encoding knowledge are still performed constantly by men who move to a private space at night where they are less likely to be seen or heard. He explained that they 'use language that women would not understand if they heard it anyway'. I watched Puebloan dances, listened to songs, ate the most extraordinary food and fell in love with the art. In particular, I started collecting the kachina dolls made by contemporary Pueblo artists. The 'kachina cult', described in Chapter 2, describes the pantheon of mythological characters who tell the stories that define most of the Pueblo oral tradition.

In my memory experiments, I used playing cards from two different decks to represent 130 'mythological' characters, far fewer than contemporary Pueblo culture. My 'ancestors' populate my Journey Through Time. It is very hard to explain just how powerful these 'ancestors' have become within my memory spaces. Their stories not only relay practical and historical facts, but also ethical issues that arise from the stories of these real people, some admirable, others not. I had not expected that I would so often ponder the moral implications and ethical lessons to be learnt from their lives and relate them to my own. I found that this complex of roles the mythological characters play in my life resonated with the descriptions of contemporary Pueblo when they explained kachina to me. Clearly mine is a constructed reality, theirs an inherited and lived lifestyle. It must be so much more intense than anything I can experience.

Critically, kachina perform the public ceremonies in the public plazas and restricted rituals in the confined kivas. The archaeology of Chaco Canyon shows a similar social structure to that of the more traditional of the contemporary Pueblo villages.

The Ancestral Puebloans at Chaco Canyon

With input from contemporary Pueblo leaders, archaeologists have been looking at the role of memory in interpretations of Chaco's purpose. The interpretations tend to favour religious and ritual ceremonies, while my focus is the practical knowledge and the memory methods used to maintain that knowledge. Although this understanding of the pervasive importance of memory spaces offers a radical new interpretation for the monuments of Neolithic Britain, it is more akin to a refinement of contemporary theories about Chaco Canyon.

Once archaeologists recognised that the great houses were not residences, it was assumed that they served as a redistribution centre for the San Juan Basin. Researchers now consider that to move perishable goods over great distances to be stored and then transported out again is not consistent with reason or with the archaeology. They have concluded that the great houses were most likely ritual structures with a small proportion of ritual leaders living there permanently.

I would agree with this concept, but add that these ritual leaders were the knowledge specialists and the rituals they oversaw involved, among other things, the maintenance and transmission of critical, rational, practical information. If this is so, then we should be able to see many of the signs identified in previous chapters indicating that the monumental constructions formed a memory space.

The great houses were usually located in prominent topographical locations, even if this meant being exposed to extremes of weather, which could have been avoided by building in less striking sites. The position was often deliberately set to enable lines of sight to significant landforms, which were marked with shrines and rock art. The wide canyon offered an excellent vantage point to see dramatic landmarks, such as the volcanic plugs, buttes, mountain peaks and mesas visible along the horizon, many of which still figure prominently in the oral traditions of Pueblo and Navajo people. Although it would not be valid to assume that the meanings ascribed to the landscape locations have remained static, the fact that the landscape is still used as a reference to knowledge is an indication of the role it had a thousand years ago.

Intriguingly, there were roads. The Ancestral Puebloans had cleared numerous stretches of landscape, averaging about nine metres wide, leading in and out of the canyon. The builders cleared the pathways and created staircases, causeways, ramps, grooves and mounds of earth on either side of over 300 kilometres of roads.

There is no rational reason to construct these roadways when footpaths could have been made with much less effort. There were no wheeled vehicles and no pack animals to move goods. The straight Chacoan roads climbed steep slopes when much easier, flatter routes were available nearby. The longest straight section is the 50.5-kilometre North Road, although it is not continuous; there are gaps as long as 12.5 kilometres. At times, the road splits into double and even quadruple parallel segments. The roads do not run between communities or lead to resources. These roads were simply impractical for trade or transport.

They were not impractical, however, if road segments were used as memory tracks designed to enable knowledge specialists to recall songs and stories associated with the shrines and landscape features dotted their length. Most of the Chacoan roads were short but appeared to lead towards dramatic landforms. There were small stone cairns located on pinnacles or ridge crests along the ancient routes, similar to the shrines on contemporary Pueblo pilgrimage pathways.

For contemporary Pueblo people, rituals performed at sacred sites are associated with retracing ancestral journeys. The Pueblo still recite the names of shrines along the ancient migration routes in their esoteric narratives. Puebloan religious leaders told me that pilgrimages are constantly made to the sacred mountains where community elders still spend a great deal of time performing the chants.

It is reasonable to consider the roads as processional memory tracks, much like a formalised version of the songlines or singing tracks of Australian Aboriginal cultures. Nungarrayi, my Australian Warlpiri advisor, reminded me often of the tradition of walking across a symbolic landscape in rhythm to the chants as they were being repeated. Shrines in the form of stone markers along the

Ancestral Puebloan roads would create an effective and evocative memory space.

Great houses

Archaeologists have estimated that over 200,000 work hours were required to construct one of the great houses, Chetro Ketl, yet no more than a hundred people were resident there. It required around 50 million pieces of sandstone and the wood of over 200,000 trees, which were transported from up to 80 kilometres away.[5] Why would such an immense investment of energy have been put into buildings that housed so few? The obvious answer is that the Chaco great houses served as the focus of rituals that stored, transmitted and taught the corpus of songs encoding the entire formal knowledge system of the culture. Consequently, the labour input would have been justified in the eyes of all members of the society.

Critical to the teaching of the initiates and elders from smaller communities would have been the kivas. These circular, enclosed ceremonial spaces provided the restricted space so necessary for the maintenance of knowledge systems in oral cultures. Some of the kivas at Pueblo Bonito were semi-subterranean, located in the plaza area in front of the room blocks. Others were elevated, embedded among the rectangular rooms, which is a significantly difficult achievement given that the Puebloan builders would have worked without architectural plans.

In Chapter 2, I mentioned Richard Ford's research into the corn rituals of contemporary Pueblo. Rituals conducted in contemporary kivas dictate methods by which corn varieties are kept pure and planting optimised for production in unpredictable climate conditions. Ford argued that the system of classification that guides Pueblo agriculture today is the result of methods evolved in the prehistoric times in the southwest, in Chaco times.

The kivas got larger as the period progressed. By around 1050, great kivas had been added to the plazas of most great houses. Great kivas are twice as large as other kivas, some over twenty metres in diameter and up to four metres deep. Four isolated great kivas had been constructed on the south side of the canyon, independent of any great house. I visited one of the huge isolated kivas, Casa Rinconada, and was shown the way it was designed for lively performances. A subterranean passageway led into a screened area, which would have facilitated surprise entrances at dramatic moments.

Less obvious architectural structures would also serve as a set of ordered locations to store items related to the knowledge system. Recessed niches were placed at regular intervals around the walls of the great kivas. These can be seen in Plate 9.3, the great kiva at Chetro Ketl. At about a foot square each, the niches could have held the artefacts used as a memory aid to one ceremony in the annual cycle.

The theatrical atmosphere of great kivas must have been extraordinary. Knowledge is performed; as in contemporary kivas, there would have been songs, chanting, dance and movement, all re-creating the stories of the ancestral beings.

One of the Chacoan outliers is mistakenly called 'Aztec Ruins'. The settlement was certainly the work of Ancestral Puebloans not the Aztecs. At the Aztec Ruins National Monument, I stood in the centre of the reconstructed kiva. Anything I said, even quite softly, could be heard clearly at the edges. If I stood at other locations in the circular room, the tone did not carry. On either side of that central position were floor vaults. Although it has been hypothesised that these contained corn, it is now thought that they were originally used as foot drums. Sarah Margoles, a Park Guide at the National Monument when I was there in 2009, wrote to me describing the experience of talking within the kiva:

The acoustics are amazing. I give ranger talks in the Great Kiva once, sometimes twice a day. I cannot stand in the center of the kiva because the sound echoes in my ears ... in the center, I can't hear anything but my own voice surrounding my entire head (and everything sounds so much louder in the center too).

A couple months ago, National Geographic came and videotaped pueblo dancers using the vaults in the Great Kiva as foot drums. They placed wooden planks over the vaults and stomped on the drums (3 men on each drum) in unison ... aww, the sound was amazing!

Enigmatic decorated objects

It is not only the landscape and buildings that serve the knowledge system. Elders use a large number of objects, sometimes described as 'ceremonial paraphernalia'. It is likely that a significant percentage of these aided the memory of the songs and mythology that encoded critical practical knowledge. Within the great houses, there are numerous carved and painted wooden objects, many brightly coloured, often representing birds. There are also wooden staffs, clay pipes, carved and inlaid stone and bone effigies, horns, hoops, discs, prayer sticks, lightning lattices, plume circles, a basket covered with shell and turquoise mosaics, and cylindrical vessels. In rooms within Pueblo Bonito, many cages were found; they had once held large numbers of macaws of two species, scarlet (*Ara macao*) and military (*Ara militaris*) macaws, both native to Mexico and South America. Artefacts using macaw feathers were elite objects with a very restricted distribution.

Particularly intriguing are a range of painted wooden artefacts found at Chetro Ketl.[6] The intact roof of one of the rooms within the great house ensured near perfect preservation of hundreds of apparently non-utilitarian wooden artefacts. Most of the wooden objects are flat and painted on both sides with decorations varying from simple colouration to quite complex designs. Quite a few had been mended, which indicates their importance. Some of the wooden objects represented animals, with many resembling memory aids from historically documented cultures.

Equally intriguing are the cylindrical black-on-white ceramic vessels. Usually referred to as cylinder jars, they are only found in Chaco Canyon (see Figure 9.1). The cylinder jars are on average 24 centimetres tall and 11 centimetres in diameter, with the decoration painted in a range of abstract styles. Although painted cups have been found all over the site, the cylinder jars were

FIGURE 9.1 Cylinder jar designs. (LYNNE KELLY)

almost all found in just a few rooms of great houses. Of the 210 known jars, 192 were found at Pueblo Bonito in the same rooms as other prestige items. One of those rooms contained an unusual wooden crypt incorporating one of the two elaborate burials in the canyon.

Cylinder jars were redecorated repeatedly. Touching up or decorating over existing motifs is common among oral cultures. The process of applying sacred designs and chanting the associated songs reinforces memory of the knowledge and practices. Traces of chocolate have been found in the jars, but nowhere else in the Chacoan archaeological record. As chocolate was a very rare substance at that time, these were certainly elite objects. The source, the cacao plant, comes from southern Mesoamerica, thousands of kilometres south of Chaco Canyon. Its consumption is historically linked to elite ceremonies.

In studying the markings on the cylinder jars, I could see that they were neither regular nor symmetrical. Each jar was quite different, implying that each design may reference particular stories or song cycles.

The art of a nearby culture active around the same time, the Mimbres people, offers a more salient lesson on the link between knowledge and indigenous art. Mimbres bowls are famous for their stunning decorations, which have a contemporary artistic feel despite being nearly a thousand years old (see Plate 9.4). I was introduced to Mimbres art by a curator at the Peabody Museum of Archaeology and Ethnology at Harvard University, where one of the major collections is held. I found the designs some of the most entrancing art I have encountered. Of course, for the Mimbres people, their primary purpose may well have been as a representation of stories that encoded their practical knowledge, although I am sure they appreciated the aesthetics as well.

An apparently stylised bat dominates a bowl that has been dated to about 1050–1150 CE.[7] It is now clear that the image included species-specific details of the Townsend's big-eared bat (*Corynorhinus townsendii*) such as the shape of the thumb, feet, teeth and elongated ears. The Townsend's big-eared bat is a species found in the caves used by the Mimbres for ceremonies. Was it a mnemonic for the stories in which the bat was a totem? Did it encode information about the bat itself? Many of the designs on the Mimbres bowls I studied appeared to represent stories rather than being purely decorative.

The Mimbres decorated bowls were deliberately destroyed by breaking or by smashing a hole in the base. It would require a great deal more work to claim that these beautiful bowls were primarily portable objects used to act as memory aids to the oral tradition, but the indicators are certainly there.

Buying knowledge at Chaco Canyon

Valuable material goods were brought into Chaco Canyon in huge quantities yet nothing appears to have been traded for them. There is no evidence that any material goods were being manufactured in Chaco Canyon or that there was any surplus of food. Turquoise, in great quantities, came from the Santa Fe area of New Mexico, Colorado, Arizona and Nevada. Macaws, other parrots and copper bells were brought over a thousand kilometres from Mexico. Thousands of pottery cooking vessels, wood, lithic materials and corn came from the Chuska Mountains, 75 kilometres to the west. There was shell from the Pacific, the Sea of Cortez, California, Texas and Arkansas. Stone used for flaking originated around the fringes of the San Juan Basin. Those who attended the gatherings in Chaco Canyon probably contributed material goods and labour in return for access to ceremonies, ritual and prestige. It is reasonable to assume that the knowledge traded encoded a great deal of pragmatic and scientific knowledge on which survival depended. The knowledge specialists throughout the Chacoan world would attend Chaco Canyon for the highest level of training available and then take their learning back to their great houses in the Chacoan outliers.

The training would have included astronomical knowledge, a feature of all oral cultures, but known to be particularly strong in the Puebloan tradition. The knowledge specialists in every Chacoan village would have needed to maintain a calendar. Those who attended the ceremonies at Chaco Canyon must have known when to leave home and how to navigate in order to arrive at the canyon at the correct time. There is ample evidence of advanced astronomy both in the canyon itself and in the outliers.

Puebloan sun-watchers in recent times are well known for the accuracy of their astronomical observations and their cultural power. One Hopi sun-watcher recited twenty verses during a ritual that named the rising and setting points of the sun mapped against named points along the horizon. These were linked to the agricultural cycle and ceremonial cycles. Stellar, lunar and planetary observations served to complement the solar observations. The rising and setting of Venus, for example, was used for the timing of ceremonies.

Archaeologists believe that this is the continuation of a very old tradition. The maintenance of a calendar based on solar observations along the horizon can be dated back at least a thousand years. The Ancestral Pueblo etched stellar and lunar markers into the rocks right across the Chacoan domain. They also used their architecture as part of astronomical observatories. For example, the walls in Pueblo Bonito align with light and shadow movements at the equinoxes as well as with the daily east–west passage of the sun. An oddly angled exterior window in Pueblo Bonito, as shown in Plate 9.5, aligns with the winter solstice sunrise. The rear wall of Chetro Ketl aligns precisely with the rising full moon at the minor lunar standstill, when the angle of the moon's orbit to the earth's equator reaches its minimum. This occurs halfway through the 18.6–year cycle of the major lunar standstills.

The Chacoans were aware of the lunar standstill cycle, which is an impressive astronomical feat. At the Chacoan outlier Chimney Rock, in southwest Colorado, the full moon rises dramatically between the natural twin pillars every 18.6 years (see Plate 9.6). I was overawed by the walk up the narrow ridge leading high into the mountains to the ruins of the great house, which provided an ideal location from which to observe the major lunar standstill.

At another of the outlying Chacoan great houses, now referred to as Salmon Ruins, archaeologist Larry Baker described his experience when watching the solstice sunset. He was excited to realise that the unique ceramic plaque he was standing on marked the exact position from which to observe the setting of the solstice sun as the light moved down one of the walls. Dating using tree rings in the wood at Salmon suggests that construction at the outlier may have coincided with lunar events.

The petroglyph known as 'the sun dagger' can be found at a very restricted location at the top of Fajada Butte, at the entrance to the canyon (see Plate 9.7 and Figure 9.2). The etchings indicate that Chacoans were tracking solstices, equinoxes and lunar standstills.

It wasn't only astronomical knowledge that was indicated in the rock art. There is a significant repertoire of motifs etched into rock in the American southwest, such as those at the National Petroglyph Monument near Albuquerque. These petroglyphs date from between 700 and 400 years ago and are believed by Native Americans to emphasise the continuity of tradition in the southwest.

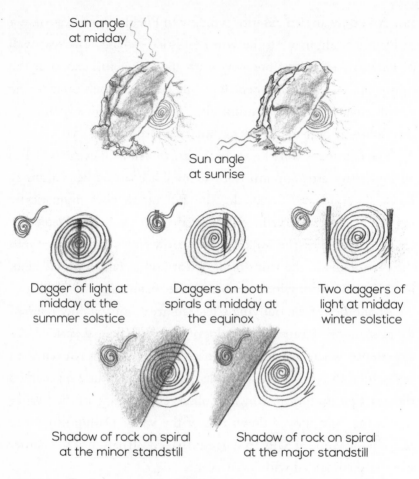

FIGURE 9.2 The 'sun dagger' light and shadows as they fall on the spirals etched into the rock on Fajada Butte. (ADAPTED FROM A RANGE OF IMAGES IN SOFAER [2008][8]. LYNNE KELLY)

I spent hours alone there one summer's day. I knew I was walking sacred knowledge paths as I wandered the trails, coming across petroglyph after petroglyph, but never with the presence of one impacting on another. They were to be viewed individually.

Among the petroglyphs in Chaco Canyon, there are representations of the humpbacked, flute-playing kachina, Kokopelli, a character who continues into contemporary Pueblo stories and art. Kokopelli is always represented playing the flute, an instrument that is used to accompany the songs of the Pueblo today as it was long ago. The wooden flutes at Chaco Canyon were decorated with designs similar to those on the cylinder jars.

Kokopelli has many roles, including that of a storyteller who conveyed information from afar with the goods he traded. But Kokopelli is primarily about procreation. Stories detail the way he tricked a beautiful village girl into having sex with him and her pleasure in the experience. An early Pueblo ethnographer, Mischa Titiev, who lived with the Hopi early last century, described a kachina dance in which six masked Kokopelli dancers entered the kiva.

Chacoan archaeology is informed by contemporary Pueblo cultures that resonate strongly with the archaeology of the canyon. Although no cultures are static, a glimpse into contemporary Puebloan life enabled me to imagine very vividly the dances, the songs and the stories that once filled the great houses with life and made Chaco Canyon the heart of the ancient Puebloan world.

The importance of the kachina and the stories they tell cannot be overestimated. It is why I treasure my small collection of modern kachina, including Kokopelli. It is why I chose the kachina as my model for ancestors in my memory experiments. I fell in love with New Mexico, with contemporary Puebloan culture and with Ancient Puebloan archaeology. I fell in love with Chaco Canyon.

CHAPTER 10

Giant drawings on the desert floor at Nasca

▌▐

The Nasca people created the most extraordinary shapes some 2000 years ago on a stark stony desert in Peru. Some are recognisable animals and plants; some are less recognisable. There is a fish with the head of a cat and a human figure standing 30 metres tall, staring from the hillside with owl-like eyes. There's an animal that is also partly a plant. There are foxes, pelicans and condors, a spider and an insect. A hummingbird hovers permanently (see Plate 10.1) while a monkey has a coiled tail nearly 70 metres across (see Plate 10.2). Half of the length of a huge bird consists of its zigzag neck. It is close to the size of the largest animal, a 285-metre-long pelican. But the vast majority of the shapes are geometric figures and straight lines. There are dozens of spirals, zigzags, triangles and trapezoids. One of the trapezoids is over 800 metres long and nearly 100 metres wide. There are well over 1000 kilometres of long straight lines. The animals, geometric shapes and straight lines are known collectively as the Nasca Lines.

All the shapes display one amazing feature: no matter how complex the glyph, the outline of the figure can be traced using a single continuous line. On the ground, this means that any shape can be walked from beginning to end without ever retracing any portion of the path. Given the care needed to ensure the images all display this feature, it is certainly no coincidence.

One of the most complex of the images is a creature that has been identified as a pelican (see Figure 10.1). It is extraordinarily intricate and yet can be traced from start to finish with a single line. The pelican was designed to be walked. It is a footpath with twists and turns in a path just wide enough for one person. As you walked around the entire intricate shape there would be people behind you, people in front, people moving parallel but no one ever crossing your path. There would be nothing to distract you from your chanting and rhythmic movements. It must have been an incredibly powerful experience.

The Nasca civilisation flourished between 200 BCE and 600 CE on a desert plateau near the present-day town of Nasca. The plateau is triangular in shape and well over 200 square kilometres in area,

FIGURE 10.1 The square pelican which, like all Nasca glyphs, can be walked without retracing steps. (LYNNE KELLY)

surrounded by the foothills of the Andes and low-lying farmlands. It is bounded by the Nasca River to the west and south and by the Ingenio River on the north. It is a desert where it almost never rains. It is, however, crisscrossed by small mountain streams or ravines, known as *quebradas*, which flow when rain falls high in the Andes. The Pan-American Highway runs right across the plateau.

Photographs of some glyphs look chaotic with shapes lying on top of others. This confusion is because we view the pampa from the air (see Figure 10.2). The Nasca people saw the shapes as paths. They continuously created the huge designs, many of the newer

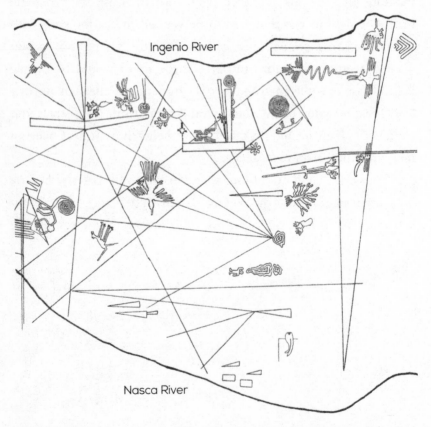

FIGURE 10.2 Overview of the portion of the plateau containing animal glyphs. (LYNNE KELLY)

PLATE 9.2 An artist's digital reconstruction of Pueblo Bonito, Chaco Canyon. (NIC CHANCELLOR)

PLATE 9.3 The great kiva at Chetro Ketl, New Mexico, showing a central hearth, post holes for roof supports, and what are thought to have been storage vats or foot drums. The regular niches around the walls are found in all great kivas. (LYNNE KELLY)

PLATE 9.4 Mimbres Bowl with depiction of Townsend's big-eared bat, c. 1050–1150 CE. Mimbres Bowl, earthenware with slip and pigments (10.8 cm x 25.7 cm). (COLLECTION OF THE FREDERICK R. WEISMAN ART MUSEUM AT THE UNIVERSITY OF MINNESOTA, MINNEAPOLIS. TRANSFER FROM THE DEPARTMENT OF ANTHROPOLOGY. 1992.22.1154)

PLATE 9.6 The natural twin peaks at Chimney Rock, a Chacoan outlier, offer a lunar standstill alignment when viewed from the great house. (LYNNE KELLY)

PLATE 9.5 One of the oddly positioned exterior windows at Pueblo Bonito; this one aligns with the winter solstice. (LYNNE KELLY)

PLATE 9.7 Fajada Butte, showing the location of the sun dagger. (LYNNE KELLY)

PLATE 10.1   The Nasca hummingbird glyph. (MATYAS REHAK)

PLATE 10.2   The Nasca monkey glyph. The spiral tail indicates a spider monkey, which is not indigenous to the area. (CHRISTIAN VINCES)

PLATE 11.1 Miniature decorated Poverty Point Objects on display in the Poverty Point Visitors' Centre. (LYNNE KELLY)

PLATE 11.2 A facsimile of the pre-Columbian Codex Zouche-Nuttall from the Mixtec culture, probably dating from the 14th century, on display in the British Museum. (LYNNE KELLY)

PLATE 11.3 *Top:* The west and north faces of the Pyramid of Kukulkan at Chichén Itzá. The serpent head at the base of the nearside balustrade of the western stairway is the one that connects with the moving shadow on the spring and autumn equinoxes. *Bottom:* The serpent head at the base of the balustrade. (RUDI HEITBAUM)

PLATE 11.5   The Bighorn Medicine Wheel in Wyoming. (US FOREST SERVICE)

PLATE 11.4 An artist's impression of Cahokia, 1100–1200 CE, with Woodhenge in the foreground. (CAHOKIA MOUNDS STATE HISTORIC SITE, PAINTING BY LLOYD K. TOWNSEND)

PLATE 11.6 The Incan khipu I examined at the Peabody Museum; it became the basis for my own khipu. (© PRESIDENT AND FELLOWS OF HARVARD COLLEGE, PEABODY MUSEUM OF ARCHAEOLOGY AND ETHNOGRAPHY, PM # 42-28-30/4532 (DIGITAL FILE # 60743280))

PLATE 12.1 The Great Ahu of Tongariki on Easter Island. (IAN ROWLAND)

PLATE 12.2 Moai on the mountainside. (IAN ROWLAND)

designs overlapping others, which may have been already centuries old when they were superseded. Like all cultures, the Nasca would have been constantly changing. They would have developed new stories to accommodate new knowledge while some of the old stories would have lost their relevance. The need for a new glyph could easily be satisfied. The elders could choose the space of an old glyph that was no longer used, the ceremony having lost its relevance. As long as the new path was clearly detectable there was no reason to erase the underlying glyph because it would be effectively invisible to those walking the newly constructed sacred path. From the ground, as the Nasca saw it, the path to take was clear. The old lines, which may have been still visible to the side, were just that—old lines.

The Nasca weren't the only Andean culture to create massive images—they are just the best known. Before them, the Paracas people created geoglyphs in the same region. They created ceremonial mounds, one at least that aligned with the winter solstice. They lived in small villages on hillsides into which they carved terraces that they irrigated and farmed. The Paracas farmed the productive zones and created their ceremonial landscape on the unproductive zone between. Many Paracas glyphs were stylised human figures, carved into the hillsides where they could be viewed from the pampa. The Nasca moved the canvas from the hillsides to the desert floor and created fewer human figures but more animals. Neither the Paracas nor the Nasca were dominated by large centralised power bases nor was there a wealthy hierarchy. Burials included grave goods of textiles and pottery but no distinction was made for gender or individual status. There is every indication that power in both the Paracas and Nasca cultures was linked to the control of knowledge.

The pattern of glyphs created by a range of cultures in the Andean region continued after the Nasca civilisation had faded from view around 600 CE. The glyphs in the Atacama Desert of Chile are far more numerous and varied in style than the Nasca Lines and cover a much larger region. They were built between 600 and 1500 CE. The Atacama glyphs frequently illustrate llama caravans with one image showing 80 animals in a row, reflecting information that would have been of critical importance to the culture for which long-distance trading and llama trains were an integral part of daily life. One of the archaeologists studying this site, Luis Briones, considers that a vital function of the images was to encode knowledge for llama caravans about the location of water, salt flats and food for the animals.[1]

But the Nasca Lines are the most famous. This is probably due to the entrepreneurial skills of a Swiss hotelier with a criminal record for theft and fraud. Erich von Däniken's bestselling 1968 book, *Chariots of the Gods*, drew the world's attention to the images etched into the pampa. Von Däniken was best known for his ideas about ancient astronauts who apparently visited the earth and influenced ancient cultures, including those that built Stonehenge, the statues of Easter Island and the Egyptian pyramids. He popularised the idea that the Nasca Lines represented alien landing strips and that the glyphs were drawn by the Nasca to attract the aliens back again. Von Däniken's writings do not stand up to even the briefest of scientific scrutiny, but that did not stop his ideas gaining him a massive following. Reading *Chariots of the Gods* as a teenager awakened my interest in the lines, but I had no idea that one day I would be writing about them myself.

The giant ground drawings were first noticed from the air in the 1930s by commercial pilots flying over the desert. Writers who prefer mysteries to reality, such as von Däniken, claimed the images could only be seen by flying over them. Explorer Jim Woodman wrote a number of books, soon after *Chariots of the Gods* was published, claiming that the Nasca must have created manned hot air balloons to view the glyphs from the air. In fact, the images on the desert floor can be seen from the top of small hills around the pampa.

Astronomy

Some researchers argue that the monument is an advanced observatory. American geographer-historian Paul Kosok noticed the sun set in perfect alignment with one of the lines he and his wife were observing at the time. From this he concluded that the pampa was a massive astronomical record. In 1941, Kosok began collaborating with Maria Reiche who took over his role of promoting the idea that the Nasca Lines were all about advanced astronomy. Born in Dresden in 1903, Reiche arrived in Peru to tutor a German consul's children in Cusco. She spoke five languages and had studied mathematics and astronomy. Reiche spent the rest of her life obsessed with her belief that the Nasca Lines formed a complex astronomical observatory demonstrating advanced levels of mathematical skill among the prehistoric Nasca. She likened each of the animal glyphs to constellations and found alignments for the lines. Reiche's 1949 book, *The Mystery on the Desert*, became a huge success. She was personally responsible for protecting the lines, using her own funds to ensure they were not destroyed by the trampling of thousands of tourists. Reiche jealously guarded her privileged position as resident expert on the lines until her death in 1998. Her theories about a giant astronomical map on the pampa are still widely accepted today, although not by archaeologists.

Archaeoastronomers Anthony Aveni and Clive Ruggles consider that some of the lines do have an astronomical alignment but that there is no evidence that the entire suite of motifs was a giant observatory. Aveni, along with archaeologist Helaine Silverman, argued that the concept that the Nasca Lines were purely about astronomy had left the people who built them out of the interpretation completely. I find their arguments very convincing and rely heavily on their detailed mapping of the lines and excavation at the ceremonial site of Cahuachi for the rest of this chapter.[2]

Observations of astronomical events are used in indigenous cultures all over the world to run the hunting, gathering, fishing, agricultural and ceremonial calendars. Contemporary indigenous Andean calendars include timing from the flowering of plants and other terrestrial events along with astronomical observations. Historical cultures in the region around Nasca use the appearance and disappearance of Pleiades, the last appearance of Orion's belt, the position of the Southern Cross, and constellations created out of the dark spaces in the Milky Way in their calendars.

Some of the Nasca Lines point in the direction of the sunrise and sunset on the days when the sun passes directly overhead. This event is well known in Andean cultures and is particularly useful as an indicator that the water from the Andes would soon appear in the canals. Not surprisingly in the parched desert, the arrival of the water is the most important event in the agricultural cycle.

Aveni and Silverman have reassessed previous evidence and argue that the Nasca Lines are more about water than astronomy. Lines are oriented to geographic landmarks, many related to the way water moves under the pampa. They liken the function of the Nasca Lines to the straight ceques of the Inca at Cusco, built a thousand years later and 350 kilometres to the northwest. As I will discuss in the next chapter, the Inca conceived their landscape in terms of imaginary straight lines called ceques, which function in a similar way to the songlines of Australian Aboriginal cultures and the pilgrimage tracks of the Native Americans. Unlike the Nasca, the Inca were documented by the Spanish chroniclers, who wrote that the ceques served partly as a guide to water rights and water rituals.

I do feel, however, that none of the archaeologists have recognised the breadth and depth of indigenous oral tradition and still place too much emphasis in a few domains—astronomy, water, religion—essential though they are. As shown in the early chapters of this book, all oral cultures maintain a broad range of practical knowledge in a huge range of genres and using a complex of memory technologies. I am certain that the performances enacted on the pampa would have told the stories of the mythological beings, and in doing so encoded a vast corpus of knowledge, including astronomy and water, calendar and agricultural rights and responsibilities, along with detailed natural history, navigation, trade agreements, marriage rights, genealogies and all the other practical information that is in encompassed in oral tradition.

Unfortunately, the oral tradition of the Nasca is no longer available for analysis. By about 600 CE, their homelands had become so dry that the culture could not survive. Around the same time, the more militaristic Wari (Huari) Empire moved into the Nasca territory. The culture that had created the extraordinary glyphs on the pampa disappeared.

Making the lines

The lines that form the animal and geometric shapes, as well as the simple straight lines, were all constructed the same way. The desert floor is covered with flat broken pieces of rock. Over the millennia, exposure to the sun and the action of bacteria has created a purplish coating known as desert varnish. To create the lines, the Nasca simply removed dark rocks from the path to expose the pale desert pampa floor beneath. The stones were then piled along the edge of the lines to emphasise the shape, and the wind ensures the continual exposure of the clay. The clay beneath the lines has been heavily compacted. The Nasca had frequently walked their sacred pathways.

Aveni and his team created lines on an unused area of pampa. They concluded that a hundred people working ten hours a day could create a figure with around 400 metres of path in about two days. The labour needed was not excessive nor the geometry complex.[3] As Aveni concluded, the lines were designed to be walked. I have no doubt that the Nasca chanted their sacred songs during a ceremonial procession; songs which told the stories encoding the knowledge—practical, rational, spiritual and ethical—on which their physical and cultural survival depended. It makes total sense that the animal glyphs represent the animals of major importance in the Nasca oral tradition, many of which will have had a practical as well as spiritual significance.

The animal glyphs

It was Patricia Jollie, from the Native American Confederated Salish and Kootenai Tribes, who first suggested that the Nasca animals might fit with my ideas; she asked me whether I had considered that the Nasca Lines might have been made by the ancestors of the Navajo. Jollie, a researcher at the Smithsonian National Museum of the American Indian in Washington, had been struck by the fact that many of the images on the Nasca Plain, the spider in particular, reminded her strongly of the mythological creatures she knew from Navajo tradition.

Until that moment, I had not considered the Nasca Lines at all. I was immediately excited by both her ideas and the realisation that the Nasca pampa might provide me with another example of monumental form and one that was completely different from those I had studied to date. We had just sat down to lunch after a morning's intensive discussion while exploring the First Nations displays at the museum. Although I could find no support for the idea that there was any link between the Navajo and the Nasca, Jollie's question resonated with something another curator in another museum had said to me only a week or so earlier: 'When I began to work here, I was shocked to see a basket from Africa that looked exactly as if it had come from the American southwest. Same shapes, same designs. Our brains are wired to like certain designs so that the same ones show up in people that have never met each other. This shows up again and again.' Susan Haskell was a curatorial assistant at the Peabody Museum of Archaeology and Ethnology at Harvard University. We'd spent three days in the bowels of the museum looking at indigenous objects, and the pattern she described had become apparent to me, too. Was the spider at Nasca another example of the same shapes and same designs? The Navajo are renowned weavers and the Spiderwoman is the mythological character who teaches them to weave. Was the link simply that the Nasca people were also superb weavers and, logically, had created a similar motif using the best-known weaver of the animal world?

The idea of the animals representing stories that formed part of the critical practical knowledge of the Nasca people continued to develop. The Andean condor reaches a wingspan of over three metres, one of the largest birds in the world. Its presence could not be ignored so it is not surprising that another of the well-known Nasca glyphs represents the bird. The stylised image on the pampa has a wingspan of about 140 metres. A similar image is also found on pottery and textiles, indicating the importance of the bird in the oral tradition. The arrival of the condor has been used by the local cultures to predict the coming of the rain on the highlands, and still is today. The Nasca people had made their home in one of the driest places on the planet. Although ten rivers descend from the Andes, most of them run dry for some of the year. There is essentially no rainfall to supplement the water collected from the rivers. The Nasca people lived in the narrow coastal strip between the highlands and the Pacific Ocean. They were totally dependent on collecting water that flowed from the Andes, 3000 metres above their coastal plain. Any help with predicting rain on the Andes would be invaluable. It is apparent that was at least one of the roles of the condor.

It is easy to imagine the way the other animals represented on the pampa, to be walked and celebrated, were also part of the knowledge system of the oral culture who created them. But the animal glyphs only occupy a small portion of the Nasca pampa, a 25-square-kilometre strip along the southern bank of the Ingenio River.

Trapezoids, squares and rectangles

Geometrical figures were created all over the pampa. There are over 200 geometrical shapes, known as geoglyphs. The most common are trapezoids, four-sided figures with only one pair of sides parallel. The trapezoids on the Nasca pampa tend to be about ten times longer than wide and taper to one end. They are cleared of stones rather than simply outlines. Archaeologists have concluded that they were probably used as plazas on which dances and songs were performed. The trapezoids could be viewed from nearby hills, but also as defined spaces from ground level. The ground around the wide trapezoids was also beaten down, even more so than the space in the middle. People had clearly gathered to observe the ceremony on the trapezoids.

On the end of the large trapezoidal geoglyphs, archaeologists have found stone platforms and small buildings with evidence of what they have identified as 'sacrifices', including textiles, guinea pigs, corn, llama bones and crayfish claws. Even more significantly, they have found the shells of the thorny oyster (*Spondylus princeps*). Although the rose-coloured mollusc is normally found around a thousand kilometres north of Nasca, El Niño rains can drive it further south. In Andean cultures, the seashell is linked to calls to the gods for rain. It is highly likely that two millennia ago, the Nasca people also linked these seashells to precious water.

Another common structure on the pampa is the spiral. These are constructed in the same form as the animals, in that they are designed to be walked in one continuous line. It is easy to imagine walking around the huge spiral from the outer edge, constantly turning, at one moment facing the coast, at another time facing the farmlands, turning to the mountains and each of the bounding rivers, the source of the precious water. You would be constantly passing other Nasca also walking the spiral, but at no time would your paths cross. In most cases, you would spiral to the centre and then, continuing on the same path, spiral out again.

Then there are the geoglyphs of mixed shapes, such as the one combining a triangle, zigzag and spiral, the whole shape designed to fit into the natural contours of the pampa. Steep cuttings from small streams border the geoglyph on either side. It has been interpreted as a needle with a ball of wool, and alternatively as a fishing rod. The thin triangle is nearly a kilometre long. From the tip, a line zigzags back across it, ending in a double spiral back at the base of the triangle. A person would cover over three kilometres walking the entire glyph.

The proliferation of abstract shapes is no surprise. In historically documented oral cultures there is also an emphasis on geometric forms because these can be encoded with level upon level of information learnt through initiation. Abstract designs also enhance the restricted nature of the knowledge taught only to those who have the right to it.

Straight lines dominate the pampa

Although the animals are the most famous of the glyphs, with the geometric shapes attracting a great deal of attention as well, most of the features etched onto the pampa are straight lines.

The straight lines form complicated networks, crisscrossing each other. From short spans to a straight twenty-kilometre length, there are well over a thousand kilometres of lines. Some are only a metre or so in width, while others are much wider. Some extend for a few metres while others continue in perfectly straight lines for long distances, the longest being twelve kilometres. Some end at landscape features, some feed into zigzags or other geoglyphs, while others end up at points of convergence known as line centres.

There are nearly 800 straight Nasca Lines attached to over 60 line centres. In European cultures, we think of the landscape being divided into rectangular plots of fields and personal properties. In Andean cultures, however, land is typically divided radially from a central point, each plot taking the form of an elongated triangle. This shape is reflected in many of the trapezoids and triangles on the pampa, hinting that the ceremonies performed on them may relate to agriculture. Responsibility for land, both agricultural and ceremonial, tends to be allocated according to kinship lines, which are also reflected in the radial pattern.

The line centres were situated on natural headlands that offered a view across the pampa. These natural hills were often topped by cairns consisting of piles of boulders. Further cairns were found on the lines and on the corners of zigzag features. Aveni's team found that the sighting of the cairns enabled them to orient themselves and navigate across the pampa.

Time and change on the pampa

The images on the pampa were not all made at the same time, nor can it be assumed they all served the same purpose. A firm chronology of the creation of the Nasca Lines is still a matter of debate, so only broad generalisations can be made.

Using changes in pottery styles, archaeologists have developed a chronology for the cultures of coastal Peru starting from about 2000 BCE. Some of the ceramics were undecorated and apparently only for domestic use. There were also stunning and colourful painted vessels that were almost certainly representations of the oral tradition. The Nasca decorated the pottery with the plants and animals that they etched into the desert surface. They also depicted harvest scenes with maize and beans. Critically, the images on the pottery are not drawn with a continuous traceable line. That form is reserved for the pampa where the images were designed to be walked.

Geometric motifs of the animals evolved from simpler forms over the millennia. Textiles provided a medium for an array of animal images. Cotton was first farmed on the coast around 2500 BCE. The dry atmosphere of the pampa means that the ancient textiles are superbly preserved despite their age. One Nasca textile measured over 2.5 by 4 metres and was painted with over a thousand people wearing costumes, dancing with gourd rattles and holding crops, staffs, war clubs and throwing sticks. There were clearly huge gatherings. It is logical to assume that the Nasca gatherings served the same multiplicity of purposes that have been seen for large ceremonies of traditional people all over the world. The gatherings would have involved trade, finding marriage partners, social enjoyment and, critically for this discussion, the performance and transmission of songs and dances that told the stories encoding all the knowledge of the culture. Living in small villages over a wide geographic domain, these gatherings would have been a focal point of Nasca life.

As the Nasca culture reached its zenith around 100 CE, a ceremonial centre was built to complement the memory space on the pampa. The precious water carried by the Nasca River passes underground for nearly fifteen kilometres and then emerges as a spring. This location provides one of the few sources of a reliable water supply all year. It was here that the Nasca built Cahuachi.

Situated on the southern bank of the Nasca River, Cahuachi was a massive ceremonial centre covering 150 hectares. The natural hills were modified to become platform mounds, which were contained by thick adobe walls. The 40 mounds grew as the rubbish from ritual feasting was added, each having an adjoining plaza. The largest mound is a step pyramid known as the Great Temple. It is over twenty metres high with a large plaza in front. People did not live at Cahuachi, they travelled there for ceremonies.

The Nasca lived in hundreds of villages and in a major residential site at Ventilla, connected by an eleven-kilometre road to Cahuachi. There were no temples or plazas in Nasca villages. Their performance sites were on the pampa and at Cahuachi. It is at Cahuachi that we find the combination of landscape and portable memory devices so familiar from historically recorded cultures. A large percentage of the pottery is heavily decorated.

Many of the straight lines on the pampa point to Cahuachi, culminating on the northern bank of the Nasca River opposite the ceremonial centre's largest pyramid. A complex of lines and trapezoids resembling those on the main pampa are still evident on a small pampa just to the south of Cahuachi.

Plazas and mounds provided public and more restricted performance spaces, but Cahuachi also boasted a highly restricted memory space known as the Room of the Posts. The room measures a little over ten by twelve metres. The adobe walls were carefully constructed and adorned with paintings of people playing panpipes and the faces of mythological beings surrounded by rays. But what distinguishes this room in particular is the presence of twelve vertical posts embedded in the floor. Three posts formed a north–south row a metre or so from the western wall. The third of these posts was the only one of the twelve that had been planed smooth. The other nine posts were arranged in the centre of the room in three lines with three posts in each. They were not structural, just freestanding posts. All but the one planed post had been left as naturally twisting limbs of a small tree indigenous to the area, the huarango.

Naturally twisting limbs would be perfect for encoding a whole range of knowledge genres. It may seem strange that natural wood would work this way, but my experiments have convinced me that any object that has form, such as twisted limbs and wood grain, can be used as a memory device. In the centre of the room was a low platform with a circular depression in the middle. This room was all about theatre.

Tellingly, the floor was clay, compacted by foot traffic. Excavations at Cahuachi show that the Room of the Posts was far less heavily used than the rest of the site. It was a memory space restricted only to the Nasca elite. When the room was abandoned it was deliberately filled with clean sand and the entrance carefully sealed with a large boulder. This is typical of the way oral cultures will destroy restricted memory devices and deactivate performance spaces when there are no suitable initiates to take over. As the Nasca culture was lost to drought and hostile takeover, they would have felt the imperative to ensure that non-initiates could not have access to the sacred room, especially those from a hostile culture.

A huge number of burials have been found at Cahuachi, although a significant proportion probably date to the post-Nasca era.

Some of the mounds contained burials but the archaeological reports are unanimous in reporting that there was no indication of personal wealth. There have been no burials found associated with the Nasca Lines and no indication that the lines relate to death rituals. There were trophy heads, as was the practice in the Andes. Richly endowed graves were known in other Andean cultures of the time, but at Cahuachi, the ceremonial centre of those who walked the Nasca Lines, there was no sign of individual wealth, no sign of individual power.

The desire to link ceremonial centres with death rituals is prevalent in archaeological writing. The health of the living depends on burying the bodies of the dead or leaving them exposed in such a way that the flesh is removed by birds or insects away from the domestic scene where they would be both odorous and distressing. What is significant is whether some bodies were buried with valuable grave goods separating them from the masses. Individual wealth is a sure sign of individual power.

For the Nasca, all the evidence indicates that power was granted to those who maintained the knowledge system. That power justified the enormous time commitment to make the lines and to construct the magnificent memory space that was Cahuachi.

CHAPTER 11

Memory spaces across the Americas

||||||||||||||||||||||||||||||||||||||||||||||

There is a lesson to be learnt about the power of memory systems from the cultures of the Americas, which has not been replicated anywhere else in the world.[1] The Inca became one of the most sophisticated indigenous cultures in the world. In their brief 300 years, they came to rule the largest pre-Columbian empire in the Americas. Emerging around 1200 CE in Peru, their domination was brief but spectacular as they conquered lands along the Andes mountain range from Ecuador to Chile. Critically for the story being told here, the Inca never developed a written script.

So how did the Inca outshine all the other major civilisations of the Americas without writing, when the Maya and Aztecs to their north were literate? The evidence is unequivocal. They used the tried-and-true combination of the sequence of landscape memory locations, along with an associated portable device, to a degree surpassing any other culture in the world. As will be described later, their major city at Cusco was conceptualised according to over 40 imagined pathways, or ceques, which supported over 300 shrines, or huacas, along their length. The huacas were memory places formally structured throughout the city of Cusco itself. Closely tuned to the ceques and huacas was the sophisticated knotted cord memory device, the khipu.

Having implemented many experiments using a landscape dotted with sacred locations, I have no doubt about the extra-ordinary efficacy of the ceques, the Inca version of songlines. I have also mimicked the Inca khipu and similarly been astonished by how effective it is as a memory device. The combination was enough to record all that was needed to run an empire.

Until now, I haven't defined exactly what I mean by writing. This is a much-debated topic, but for the sake of the argument presented in this chapter I am using the definition preferred by Mesoamerican archaeologists. Writing is a form of visually recorded speech.[2] When reading a memory device, the actual words spoken to convey the information will differ between individuals. When reading the written word, equally informed readers who speak the same language will repeat exactly the same words. It is only when there are symbols for sounds that everything we say can be written down word for word.

The Zapotec, from the south of modern-day Mexico (see Figure 11.1) had created the first writing system in the Americas with symbols for the sounds of syllables. The Maya developed their own written script around 300 BCE. Having emerged as a distinct culture over 2000 years earlier, the Maya had passed their florescence by the time the Aztecs made their brief yet dazzling appearance from around 1300 CE in Mexico. Like most of the cultures in the region, they were literate. The Aztecs only lasted

FIGURE 11.1 Map of the location of the cultures mentioned in this chapter. These cultures were not all active at the same time. Contemporary country boundaries are shown. (LYNNE KELLY)

200 years before the Spanish invaders destroyed all that they had achieved. Amazingly, despite the Spanish onslaught, there are still large Mayan communities active today.

While the Maya and their contemporaries spent millennia developing ceremonial spaces lined with pyramids, Native American cultures did exactly the same for the length of the Mississippi. Without suitable stone, they raised their performance spaces above the plazas by building earthen mounds. The Americas provide a unique insight into a huge range of indigenous cultures, from hunter-gatherers who created massive mound structures in Louisiana to farming civilisations who built huge cities such as Cahokia in the north and Cusco in the south. While the abundant supply of stone enabled the cultures of Central and South America to create the pyramids for which they are so famous, the mound-builders of North America built very similar monuments from earth to serve a similar range of purposes. While some of these mounds were used for burials and elite residences, this chapter will show that a significant proportion served as memory spaces.

In a single chapter it would be impossible to describe in depth the vast array of cultures across the Americas. I can only highlight the most spectacular.

There is a great deal of debate about when humans arrived in the Americas, but by 10,000 BCE both continents were populated by hunter-gatherer families moving in small groups. They were probably no longer nomadic, but moved between semipermanent, resource-rich sites over the annual cycle within a defined territory. By 8000 BCE, indigenous populations had started planting maize, squash and chili. There is plenty of evidence of domesticated turkeys and dogs in their small villages. As is the case across the world, settlement was associated with the building of monuments.

The hunter-gatherers of Watson Brake and Poverty Point

The day was overcast and the rain relentless. I was having lunch with a number of archaeologists, including Dr Joe Saunders from the nearby University of Louisiana at Monroe. The meals arrived and Joe started quizzing me on my theory while everyone else ate. My lunch went cold. He gave no feedback, despite my regularly asking what he thought. At the end of an hour, he offered to take me to Watson Brake, the earliest known mound site in North America.[3] I had passed the test.

Joe and I walked the site for hours in the pouring rain, brushing aside the poison ivy as we splashed through the floods. My skirt became drenched and I was constantly brushing wet hair from my face. It was one of the most wonderful days of my life. Unfortunately, I was too excited to take enough notice of the many warnings about poison ivy, with which I had no previous experience. For the next ten days, my face was red and the itching horrible. It was well worth it.

Watson Brake was a seasonally occupied site built on the floodplain of the Ouachita River in the Lower Mississippi Valley of northern Louisiana. It consisted of eleven earthen mounds connected by ridges, creating an oval nearly 270 metres across. Mound building began at Watson Brake around 3500 BCE, although the site had probably been occupied for 500 years or so before that. The tallest mound is over seven metres high, even after millennia of erosion. As we stood at the base, it was clear that I would not have been able to see what was going on at the top. From the top of the mound, this huge pile of earth would have provided a restricted performance space in an environment that lacked caves or stone, which could have offered an alternative. We walked the site following the natural order of the oval arrangement. The mounds formed a perfect sequence around the central plaza.

This monument was built by hunter-gatherers, as was the far more sophisticated Louisiana site of Poverty Point, which emerged nearly 2000 years later. Poverty Point was the centre of a hunter-gatherer culture spreading over nearly 2000 square kilometres.

It demonstrated that a large complex monument could be created by hunter-gatherers.[4] The fact that these sites were built without any sign of agriculture challenges accepted wisdom that communities needed to settle and farm in order to free up the time required to build monuments. I believe that the reverse is true: people needed to build monuments in order to preserve the knowledge system to enable them to settle.

The iconic ridges of Poverty Point (see Figure 11.2) were constructed around 1800 BCE on the banks of a small watercourse running parallel to the Lower Mississippi River in northeastern Louisiana and are barely visible today due to centuries of ploughing. It was first comprehensively mapped as recently as 1999 and only a tiny percentage has been excavated, so there is a great deal more to be learnt. As with so many of the major prehistoric archaeological sites, Poverty Point spawned many smaller imitations across its huge territory. These outliers varied greatly; they were local implementations of the major site.

Poverty Point was established in a rich environment providing ample food sources due to the proximity of the massive river and its tributaries. Critically, the monument falls in the path of what is known as the Mississippi Flyway. Nearly half of the migrating waterbirds who pass through the Americas use this path, which narrows through the Lower Mississippi River Valley. Knowledge of these birds and their behaviour would not only help provide a varied diet but also add a reliable set of indicators to run a calendar.

The Poverty Point people were dependent on the river system, which would have been difficult to navigate and subject to floods, drought and hurricanes. During my visit, I was grateful to the staff at Poverty Point, who constantly provided me with industrial-strength insect repellent. The size and density of the mosquito swarms amazed me. The original inhabitants had to deal with the

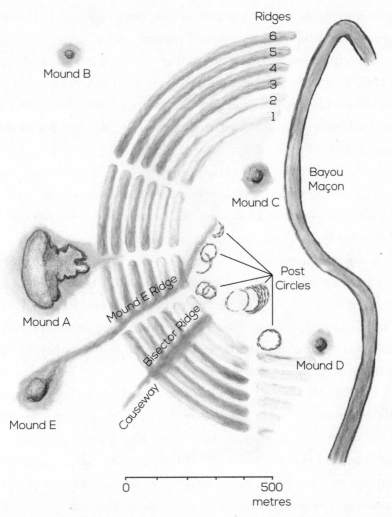

FIGURE 11.2 Plan of the Poverty Point archaeological site adapted from LiDAR data courtesy of FEMA and the State of Louisiana, and distributed by 'Atlas: The Louisiana Statewide GIS', LSU CADGIS Research Laboratory, Baton Rouge, Louisiana. Mound D was 2000 years later than the rest. (LYNNE KELLY)

challenge of pests and diseases specific to the area, along with the normal diseases and injuries that plague any human population. Knowledge of how to deal with all these aspects of their environment had to be maintained, along with knowledge of the numerous plants, astronomy, genealogies, laws, regulations, trading agreements, land management and resource rights.

Poverty Point had one huge disadvantage for a 'Stone Age' people: they had no stone, nothing bigger than tiny grains of sand. All stone had to be imported, and it was; tonnes of it from as far as 2400 kilometres away. Yet archaeologists have found no goods that were produced from that same area. Nothing seems to have been exchanged for the stone. I believe this is because it was knowledge that was being traded. To maintain a complex knowledge system requires a sophisticated memory space, and that is what was built at Poverty Point. A sequence of mounds surround the plaza. These were not burial mounds—in fact, no Poverty Point burials have ever been found. All indications are that Poverty Point was built by an egalitarian society. The consensus of opinion by Poverty Point researchers is that the monument was primarily a ceremonial site, exactly the sort of location where elders will initiate others in the formal knowledge of the culture.

I climbed the largest of the mounds, known as Mound A. After all these years it is still 22 metres high with a flat platform on top. It has an elongated shape with a ramp-like feature climbing to the summit. From the top, looking down to the plaza, I could see that this mound would have provided a superb restricted performance site in a landscape that provided neither caves nor hills and had no stone to build the flat-topped pyramids found further south in the Americas.

A unique set of six semicircular earthen rings curve round a huge open semicircular plaza nearly 400 metres in diameter. The ridges are estimated to have been originally up to three metres high and between 20 and 40 metres wide, with a total length of around twenty kilometres. There are gaps through the rings forming aisles that enabled performers and audiences to enter the plaza. Archaeologists have estimated that the earthworks required moving anything between 700,000 and one million cubic metres of soil, basketful by painstaking basketful. One of the most influential writers about Poverty Point, Jon Gibson, estimates that over seven million work hours were required to construct the site.

Hundreds of post holes have been found on the ridges. Although some researchers have speculated that these supported buildings, no evidence of such buildings has been found. It is possible that these were totem poles, offering a structured set of locations in the memory space. Nothing can be concluded without a great deal more excavation. The post holes in the plaza are far more telling.

The site archaeologist, Dr Diana Greenlee, told me about circles of post holes that had been discovered in the plaza and just been excavated. She described the post holes as 65 centimetres wide, with evidence that the posts had been sunk two metres into the ground. She suggested that the circles were renewed and rebuilt, but were unlikely to have all been present at one point in time. The layout of the circles in diameter and spacing are reminiscent of the post circles of Neolithic Britain, even though there can have been no contact between the cultures. This outcome is a natural implementation of the memory methods that work so very well in the modern human brain.

I stood in that central plaza on a hot October day, surrounded by swarms of mosquitoes kept at bay by the repellent, and tried to imagine what it would have been like as an elder in this extraordinary space. I drew on an experience of tall totem poles a few years before. The Hall of Northwest Coast Indians at the American Museum of Natural History in New York had given me a fortuitous experience which I simply couldn't have planned. Throngs of school groups and adults speaking languages from across the globe all suddenly and unexpectedly departed, leaving me alone with the extraordinary carvings. In the silence, I stood at the base of each pole, focusing on each character in turn. I had no problem imagining the way each character told their stories, the way I'd heard them described by the Haida and Tlingit people of the northwest shores of the United States and Canada. It was an overwhelmingly emotional experience. That was something I had not expected.

I can't create a full-sized totem pole but, as I have explained, I have used a post on my verandah to experience the way the stories about a sequence of characters could encode practical information. In the cultures of the Northwest Coast, totem poles were not religious objects. They served to encode myths and legends as well as to commemorate important events, which then became part of tribal history. My experiment convinced me that even fairly simple painted and carved poles work as effective memory devices. The totem poles of indigenous cultures would be hugely effective.

With sequences of mounds and ridges, along with posts on the ridges and in circles in the plaza, Poverty Point was a perfect, yet uniquely designed, memory space.

Enthusiastic as I was about all the post holes, it was in the visitors' centre and laboratory that I found something even more exciting. In the display cases were scores of decorated objects, some only a centimetre or so in diameter. Some of these objects were human figurines while others represented animals, in particular the fat-bellied owl, which is often used as an icon for the site. There were cubes, discs, ovals, spheres, cylinders, cones and triangles, as well as a crescent, a tetrahedron and a small cup. They had no perforations and so were not beads or other objects to be worn. Flat polished stone objects were incised with the sort of abstract designs I was used to seeing on Australian Aboriginal objects that I knew were used as memory devices. Some of these objects, referred to at

Poverty Point as gorgets, had clearly been carefully repaired. The objects were highly valued. Best of all were the miniature versions of the decorated clay balls known as Poverty Point Objects or PPOs (see Plate 11.1).

At Poverty Point, clay balls dominate the archaeological record. Archaeologists estimate that many millions of these balls were made. Most take one of six shapes: cylindrical grooved, cross-grooved, melon-shaped, melon-shaped with end grooves, biconical-grooved and biconical plain. There are dozens of less common forms.

Most writers about Poverty Point refer to these clay balls as cooking balls, arguing that there may have been some kind of subtle effect on cooking due to the shape of a clay ball. Experiments backing this idea are minimal at best. I can accept that plain cooking balls would work as heat stones and that decorated ones may have been re-used for this purpose once they were no longer needed. I don't think that Poverty Point people carefully shaped their clay balls to enhance cooking.

I have discussed clay cooking balls with Indigenous Australians and archaeologists working on Aboriginal sites where thousands of clay cooking balls have been identified. These balls are all no more than a lump of clay made vaguely spherical and thrown into the fire. I would be surprised if over tens of thousands of years, not one of the hundreds of different Australian language groups had discovered that carefully shaping clay balls refines cooking. I discussed the cooking theory with American archaeologist Robert Connolly who said that he had no doubt the Poverty Point Objects served some function other than cooking, although plain balls may have been used in this way. He commented that the cooking ball theory is questionable because the decorated objects vary so much in size. The smallest would be of no use for cooking.

I knew from studying the divination systems of the West African Yoruba and the timekeeping of the Highland Maya that groups of objects, in those cases cowrie shells and seeds, could be used as a mnemonic teaching system for a hugely complex oral tradition. At Poverty Point, combinations of shaped clay objects could serve exactly the same purpose. Given the readily available clay and the rapidity with which these objects can be made, there would have been no purpose in carrying them. They could just make the shapes wherever they sat and then work with the combinations.

This sounds like a difficult system. As has been described in Chapter 2, the Yoruba toss their sixteen cowries or palm nuts and respond to the number that land face-up and the Highland Maya create patterns in seeds, to maintain their complex calendar and associated knowledge. Given how thoroughly both the Yoruba and Maya practitioners have explained their systems to anthropologists, I was loath to doubt the efficacy. The Poverty Point Objects are larger and fragile, with six specific shapes providing over 80 per cent of the objects. This would allow them to use a series of permutations and combinations. As mentioned in Chapter 3, I am using six objects in various combinations to represent the pantheon of gods from Greek and Roman mythology. The more I work with my six objects, the more convinced I am of how effective the system would be.

It is logical to think that the Poverty Point elders used the basic set of six objects for the lower levels of initiation, and the rarer shapes were reserved to add further layers for the very highest of their elite knowledge keepers. Secrecy is retained in the knowledge of the verses associated with the combinations, not in the objects themselves.

The archaeology of the Poverty Point monuments demonstrates that essentially egalitarian hunter-gatherers attained levels of organisation and integration once only attributed to advanced farming cultures. Hunter-gatherer people may be less complex in terms of their hierarchies, cities and politics; it should never be assumed that they are less complex intellectually.

Memory spaces grow more complex

The ethnographic record is consistent the world over: hunter-gatherers use the broad landscape to structure their knowledge while some, such as at Poverty Point and the Göbekli Tepe site described in Chapter 4, used monuments as well. To settle, they need to localise their memory spaces, which is exactly what they did.

A thousand years after Watson Brake, the earliest city in the Americas was being built. Around 2600 BCE a city designed around pyramids emerged about twenty kilometres inland in the Peruvian desert. The people of the Caral-Supe civilisation had already settled and were farming squash, beans, nuts and cotton using sophisticated irrigation systems. In the city they made nets from cotton, which they traded for fish with the coastal fishermen. Caral was part of an extensive trading network.

At Caral, there was no sign of writing, ceramics or metalwork, yet a complex society emerged and created one of the earliest ceremonial centres, with a huge plaza surrounded by six large platform mounds. The largest of the mounds was around twenty metres high and had a base measuring approximately 140 by 150 metres. There were three sunken plazas among the courtyards, stairs and rooms. There is no sign of warfare, defensive structures or weapons, and no signs that the population was coerced to construct the public monuments. The site offers all the performance places needed for a non-literate culture to memorise and teach both public and restricted knowledge. To date, eighteen other sites nearby have been found with public architecture reflecting that found at Caral. The pattern is the same as seen in the British Neolithic and the American Ancestral Pueblo sites. Large central memory spaces were replicated on a smaller scale in outliers. Elders from outliers would have come to the major site, in this case Caral, to exchange knowledge and take it back to their local communities. It is at Caral that the earliest known khipu was found, the knotted cord memory device so critical to the Inca dominance throughout the Andes nearly 3000 years later.

For the next 4000 years, various civilisations in South America would continue to expand on the theme of platform mounds and plazas, but meanwhile in Mexico, the most long-lived of all the cultures was emerging.

The Maya can be dated back nearly 5000 years. Current thinking is that the Maya gradually spent more and more time in a number of seasonal locations. From about 1800 BCE, it is thought that they started living in villages all year. Non-literate for over 2000 years, the Maya are one of the few cultures in the world to develop writing and therefore cross what is known as the 'orality/ literacy divide' around 300 BCE. Initially, writing was used to record names and trade figures. It would only erode the dominant role of the oral tradition when literacy started being used to recall the genres of information that had traditionally been stored in memory.

The Maya can be imagined as loosely associated groups of people speaking related languages but mutually unintelligible dialects. The lowlands formed the major part of their territory, including the Yucatan Peninsula of modern Mexico. As the rainfall is low and there are very few rivers feeding the Mayan lowland, from very early times they excavated and constructed thousands of under-ground cisterns. The lowlands were also affected by series of long droughts often lasting years. Many archaeologists believe that the collapse of this civilisation from about 820 CE was due to a severe drought.

The theme of this book has been very much that of the way knowledge is stored in oral cultures. The need for memory spaces disappears when writing replaces the mnemonic technologies used. Mesoamerica is one of the few places in the world where writing was developed independently. Mesoamerica is a cultural region extending from central Mexico to northern Costa Rica encompassing Belize, Guatemala, El Salvador, Honduras and Nicaragua. Increasing city populations, the emergence of specialist experts and the introduction of writing would have eroded the ability of the elders to control information. The elder who could memorise a thousand songs and all the knowledge of the culture was now long gone. The archaeology of these cities provides only glimpses of the monumental structures and portable memory devices that were once the domain of the knowledge keepers.

Oral tradition is malleable. It is not written down and can be constantly adapted to the social and political needs of the time. Across Mesoamerica, hieroglyphic representation of information started to evolve and provide a permanent record. For the first time in the Americas, history, beliefs, genealogies and mythology were cast in stone.

One of the first cultures known to use hieroglyphs was the Olmec, who greatly influenced the Maya with whom they had significant contact. The Olmec emerged in southwestern Mexico as a distinct culture sometime before 1400 BCE and spread widely across Mexico. Along with the hieroglyphs, it is believed that the Olmec developed the long count calendar, which became widely used across Mesoamerica and is best known from the Maya. The date corresponds to the number of days that have passed since a mythological origin, which has been calculated to be 13 August 3114 BCE in the Gregorian calendar.

The Olmec civilisation lasted about 1000 years and is distinguished by the colossal heads that they carved from stone. Their cities were centred on public plazas surrounded by mounds and platforms, some of which served as public and restricted performance sites. Over time the Olmec constructed ever more complex ceremonial centres until at San Lorenzo they created the first 'urban capital'. Here the largest of the colossal stone heads weighs about 28 metric tons and is nearly three metres high. Stone sculptures, figurines and pottery all include the sort of images that would be expected when acting as a memory aid to the knowledge encoded in oral tradition: humans, cats, birds, crocodiles, supernatural creatures and a multitude of abstract designs. These ideas were replicated at smaller Olmec sites.

After 900 BCE, the influence of San Lorenzo had declined and another Olmec site, La Venta, gained prominence and dominated for a further 800 years. It consisted of various groups of mounds, platforms and plazas, some public and some with restricted access. Four colossal heads were placed in prominent positions. Each head is different, although conforming to a distinctly Olmec style. Dating indicates that these heads were carved hundreds of years after those at San Lorenzo. This was a continuous culture.

The Great Pyramid, one of the earliest pyramids known in Mesoamerica, was built quite late into the life of La Venta. The pyramid was a rectangular mound with stepped sides and inset corners. It has never been excavated. In the ceremonial centre of the city, huge basalt slabs, a few metres high and around four metres wide, were elaborately carved with abstract and representational designs surrounding a sculpted figure crawling from beneath. Usually referred to as 'altars', there is no indication that they were used for sacrifice or worship. One of the carved stone monuments at La Venta is considered to be the earliest representation of one of the most widespread mythological characters in Mesoamerica, the feathered serpent. He appears in various incarnations across a range of cultures, including the Maya, but he is best known as the Aztec god, Quetzalcóatl.

The Olmec ceremonial centres would have been far more than memory spaces, although it is still highly likely that elements of the knowledge system would have been performed for a largely illiterate community, as was the case in ancient Greece and Rome long after writing had become commonplace.

Around the same time as La Venta was dominating the Olmec culture, the first signs of what would become the Inca Empire were appearing in Peru. There is no sign of writing; this was still a non-literate culture. Chavín de Huántar was a city constructed by the Chavín culture. It was located north of modern-day Lima on the slopes of the Andes Mountains over 3000 metres above sea level. The agricultural economy was supplemented by trade between the coast and the jungle carried by llama trains. At Chavín de Huántar there is evidence of burials with valuable grave goods, so the egalitarian structure of small-scale oral cultures had dissolved. Public performance spaces were provided in a U-shaped plaza with a sunken circular court in the centre. A massive flat-topped pyramid with lower platforms surrounding it provided a further array of spaces, with highly restricted spaces available inside buildings referred to as 'temples'. Along narrow corridors, an extensive network of underground galleries was found in small rectangular alcoves of artworks. Extraordinary acoustic effects have been produced when researchers played the Strombus shell trumpets found at the site.[5] Relief carvings of animals, such as jaguars, eagles, snakes and caiman, were found on stone monuments. Some were depicted with human features as is typical of mythology the world over. Three-dimensional heads stood out from the walls of the temples. Stelae were covered in complex designs, much of which was abstract. Pottery, shells and textiles were found decorated in the distinctive Chavín style. There is an abundance of possible memory spaces.

By 1000 BCE the Chavín were pre-empting the non-literate Inca in South America, and the Olmec were influencing the Maya on their way to eminence with hieroglyphics and the long count calendar. Plazas, mounds, pyramids and ceremonial buildings were defining memory spaces across the two continents. In North America, the mound-builders were in the transition to agricultural communities. One such culture was the Adena in what is known as the Early Woodland Period. Their territory surrounded the Ohio Valley from which they traded over great distances. Some of their mounds were for burials while others were ceremonial sites. Along with the monuments, the Adena also used small stone tablets as portable devices; these greatly resemble the memory aids known from contemporary cultures. The tablets were perfect to hold in one hand and featured sophisticated artwork of animals and geometric designs.

And so the pattern continued as the transition to cities and wealthy powerful rulers became more common. Major resources were no longer devoted to building monuments that served primarily as memory spaces. Cities serving the rulers and their gods evolved into complex political arenas, but within the cities there were still memory spaces. The Mesoamericans had yet to develop a written script.

By 800 BCE construction had started on the huge Mayan site of El Pilar on the border between modern-day Belize and Guatemala. Well over twenty plazas have been found surrounded by pyramids, ball courts, underground tunnels, stairways and elite residences. Around 600 BCE, the Maya used a unique grid system to lay out the city of Nixtun-Ch'ich' in Petén in Guatemala. Flat-top pyramids almost 30 metres tall lined the main ceremonial route. The residential area was also designed on the grid. The city was entirely oriented almost directly east, enabling the time-keepers to observe the sun's movement with ease. Astronomical alignments, not surprisingly, have been found throughout the Mayan world. Around the same time, the Mayan settlement at El Mirador in Guatemala was established. By 200 BCE the population had climbed to over 100,000 people. One of the largest pyramids in the world by volume, La Danta, was about 70 metres tall and filled with nearly three million cubic metres of soil. It was not a burial site; pyramids were still being constructed with massive platforms for performance.

Writing represents sound in Mesoamerica

By 500 BCE the Olmec culture based on the Gulf of Mexico had declined. To the south, on the Pacific Ocean coast, a new civil-isation reached its peak. The Zapotec was the first Mesoamerican culture to introduce symbols representing the sound of syllables. The importance of this innovation in the evolution of writing cannot be overestimated. Symbols initially represented objects and ideas. It is only when signs for sounds are introduced that the entire repertoire of human speech can then be written down.

The major city of the Zapotec was Monte Alban, located about 200 kilometres south of modern-day Mexico City. Archaeolo-gists have estimated the population was over 5000 people by about 300 BCE. The hieroglyphs carved into many stone slabs told the stories of powerful leaders and their territorial warfare. Around the massive main plaza, monumental staircases lead to large platforms at either end with mounds and smaller platforms along the sides, some supporting temples and elite residences. Many of these are believed to be ceremonial. It is likely that a great deal of practical knowledge was still being maintained through the medium of mythology and conveyed through performances on the many platforms found on the site. But it is also likely that much of the ceremonial content played out on the platforms was now more related to religion and offerings to gods.

The Zapotec continued to be hugely influential in the region for a thousand years. Even after the decline of their culture, Zapotec artisans settled in the Aztec capital of Tenochtitlan. The different cultures across Mesoamerica were trading not only material goods but also knowledge technologies, including writing. Archaeologists have decoded some of the Zapotec script, which indicates that the writing provided information on the calendar and placenames of cities ruled or conquered. The Zapotec innovation was later adopted and enhanced by the Maya and Aztec, among others in the region.

The Maya were never a single people but a network of related city-states. Along with their stunning architectural achievements, the Maya are also famous for developing a hieroglyphic script around 300 BCE. The Mayan script is known as a logosyllabic system, that is, the glyphs were symbols that could represent either a word or a syllable. Numbers were written using dots and bars, a vigesimal system based on twenty, not our familiar decimal system based on ten.

The Maya developed the most advanced script in Mesoamerica. They could write everything that they could say. That doesn't mean that they wrote everything they knew. Even today, as will be described below, the Highland Maya retain their calendars in the original oral form.

I find the hieroglyphs of the Mesoamerican cultures stunning artistically, more so than any other writing system. I often wonder how much the aesthetics impacted on the design of the symbols in a way that cannot be seen in the Roman script. Although the script appears on pottery and stone monuments, it is in the folded barkcloth books known as codices that the skill reached its stunning apex. It is believed that thousands of Mayan codices were written by scribes, a role not unlike the scribes in the monasteries of medieval Europe. The scribes were the knowledge keepers of their time. Subservient to the leaders, they were still important people in their culture, but no longer earned the power that the control of information had afforded the elders of simpler, non-literate times.

One of the great tragedies of history is that Spanish Bishop Diego de Landa ordered the destruction of large numbers of exquisite Mayan works, including the codices. His goal was to extinguish the ancient ways and convert the Maya to Christianity. The Spanish destroyed all but four Mayan codices. Surviving Mayan texts were either the few hidden codices or the hieroglyphs found on pottery, painted on walls, molded in plaster or carved in wood or stone. Most have been found in tombs or sites that were protected by ignorance; they had already been abandoned before the Spanish arrived.

Codices from other Mesoamerican cultures did survive, some of the most famous being the pictographic histories and genealogies of the Mixtec culture created in folded books made of deerskin. The Codex Zouche-Nuttall, for example (see Plate 11.2), tells the epic story of Lord Eight Deer, one of the most successful leaders of the Mixtec people.

Genealogies were also painstakingly recorded in Mayan inscriptions. Around the world, genealogies have been maintained by every non-literate culture I have explored. Extensive genealogies are still held by the West African *griot*, whose job is to sing the information. As will be discussed more fully in the next chapter,

Pacific cultures use their genealogies along with the landscape as a way to structure the knowledge system.

The Maya recorded their dynasties in hieroglyphs. Historians have now decoded a very long sequence of the ruling dynasty of the Mayan city of Palenque in southern Mexico. So extensive is the iconography and text at this site that it has been a primary resource for decoding the Mayan script. Although Palenque was probably established around 200 BCE, it is the inscriptions from centuries later that detail leaders and history, rivalry with neighbours, mythology and ritual practice.

With literacy, the lowland Maya recorded the histories of their ever more impressive cities filled with public buildings, platforms and plazas and decorated with murals and friezes depicting animals and geometric shapes along with human-like figures. The Great Pyramid of Cholula is the largest pyramid by volume known in the world, at over 4.45 million cubic metres. Started in around 300 BCE, with constant additions over the following 500 years, the pyramid grew to a height of 66 metres. Archaeologists have excavated around eight kilometres of tunnels within the pyramid. A codex from the Cholula region of Mexico talks about an Olmec-Xicalanca lord who resided at the Great Pyramid. Public memory was now recorded in writing.

It is impossible to mention all the extraordinary sites in Meso-america but it is worthwhile to note some of the most spectacular, and the remnants of the memory spaces that may well have still served their ancient purpose as writing slowly gained dominance. That transition did not happen quickly.

The massive site of Teotihuacán in Central Mexico had once been the home of people from various cultures, including the Zapotec, Mixtec and Maya, all living and working alongside the indigenous Teotihuacáno. Despite reaching a population estimated at well over

100,000, the city had no fortifications or military structures. Few burials have been found nor is there indication of a wealthy elite. But there are huge plazas, a broad central avenue, ceremonial platforms and the two immense pyramids of the Sun and Moon. The maintenance of calendars was, as always, critical. There are also thousands of spectacularly beautiful, coloured, intricate murals at the site. Over a thousand years later, the Aztecs would name the city Teotihuacán and claim that it was here that the gods created the universe.

One of the most remarkable Mayan pyramids was constructed towards the north of the Mexican lowlands on the Yucatan Peninsula. Chichén Itzá was in use from around 550 to 800 CE. On the spring and autumn equinoxes, the most extraordinary visual effect can be seen as a result of the design of the square-based stepped Pyramid of Kukulkan, which stands about 30 metres high (see Plate 11.3). Mid-afternoon, the northwest corner of the pyramid casts a shadow in the sunlight which falls on the western balustrade of the main stairway. The shadow forms a series of triangles which resemble a serpent over 30 metres long moving in a creeping motion down the balustrade. When all seven sunlit triangles have been formed, the serpent completes its movement by joining to a huge stone serpent's head at the bottom of the stairway.

But it gets even more amazing. The Pyramid of Kukulkan reflects sound and a brief handclap can be transformed into a longer sound reminiscent of the melodious and harmonic-rich chirp of the quetzal. The quetzal is a genus of spectacular native birds. Many Mesoamerican cultures associated the quetzal with the plumed serpent often referred to as Kukulkan but best known by its Aztec name, Quetzalcóatl. Research by physicists has shown that the sound effect is due to periodic reflections from the faces of the steps that climb the sides of the pyramid. Another building at the spectacular site of Chichén Itzá was used as an observatory and enabled the Maya to record the rising and setting positions of the sun, moon and the planet Venus.

So far, I have only talked about Mayan sites from the lowlands. Kaminaljuyu is the major highland site. It has been mostly demolished through the growth of Guatemala City. The region is known as the central highlands with an altitude of about 1500 metres. There were approximately 200 mounds at Mayan Kaminaljuyu, which were made of earth as they were in North America. Although we have only glimpses of the oral technologies in the massive cities of the Lowland Maya, we have an insight into the exact methods they used in the highlands where some Maya still use oral technologies to maintain their complex calendar.

Starting in 1975, anthropologist Barbara Tedlock was formally trained and initiated in the calendar divination tradition of the contemporary Quiché-speaking people of Highland Guatemala.[6] Substantial payment was required for training—knowledge, as always, is a tradeable commodity. In a method remarkably similar to the use of divining cowries and nuts of the West African Yoruba described in Chapter 2, Tedlock learnt to use the systematic arrangements of seeds as a memory aid. These were used to supplement the constant repetition of verses that had to be committed to memory. Long genealogies were also recited as part of rituals in the initiation of the Mayan 'daykeepers' who maintained the complex 260-day and 365-day calendars. As will be described for the Inca later in the chapter, the elders visit shrines where they repeat verses. Tedlock wrote that the shrines were described to her as 'like a book where everything—all births, marriages, deaths, successes, and failures—is written down'.[7]

Tedlock noted that many of the shrines were just simple pits in the ground. The Maya also made pilgrimages to various mountains, which were visited in a strict order. Both pits and mountains are sacred memory locations. The daily practice can be found encoded by mythology in the narratives of the Guatemala Quiché speakers, the *Popol Vuh*.

The earthworks of North America gain complexity

While the Maya were building their mounds and pyramids and establishing ever more sophisticated cities, the same trend was happening in North America. The major difference was that the Native Americans of the north, like the Inca in the south, did not use writing. They did, however, develop spectacular civilisations.

It was over a thousand years after the hunter–gatherers had built their mounds and post circles at Poverty Point that some of the most impressive sites of all were being constructed on the Ohio River Valley. The Hopewell culture built mounds in various shapes reaching a height of over nine metres. They also constructed geometrically shaped enclosures hundreds of metres across surrounded by earthen walls. The Hopewell constructed their monuments by carrying basketful after basketful of soil by hand.

It is only in the last twenty years or so that archaeologists have discovered that the Hopewell people not only built platform mounds but also constructed post circles.[8] Sometime between 150 and 200 CE, a large rectangular enclosure was connected to a semi-circular form at what is known as the Stubbs Earthworks. Here the Hopewell built a monument known as The Great Post Circle. The 151 posts in the 75-metre diameter circle were placed at an average of 1.4 metres apart. Eight kilometres away, the Moorehead Circle consisted of three concentric rings of posts with a formal entrance on the north side. Some posts are quite close together, while others are almost a metre apart. The outer ring is about 60 metres in diameter. The Moorehead Circle has been nicknamed

'Woodhenge' like so many posts circles in North America, making reference to the British Neolithic site on Salisbury Plain. Archaeologist Robert Riordan has shown that at the end of its life, around 150 CE, the posts at the Moorehead Circle were carefully removed and the post holes filled. As we have already seen, indigenous cultures around the world will destroy a memory space or restricted memory objects if there is no fully initiated elder to take them over.

One of the most spectacular Hopewell creations is the earthworks at Newark, Ohio, built between 250 and 500 CE. Along with many earthen mounds, here the Hopewell built a huge circular earthwork, 321 metres wide. The circle is linked by passage to an octagonal earthwork that is thought to have acted as an observatory for tracking the 18.6-year lunar cycle. Like other geometric enclosures at the site, archaeologists have concluded that the earthworks were ceremonial spaces.

Some mounds take the shapes of animals. Referred to as effigy mounds, dating of them has proven difficult. Given that a significant proportion of oral tradition involves mythological characters who take animal form, to have mounds that can be walked much like the Nasca animal glyphs makes perfect sense when constructing a memory space. Effigy mounds were a widespread phenomenon in the region around the present-day states of Iowa, Ohio, Wisconsin and Illinois. Best known are the effigy mounds in Ohio, which are thought to have been constructed by the Fort Ancient people who followed the Hopewell. The Great Serpent Mound is a six-metre-wide mound that winds back and forth for over 400 metres before ending in a triple-coil tail. The head appears to be eating an egg. The Alligator Effigy Mound is also considered to be a Fort Ancient culture creation. At over 60 metres long and up to two metres high, it looks more like an opossum or some other mammal able to curl its tail than it does an alligator. It is considered a purely ceremonial site because no burials have been found.

By 700 CE, the Coles Creek culture in the Lower Mississippi was using flat-topped platform mounds that were built around central plazas. The pyramid shape had buildings on the top. The culture was in the transition from a hunting-gathering lifestyle using some domesticates, but was not yet dependent on the maize plant, which had been imported from Mexico.

Around the same time as the Chaco Canyon culture dominated the southwest, the mound building would reach its most impressive manifestation in the east. The Mississippian culture built its largest cities at Moundville and Cahokia and traded across extensive networks from the Great Lakes in the north to the Gulf of Mexico in the south. Maize became the primary crop but a wide range of foods were eaten. Social inequalities were now apparent as population centres grew and social complexity increased.[9]

Moundville in Alabama featured 26 platform mounds and a rectangular plaza. Occupied from about 1000 CE, the mounds had rectangular bases and pyramidal shapes with buildings serving various functions on top. The tallest reached nearly twenty metres in height. At the peak of influence, Moundville had a population estimated in the tens of thousands. Along with their landscape modifications, the Mississippian cultures created stone discs, the majority of which were found in Moundville. Many had notches carved into them evenly around the side, which would work well as portable memory devices. The most famous of the Moundville discs is just over 30 centimetres in diameter, perfect to use as a handheld memory aid. Known as the Rattlesnake Disc, the sandstone is inscribed with entwined serpents, an open hand and other symbols.

The only Mississippian site larger than Moundville was Cahokia in Illinois. It was occupied from around 1000 CE and thought to have supported a population of up to 20,000 people. The Grand Plaza covered an area of about twenty hectares surrounded by at least a hundred mounds, some circular, some rectangular, some large and others small. The dominant structure, Monk's Mound, was constantly increased over its life until it became a 30-metre-high flat-topped pyramid built in four stepped terraces on a 290-by-236-metre base. The variety in the functions of the mounds at Cahokia adds a great deal of complexity to the site. Mound 34 was the only known Mississippian copper workshop. Mound 72 covered the remains of a man in his forties resting on a bed of over 20,000 marine-shell disc beads that had been arranged in the shape of a falcon. Within the same mound there were over 250 other skeletons. Researchers believe these are the remains of sacrificial victims. This site is far more than just a memory space. However, the signs are still there. Apart from the performance spaces, the public plazas and restricted buildings atop pyramidal mounds, there is a Woodhenge (see Plate 11.4).

Like other post circles in North America, the circle of posts at Cahokia was constantly rebuilt over its life. The number of posts and the diameter of the circle varied with the constant restructuring, but the circle itself was usually around 120 metres in diameter. The number of posts increased as it was rebuilt, ultimately reaching 60 posts. Posts were positioned to mark solstices and equinoxes, but that would only explain the presence of a few critical posts. The presence of red ochre pigment in the pits of some other posts indicates that they were likely to have been painted. It is also highly likely that they were carved. A circle of totem-like poles, like post and stone circles the world over, would have functioned as a memory space. Stone disc palettes like those found at Moundville have also been found at Cahokia. With no sign of writing, the combination of large memory spaces and portable memory devices is a strong indication that the study, maintenance and transmission of knowledge were certainly some of the purposes of the site.

Scattered across the great plains of Canada and the United States are thousands of 'stone circles'. A stone circle, however, does not necessarily imply a memory space. Most are simply the stones that once held down the conical tents of the Indigenous tribes of the Great Plains, their famous tipi. Much bigger and much rarer than the tipi rings are the stone circles referred to as 'medicine wheels'. At the centre is usually a cairn of stones, while the spokes are usually enclosed by an outer circle. The designs of the hundred or so medicine wheels found across the Great Plains vary greatly in terms of size, number of spokes, number of outer circles, the existence or not of a path through the circle to the centre, and the presence of features such as smaller cairns around the outer circle. A variety of astronomical alignments have been claimed for the circles.

The most famous medicine wheel is at Bighorn Mountains in Wyoming (see Plate 11.5). At 23 metres in diameter, the wheel has 28 spokes emanating from a central cairn, which is itself three metres in diameter. There are six smaller cairns dotted around the outer circle. Dating is difficult, but archaeologists believe that the Great Plains tribes created the monument at least 300 years ago, and possibly as early as 1200 CE. It did not stand alone but was part of a complex of landscape adaptions. The cairns appear to mark the rising and setting points of the sun on the summer solstice. Other alignments have also been claimed, but none can be certain. There is simply too little information.

The literate Aztecs and non-literate Inca

By the time the Aztecs came to power in Central Mexico, around 1300 CE, their culture invoked grotesque displays of violence in public spaces, including human sacrifice. They were ruled by an extremely wealthy elite. They adapted their writing from earlier Central American cultures using phonic elements. Their gods had become all-powerful creatures that were worshipped and could wreak revenge on those who did not obey the priests who claimed a unique communication with them. Those who retained the practical knowledge by this time served the powerful leaders. Memory spaces were no longer significant. Their biggest city, Tenochtitlan, was founded in 1325 CE on an island in Lake Texcoco in what is now Mexico City. Population estimates for Tenochtitlan tend to peak at around 200,000 people. Although memorising a vast corpus of knowledge about wild animals, plants, genealogies and navigation would no longer have been an important task, the role of the timekeepers was still evident. An intricately carved calendar stone, four metres in diameter and weighing over twenty tons, was located in the ruins. The Aztecs used a solar calendar of 365 days.

While the Aztecs dominated Central America, and North Americans were building cities with pyramidal mounds along the Mississippi and massive great houses in the southwest, the Inca started creating the greatest empire of all from their heartland in the mountains of Peru. The civilisation eventually had a population of around sixteen million people in a territory stretching 4000 kilometres from Ecuador down the Andes Mountains into Chile. They built one of the most spectacular cities in the world, Machu Picchu. And they did it all without writing.[10]

The Inca turned their major city, Cusco, into a massive memory space, the details of which were documented by the colonising Spanish. Radiating from the Coricancha temple in the centre were over 40 pilgrimage pathways known as ceques. The ceques divided the land into wedge-shaped political, agricultural and irrigation zones, each assigned to a specific kinship group. It is still unclear the degree to which the ceques were physical paths and how much they were purely imagined. To form a city-sized memory space, it does not matter as long as the pathways could be followed in the minds of the users.

At regular intervals along the ceques were 328 huacas which Spanish priest Bernabé Cobo carefully described in his detailed writing about the ceque system. Journeying along the ceques ensured that the huacas were visited in order. The huacas were often natural landscape features such as caves, springs, rock formations, river bends and even trees. Some were man-made buildings, some watercourses and some simply small, nondescript places marked with stones. Each huaca had a specific aspect of the knowledge system associated with it. Some huacas encoded information to do with irrigation, the calendar, spiritual beliefs or rituals. This is exactly how I would imagine Australian Aboriginal songlines or Native American pilgrimage trails enmeshed in a built environment. It was the ancient Greek method of loci on a grand scale.

Some huacas functioned as astronomical observatories linking the agricultural calendar to the solar cycles. For example, Q'enqo Grande was a prestigious huaca built by Inca king Pachacuti Inka Yupanki. Various visual effects occurred at the summer solstice and the equinoxes. In particular, a cave was sculpted from the limestone that included three stairs—a religious symbol representing the underworld, the present and the world above. As the summer solstice approaches, the sun enters the cave, illuminating the stairs in order. A similar effect was built into a cave known as Intimachay at the incredible mountain-top city of Machu Picchu, also believed to have been built by Pachacuti. Like many structures in Neolithic Britain and Ireland, a stone window was carefully shaped to block sunlight from reaching the back wall of the cave except for the days around the summer solstice.

The Inca ceques were used in combination with the extraordinary memory device, the khipu (see Plate 11.6). In fact, the design of the ceque system was given to the Spanish chroniclers encoded on a khipu. It is as close to writing as a memory device can be. The khipu specialists, the *quipucamayos*, were highly trained, restricting their knowledge to those of their profession.

Khipu were made from knotted cords, usually of cotton, a resource readily available from the Andean farms. A primary cord had any number of pendant cords, which hung vertically when used. Subsidiary cords could be added to any of the pendant cords for even greater complexity.

It has long been understood how the knots were tied in order to represent numbers and calculations such as demographics, tributes, trade data and calendar references. This use was thoroughly documented by the Spanish invaders. From a more detailed study of historic accounts and the 600 or so remaining khipu in museums and private collections, researchers have recently concluded that the khipu stored a great deal more than numerical information (see Figure 11.3). Colonial texts refer to the use of khipu for recording laws, censuses, tributes, trade, rituals and songs, genealogies and histories, as well as for transmitting messages across the huge empire in the hands of runners, much as memory sticks have done for millennia in smaller cultures. Documents also reveal that each category of information had its own official functionary, with their khipu designed and encoded for their area of specialisation.

A huge variety of knots were used in many different combinations along the cord. With different lengths of cord, different colours, twists, plaits and extra threads woven into the khipu, the coding possibilities are immense.

I have replicated the concept to store the history of art on a khipu, which I made incorporating the properties described above.

FIGURE 11.3 Khipu illustration by Inca nobleman Felipe Guaman Poma from his 'El Primer Nueva Coronica y Buen Gobierno' (1615/1616), known as the Inca Chronicle.

Numbers, and therefore dates, were easy to add. I structured the history into eras, locations and artistic media, then added individual artists. The beauty of the khipu was that I did not have to worry too much about leaving something out because it is so easy to add a subsidiary string. It is also easy to add knots, or even replace a string when adding complexity to the data. I still found I had to use vivid stories and memory tricks to link the cords to the actual information. I added different colours for female or male artists, plaits and twists in different combinations to denote whether this was indigenous artwork, traditional or contemporary, sculpture or painting and so on. Given the success of the Inca Empire, I had no doubt that I would find the khipu extremely effective. What I had not understood until I used it was just how flexible this device could be. It really is as close to writing as it is possible to get with no images and no alphabet.

The first khipu date back to the Caral-Supe culture, nearly 4000 years before the Inca perfected this incredible device. The Spanish arrived in Cusco in 1532. The conquistadors destroyed thousands of khipus. The Inca culture could not survive their onslaught.

CHAPTER 12

Polynesian navigators create a unique world on Easter Island

¦ ¦

The most famous statues in the world must be the monumental moai on the most remote inhabited place on earth, Easter Island. Nearly a thousand magnificent sculptures were carved on the island, each different, yet each conforming to a common style. Well over 200 moai stood majestically on platforms, their backs to the sea and their faces towards the volcano crater from which they emerged. Why did the islanders put so much effort into carving, transporting and erecting these massive creations? Why were they the only people on earth to adorn their landscape so spectacularly?[1]

There is little doubt that the original Easter Islanders were Polynesians. An expert Polynesian navigator, Tupaia, had joined

Cook's crew in Tahiti in 1769. When they arrived on Easter Island in 1774, Tupaia had no trouble chatting with the Easter Islanders. Linguists have concluded that the language was most likely from Mangareva, or the Marquesas Islands, both part of modern-day French Polynesia, a journey of 2600 or 3200 kilometres respectively.

Given the Polynesian origins of the culture on Easter Island, it is essential that any interpretation draws on Polynesian priorities. There is a significant difference between the Polynesian cultures and those I have used to understand non-literate knowledge systems in the previous chapters. Australian and American indigenous cultures maintain genealogies, but their method for organising the knowledge system tends to be based in the landscape. In Polynesian cultures, although the landscape is marked by sacred locations, the fundamental mechanism by which the knowledge system is structured is a complex of genealogies. Once this is understood, it is possible to shed light on the reason for the way the Easter Islanders set up their platforms and distributed their massive statues.

Easter Island is about 2000 kilometres from its nearest neighbour, the tiny Pitcairn Islands to the northwest. Chile is 3600 kilometres to the southeast. With an area of 171 square kilometres, the island is only 25 kilometres long (see Figure 12.1). It was named Easter Island by the Dutch explorer Jacob Roggeveen, who landed there on Easter Sunday in 1722. Tahitian sailors named the island Rapa Nui, meaning 'Big Rapa', due to its similarity to Rapa, a Polynesian island 2400 kilometres to the west. Consequently the indigenous people are referred to as Rapanui. I shall stay with the more familiar name of Easter Island, but use the name Rapanui for the indigenous inhabitants.

Easter Island is the peak of a volcano rising 3000 metres from the ocean floor. Only 500 metres of the volcano is above sea level, forming the island. High up on the steep cliffs that surround most

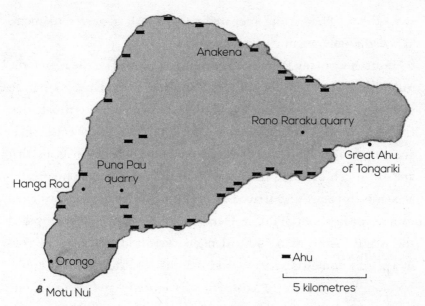

FIGURE 12.1 Map of Easter Island with the locations referred to in the chapter.
(LYNNE KELLY)

of the island are numerous caves formed by lava flows, which serve
to drain any rain away leaving the landscape arid. There are three
freshwater crater lakes but no permanent streams or rivers. There
is ample good soil, which once supported a dense forest of palms,
but there has been only a barren and treeless landscape for the
last few hundred years. There was obsidian for making tools and,
most important for our story, Easter Island had lapilli tuff stone in
abundance, perfect for making statues.

The original settlers

The original settlers travelled thousands of kilometres across the
Pacific Ocean to arrive at a tiny speck of land. The Polynesians were
superb navigators and gradually populated every habitable island in
the Pacific. When the first group of colonisers arrived on Easter
Island, they had tools, food, and domesticated plants and animals

with them. They came prepared to establish a new settlement, as was the Polynesian tradition.

As to how many Polynesians originally arrived on the island, the only thing we can be sure of is that the group was large enough to establish a rapidly growing population. Archaeologists estimate that the prehistoric population was at least 6000, with some researchers arguing for double or even triple that number. For reasons that are still much debated, the population then dropped dramatically. When Europeans first arrived in 1722, the population is estimated to have been about 3000. In December 1862 slave traders invaded the island. More than 1400 islanders were kidnapped to be sold in Peru as domestic servants and manual labourers. When public opinion forced Peru to cease the slave trade and return some of the islanders they had enslaved, they packed an old ship with 470 islanders from across the Pacific, four times as many people as could comfortably fit aboard. Of the 100 Rapanui loaded onto the decrepit ship, only fifteen survived the journey. They arrived home bringing smallpox with them. By 1877 there were only 111 people left on Easter Island. The few survivors told the early archaeologists that the raids stole the last of the *ariki*, or chiefs, along with those they described as the learned men.

Meanwhile, in 1864 missionaries built the first Roman Catholic church on the island and four years later they reported what they considered a great success: they had converted all the islanders to Christianity. In 1888 Chile took possession of the island, and just over a decade later rented it out in its entirety for sheep farming to Scottish ranchers. All native Rapanui were moved to the island's only settlement at Hanga Roa.

Swiss anthropologist Alfred Métraux led a French expedition to the island in 1934. He considered that so little was left of the ancient culture that it was almost worthless anthropologically.

He also felt that the few Rapanui left had been quizzed so often that there was a risk that they were now constructing answers to suit the visitors.

With the senior men and women gone, and a smaller population, the structures needed to maintain multiple levels of oral tradition could not possibly survive. Disease, religious conversion and dispossession had radically altered Easter Island; the traditional culture based around the moai was destroyed. The new cult of the Birdman arose as a reaction to the loss of all that had gone before. As will be described later in this chapter, the selection of the annual leader, the Birdman, was decided by a race to gain the first sooty tern egg from a nearby island. Christian missionaries suppressed the practice and the last Birdman was declared in 1878. The oral tradition recorded during early European contact can only offer glimpses into an enigmatic past.

There are many theories about the purpose of the magnificent moai staring across the landscape of Easter Island. Many pay scant attention to the details of the archaeology, only choosing to address the statues themselves. Erich von Däniken ascribed the moai to alien influence as he had done with the Nasca Lines. Thor Heyerdahl attributed the settlement to South Americans. To justify his claim, Heyerdahl led a five-man crew on the Kon-Tiki Expedition, sailing a hand-built raft from Peru in 1947. After 101 days at sea, the traditionally designed raft crashed onto a reef just east of Tahiti. The presence of sweet potato on Easter Island, however, has some researchers suggesting that the early islanders may have had contact with South America, possibly travelling there for trade themselves. Heyerdahl went on to lead some of the early archaeological studies of Easter Island. But it is to the Pacific we need to look to understand why the Rapanui erected their extraordinary moai.

The amazing skill of the Pacific navigators

The Pacific is huge. The skill of the Pacific navigators is legendary.[2] They could trade between settled islands, crossing thousands of kilometres of open ocean, often at sea for weeks at a time. They constantly sought to colonise new islands, and in their search would often travel against the prevailing winds until their food nearly ran out. If no island had been encountered, they would turn windward for a rapid trip home to safety. There is evidence that they visited New Zealand a number of times before finally coming equipped to settle. It is clear that the first Rapanui must have included a few of the highly trained Pacific navigators.

The navigational knowledge relied on extensive rote memorisation and mental calculations. Songs, chants, stories and mythology were used to store a vast amount of navigational data, along with diplomacy and politics relating to the different social expectations of the many islands a navigator might visit. They would memorise details of the behaviour of the ocean-going birds, enabling them to estimate the distance and direction to land at dawn or dusk. They memorised a detailed fish taxonomy, along with the behaviour of each species and where they could be found. The navigators studied how the swells and wave patterns around each island or reef would feel in intensity and at what angle they would strike the bow of the double canoe in different tidal and weather conditions. A highly skilled navigator could sense even the slightest of wave movements by entering the water and using his scrotum as a hypersensitive detector.

The navigators also trained in the use of complex star compasses, a memorised dynamic diagram that enabled them to calculate their position from the movement of the stars. One Tahitian chant told the exact position of the North Star, Polaris, although it could not be sighted until the sailor was well over a thousand kilometres north of home. Although varying between island groups, the star compass usually takes the form of a circular structure with around 30 points each named for the star that is observed to rise and set on the horizon at that point. The navigator shifted his focus from one star to the next rising over the course of a night. Within the compass, there were also individual names for hundreds of stars beyond those used as a primary focus. Star compasses were used as a set of memory locations not only for the physical star positions but also for organising the information about wind currents, ocean swells, the relative positions of islands, shoals, reefs and many other aspects of their seascape. Star compasses are still used widely across the Pacific.

Navigators could detect the presence of land long before they could sight it. They maintained a detailed knowledge of the way seasonal winds, clouds and ocean swell patterns, as well as fish and bird behaviour, were affected by land. In this way they effectively increased the size of the target island many times over. A phenomenon known as 'subsurface luminescence' allowed them to observe streaks of light 100 to 160 kilometres from land. These were used to steer on overcast nights when the star charts were of no use.[3]

Navigators took years to learn the knowledge and skills to cross the oceans. Training was only offered to the select few by the secretive navigational schools, each located in a boathouse. No one was permitted in the boathouse other than the navigators and their students. The navigators used esoteric language and commentaries to enhance the chants, mythology and stories used as memory aids. Anyone just hearing the songs could not gain sufficient knowledge to navigate.

Physical memory devices were also used extensively during teaching. Charts were constructed of sticks and shells. The points on the chart may represent real islands, reefs and sandbanks but also non-existent islands or fantastic creatures placed in the spaces between the real islands to give sufficient points on the memory path. Imaginary islands were included in the mythological origin narrative, which told of an animal or mythical hero moving along the navigational course, a songline in the ocean.

Various structures were also used for training. On the Gilbert Islands, for example, a small stone setting was just big enough for the students to sit in. Stones could represent an island or a canoe or be aligned astronomically for the student to learn the rising and setting points of navigational stars. Other stones represented major swells or the waveforms and the interference patterns when waves are mixed. Training started at quite a young age for those selected for the exclusive schools. On the Caroline Islands, boys started intensive training from the age of about five and it wasn't until they were eighteen that they were able to lead a voyage.

We can assume with reasonable certainty that the captains of the canoes that landed on Easter Island were highly trained Pacific navigators. They would have taken their understanding, their logic and their memory systems with them and adapted their mythology and skills to the Easter Island environment.

Arriving on Easter Island

The first settlers arrived somewhere between 300 and 1200 CE, depending on which researcher you read. Current thinking tends towards the later date, but this is still far from certain. The little oral tradition that survives includes the story of the first colonisers. This would have been public knowledge and the story most often told. Hotu Matu'a was a great navigator who led the first settlers in two canoes. He arrived from the west heading for the sunrise from his island called Hiva. Hotu Matu'a then circled the island twice before landing at Anakena, one of the few sandy beaches on the island. On arrival, Hotu Matu'a's family spread across the island, dividing it up into clan territories.

Archaeological evidence points to the land on Easter Island being divided into eleven tribal holdings, each with a platform holding statues. The platforms provided the public performance spaces for each clan. The archaeological evidence also indicates that the Rapanui settlers brought chickens and the edible Polynesian rat with them. They hunted seabirds, which bred in huge numbers on the various islets. They made regular trips to the breeding colonies on the small reef of Salas-y-Gómez, 415 kilometres to the northeast, to collect eggs and young birds for food. They began growing yams, sugar cane, taro, sweet potatoes, bottle gourds and bananas. They mulched their fields with stones and built rock walls and circular stone planting pits, methods that increased the soil fertility, retained moisture, regulated soil temperature and reduced weeds.

Most importantly, the newly arrived Rapanui began making statues that represented the ancestors, be they human or mythological. Although minimal oral tradition survives from the first Rapanui, we can get an idea of the way Polynesians settled new islands in similar circumstances from the oral tradition and knowledge systems of Rarotonga and New Zealand.

Settling another small Polynesian island: Rarotonga

Rarotonga, in the Cook Islands, is only 67 square kilometres so its history offers insights into how Pacific Islanders colonised a very small island.[4] The oral tradition of Rarotonga is still strong, with the story of the original settlers showing many similarities to that of Easter Island. The *Takitumu* from Tahiti, the origin story tells, was captained by Tangi'ia Nui who was fleeing from his older brother,

Tutapu. At sea, he met with another canoe from Samoa and together they sailed to Rarotonga. Tangi'ia Nui landed at Ngatangiia on the east coast. There he built a marae, a Polynesian ceremonial centre. Tangi'ia Nui proceeded around the island, establishing over 40 ceremonial centres along a road known as the Ara Metua, and divided up the land for the clans. As the Rarotongans process along the Ara Metua, they replicate the route of Tangi'ia Nui. This procession acts as a memory path, the recitation being a performance of the oral tradition. With the marae along its route, the familiar pattern emerges, that of a set of memory locations, their order fixed by the landscape.

The marae located on the Ara Metua were the sites of island-wide ceremonies, while those inland were more restricted. This is exactly the pattern that is indicated by the archaeology on Easter Island. The platforms on the shore, known as ahu, act as the public ceremonial spaces, while the crater where the statues were carved was highly restricted.

On Rarotonga, the genealogy is divided into two parts: the descent from the founding mythological ancestor and a record of births, deaths and marriages. Rarotongan genealogies are the basis of the memory system rather than being a factual record of forebears. A malleable genealogy is far more practical as it can be adapted to the current situation. Eventually unimportant names, events and stories will be forgotten while detail is added to information still valued. The practicality of these genealogies can be seen in the way land boundaries, dispute resolution and the legal system are regulated according to the information stored in the genealogies. An expert on Rarotongan oral tradition, Matthew Campbell, wrote that

> the building of monuments is a near universal activity, and their purpose is also universally bound to memory. In most preliterate

societies memory is preserved in oral tradition and genealogy, and such societies will build monuments with genealogical memorial practices in mind, as the Rarotongans did with the Ara Metua and the *marae*.[5]

Across Polynesian societies, it is the genealogies that form the strongest element integrating the culture and structuring the knowledge system, as can best be understood from the New Zealand Māori.[6]

Adapting to a different environment: New Zealand

Like the first Rarotongans and the Rapanui, the Māori of New Zealand had travelled to uninhabited islands, arriving around 1280 CE. Sufficient Māori culture has survived to offer an understanding of the way they adapted to a very different environment, yet maintained the essence of their Polynesian origins.

Mātauranga Māori is the traditional knowledge of the Māori. Critically, Mātauranga Māori takes both public and restricted forms, with performance spaces reflecting this dichotomy. The powerful role of knowledge specialists, the *kaumātua*, is found across New Zealand. They have the responsibility for research and adapting the oral narrative to new situations.

In the hierarchical Māori society, critical knowledge was restricted to the upper rank of what is often referred to as the 'priesthood'. The next rank was concerned with conducting rituals relating to issues such as warfare, agriculture, seafaring, fishing and other industries. The third grade dealt with the needs of everyday life, while the fourth grade, the lowest, were the shamans.[7]

Māori writer Bradford Haami described the memory devices used to help the elders in memorising the *waiata*, which he describes as songs. Elders constantly repeated many forms of songs in the ceremonial houses, the marae. The memory devices included rhyme, melody, structure, repetition, dancing, beating of drums, rocking, walking and playing string games (whai). Haami goes on to describe a comprehensive array of material memory devices, 'ngā pūrere whakamahara', which includes 'whakairo' (carving), 'mahi tauira' (design and weaving), 'moko' (body tattooing) and 'tohu' (physical or metaphysical signs). There is also 'tuhi', a complex concept that includes art on rocks, cliffs and in caves. Of the art forms, Haami refers to the tradition of carving as the most prominent of the memory aids. He emphasises that it is not just the finished product but the process of carving which acts to enhance memory.

Most famous of the carvings are the Māori jade tiki, representations of the first man and the hero of the creation stories that tell of the way in which the land and all the animals and plants were created, along with the laws binding the Māori to their culture. The carving designs were brought by the original settlers and then adapted to their new environment. Of all the carved objects, Haami notes that the most significant was the 'rākau whakapapa', the genealogy stick. The carved wooden staff has the ancestral figure at the top, with each knob below representing a generation. The ceremonial orator touches each knob, which acts as a memory aid for reciting not only the genealogy but the knowledge associated with each generation.

The knowledge system maintained by the Māori, as it is across Polynesia, is structured by a complex of genealogies. In this context, genealogies need to be seen as much more complicated forms than simply family trees. The Māori version, whakapapa, not only relates all people to their foundation ancestors but also relates all living things, even including rocks, mountains and all landscape features. Whakapapa is essentially the encyclopaedia that organises all knowledge into a structured format, which is essential for ensuring information is not lost when it is not written down. The ancestry provides protagonists for the stories which encode practical and spiritual information.

Whakapapa are functionally similar to Australian Aboriginal songlines, but the founding structure is based in genealogy. Haami describes whakapapa as an essential 'skeletal framework' for memorising a chronological sequence of events and giving a structure to the past, including the arrival of people in Aotearoa (the Māori name for New Zealand), their subsequent travels and the ancestral sources of knowledge. It also provides a taxonomy for all aspects of the universe, not just human events. Haami wrote that

> Genealogies of biota and environmental phenomena produce a classification system derived from the Polynesian/Maori practice of observing the connections between different entities, taking into consideration location and habitat, shape, form, texture, colour, smell, seasonality, change, human usage and adaptation ... Integral to these lists of genealogies were allegorical and analogical oral narratives which often used specialised language. Without an understanding of these accompanying narratives, the genealogies make no sense. Maori use of 'organic analogies' in whakapapa allowed them to link diverse biological phenomena.[8]

Typically, Polynesian cultures recall about 25 generations back in time. Beyond that the human and mythological ancestries are interwoven in the mythology. Haami explains that a lot of ancestors are needed in order to have sufficient stories to store enough information, but too many becomes unwieldy. This complex use of the term 'ancestors' is only problematical when a literal approach is taken to the stories. The stories attributed to revered ancestors are sacred, having both power and validity. They are known as 'kōrero tuku ihu', which translates as 'words handed down'. However, Haami notes that there was a deliberate construction of myths and legends. The ancient Polynesian stories were adapted to meet the needs of a new and very different environment. As well as the environmental knowledge, whakapapa encoded political relationships, inheritance status and the extensive family relationships of the chiefs. Given the critical nature of whakapapa, it is not surprising that the elders would examine initiates and each other on the genealogies, debate them and go to great lengths to ensure that they were memorised accurately.

Also critical to the understanding of the archaeology of Easter Island is the important role of the carved 'whare tupuna' (ancestral houses) of the Māori. Haami talks about these as akin to learning centres or libraries. The carvings within the whare tupuna are the equivalent of books; they encode the knowledge by memorialising the ancestors and then the oral tradition associated with each of them.

Across Polynesia, the open ceremonial spaces, the marae, often included wooden structures that housed carved figures, which acted as memory aids when singing the complex genealogies. In New Zealand, the culture was built around a knowledge system structured by genealogy whereby history, beliefs and the practicalities of daily life could all be associated with one of those ancestors. In New Zealand they carved their representations of the ancestors in wood. On Easter Island, they used stone.

Knowledge structured by genealogy

The purpose of the most distinctive of the monuments on Easter Island, the moai, can only make sense by understanding the way in which genealogies index the knowledge systems of Polynesian cultures. Even after all the devastation of the slave raids, disease and missionary suppression of the indigenous culture, genealogies were still maintained at the beginning of the twentieth century, with each person knowing their clan and relationships. Marriage was not allowed between relatives closer than third cousins. As Polynesian genealogies are both mythological and a tree of forebears, it is impossible to tell from the information currently available whether the statues represented real people or mythological ancestors. The islanders would have carved ancestors to populate the stories they needed to store, adapt and transmit their oral tradition. They would have started with the ancestors who taught the knowledge they brought with them, and they needed sufficient to populate their stories. They would have then adapted the stories, as required, to encode the new knowledge of their environment and the laws by which their isolated society would live. That may well have required new ancestors to be added, possibly those of the first chiefs on the island. Without reliable oral tradition, we simply cannot know.

There are over a thousand individual moai, varying in size from about two to nearly ten metres tall, all representing heads and nude torsos, the arms folded, fingers nearly meeting and the ears often elongated. The early voyagers describe 'long ears' as the fashion among many of the islanders. Although a few of the moai have indications of gender, a goatee beard or a vulva, the vast majority are sexually ambiguous, which is common in the Polynesian tradition of carving statues. On Easter Island, each statue follows the general rectangular form, which gives them their famously identifiable style. Yet each is different, as is essential for a memory system.

The majority of statues were made of tuff, a fairly soft volcanic rock. They were quarried from the crater at Rano Raraku, probably the most sacred place on the island. The moai were found right around the island, scarce at the steep headlands and clustered more thickly around principal centres of population. They were not placed in domestic sites. Many archaeologists argue that the land was divided according to tribal allegiances, but that the Rano Raraku crater was the source for almost all moai. The crater apparently served as a restricted site for the whole island. The islanders would not accompany British archaeologist and anthropologist Katherine Routledge into the crater. They stopped at what they referred to as a boundary marked by two large horizontal moai. To cross that boundary, they told her, would lead to their deaths. Despite her questions, they would say no more.

Katherine Routledge had arrived on the island with her husband in 1914 for a seventeen-month stay. She later published her detailed journal as *The Mystery of Easter Island*, which provides a comprehensive reference on Easter Island as close to the original inhabitants as we can get. The Rapanui told Routledge that some of the statues were individually named for the carvers, while a separate class of names indicated natural phenomena, such as references to water and to various birds. There is insufficient consistency or surviving oral tradition to be certain, but none of the islanders indicated that the moai represented gods. It is a logical conclusion that the moai represented ancestors and the knowledge encoded in their stories, as is the Polynesian way.

It is commonly reported in popular media that the statues were erected as gravestones or were images of chiefs buried beneath them. The evidence all argues against this role. Routledge was told by one of her Rapanui informants that the statues provided a marked place for burying the remains of those who died in the epidemics that ravaged the island after European contact. Prehistoric burials have been associated with a few statue-less platforms, but not with those holding the moai.

There are at least 360 of the platforms known as 'ahu' on Easter Island. On other Polynesian islands, the term 'ahu' refers to the altar at one end of a marae, the ceremonial enclosure. On Easter Island, however, these altars have been enhanced to become a central platform with two long wings of stone, the entire structure providing the backdrop to a plaza. Having an ample supply of easily carved tuff within the quarry and an increasing isolation from their Polynesian roots with every generation, it is not surprising that the Rapanui developed a unique style. There were just under a hundred platforms with moai on them, which are referred to as 'image ahu'. They supported over 200 statues.

The image ahu were made of a long wall that usually ran parallel to the sea. With their backs to the sea and faces gazing skyward, the moai towered over their audience below. At the Great Ahu of Tongariki, shown in Plate 12.1, there were once fifteen statues, while some other ahu supported only one. As the largest ahu ever built on the island, the central platform of the Great Ahu was nearly 100 metres long, reaching 220 metres when the length of the wings is included. The largest of its moai was 8.7 metres tall and weighed 88 metric tons.

Although over 90 per cent of the coastal platforms were built parallel to the shore, as is the Polynesian tradition, six of the platforms near the shoreline were aligned so that they faced the rising equinox. Some of the inland platforms appear to be aligned with sunrise on the winter solstice.

The figures on the ahu were fitted with hats, referred to as 'pukao'. The cylindrical hats were hollowed on the bottom to fit onto the heads, with a knot carved on top. The pukao were made of scoria, a type of red volcanic rock, quarried from a small crater, Puna Pau. It was only once they were on their ahu that the moai had eye sockets carved and filled with white coral and obsidian eyes.

Some of the platforms incorporated old moai or other previously used slabs in the construction, which indicates that ahu were modified and rebuilt over time. In front of the platform was up to 75 metres of smoothed stonework with the ground then levelled for another 50 or so metres. This was a performance space. Routledge describes the effect:

> Looked at from the landward side, we may, therefore, conceive an ahu as a vast theatre stage, of which the floor runs gradually upwards from the footlights. The back of the stage, which is thus the highest part, is occupied by a great terrace, on which are set up in line the giant images, each one well separated from his neighbour, and all facing the spectator. Irrespective of where he stands he will ever see them towering above him, clear cut out against a turquoise sky.[9]

Could you get a more perfect description of a public memory theatre?

A memory space beyond the shoreline

Many moai made a trip from the quarry in the crater of Rano Raraku to be mounted on their ahu platforms at the water's edge. Many more are along the roadways, on the side of the quarry mountain or still within the quarry (see Plate 12.2). There are differences in style for those on the ahu and those adorning the slopes of the mountain and roads around the island. Only the moai on the ahu had hats. The eyeballs of the statues on the side of the quarry mountain were only indicated by a simple line below the brow, and the backs often had a different shape.

Archaeologists have identified a network of ancient roads running from the quarry to the shores, across the landscape and around the shoreline. The many ancient tracks probably served to transport the moai and as ceremonial avenues. Routledge believed the statues had been deliberately placed on the roads. She described the section of one road approaching the quarry as having statues occurring every hundred metres or so. As a ceremonial avenue, an elder approaching the restricted quarry would have faced each standing moai individually. This would form a perfect sequence of memory locations.

Routledge described her impression:

> When the whole number of the statues on the roads were in imagination re-erected, it was found that they had all originally stood with their backs to the hill. Rano Raraku was, therefore, approached by at least three magnificent avenues, on each of which the pilgrim was greeted at intervals by a stone giant guarding the way to the sacred mountain ... One of the ahu on the south coast, Hanga Paukura, has been approached by a similar avenue of five statues facing the visitor.[10]

Many moai are still on the side of the mountain close to where they would have emerged from the quarry situated inside the crater of Rano Raraku. Some of these moai lie horizontal, possibly because they fell during transport to the ahu and had either broken or were simply deemed unsuitable to raise again. However, the majority were standing in holes dug specifically to hold them while still close to the quarry. Excavations have now shown that what appear to be just heads to modern visitors are complete statues, with torsos that have become buried by sediments up to their shoulders over time. This is hugely fortunate. The backs of the statues were carved with the belts and rings that still appear on some of the moai on the ahu. The buried backs also have abstract markings that would have served as memory aids. It is likely that the moai on the ahu also had these markings but that the soft stone has been eroded while exposed to the weather for hundreds of years.

Early reports also describe the Rapanui as being 'painted'. In Polynesian tradition, both women and men were tattooed in superbly executed designs that were highly admired by those who described them. Across Polynesia, tattoos are used to designate clan affiliations and record further complexities of the knowledge system.

Over 150 moai are still within the Rano Raraku quarry, some partially carved, with most yet to be freed from the bedrock. All but a dozen or so of the moai on the island were carved in this crater. Katherine Routledge was convinced that so many moai were still in the quarry because there was no intention to move them to the coast. If all were still in the process of being carved, she reasoned, then the number of workers involved would have been well out of proportion to the estimated population. Some of those remaining were carved in a way which means that they would not stand if extracted, others are no more than embossed faces without the access alleyways that surround those being carved for extraction. Twenty or so were already standing erect and others were simply too large to be moved. The largest, at 21.6 metres and weighing an estimated 270 tonnes, is nearly double the size of anything found outside the crater.

Routledge was told by Rapanui colleagues that the crater was a restricted place, one they still feared. Oral tradition talks of the carvers whose only job was to create the moai, with food provided to them as payment. Such specialist communities of artists are found across Polynesia.

I have no doubt that the statues in the crater were part of the memory theatre of the quarry itself, the most restricted area on the island. Restricted memory spaces are an integral part of all oral cultures. Clearly, this was the case with Easter Island as well. The

ahu, adorned with their statues and plazas, offered public performance spaces. The moai along the roadways and mountainside acted
as memory locations along the processional routes to the crater.
The crater of Rano Raraku was a restricted space.

The 'mysteries' of Easter Island tend to fall into two camps.
Why did they make the statues? How did they move them? We've
looked at the first question, but it is worth mentioning the current
ideas on the second. Some researchers believe the statues were
placed on sledges, which were then moved on wooden rollers. If
a lubricant was created out of sweet potatoes and mashed yam, as
oral tradition holds, then very few people, perhaps only ten, would
have been required to pull the sledges. However, oral tradition also
said that the statues walked from the mountain to their platforms
at the ocean. A study of the roads, according to some archaeologists, showed that the profile of the roads was V-shaped and not flat
and therefore unsuitable for sledges. Experiments have shown that
upright replica moai can be rocked and moved by teams of people
controlling three ropes tied to the statue.[11]

Once at the ahu, the moai were raised onto the platforms using
wood, with stones progressively being placed under the base. As the
stones were added, the moai stood up. And there they stayed until
they were toppled by the Rapanui themselves. Why?

The collapse of a culture

The population grew, estimates putting the peak as high as 10,000.
It then declined rapidly, long before European contact. The early
human settlers on Easter Island ate fish and shellfish and numerous
species of birds, including sooty terns, storm petrels, albatross,
fulmars, booby, shearwaters, rails, pigeons, doves, herons, parrots
and barn owls. Those first inhabitants almost certainly caused a
massive reduction in the bird population due to their hunting but

also through diseases brought with the chickens and the destruction of habitats by the rats and Rapanui themselves. No indigenous land birds exist on Easter Island today, a pattern that occurred across the Pacific when settlers colonised uninhabited islands.

The island was originally covered with palm trees, but it was completely deforested by 1650. One theory that attempted to explain the disappearance of the palms blamed the indigenous population for destroying all the trees to use in moving the moai. The deforestation, the argument goes, led to environmental devastation, which then led to a population collapse. This idea has since been discredited. Rampant warfare has been a popular explanation but has also been rejected by most scholars due to lack of evidence. Another theory holds that the Polynesian rats devoured the palm seeds, stopping any regeneration, which led to the deforestation of the island. Climate change has also been blamed for some impact on the island's agriculture, including a severe drought in 1456.

The population collapse may not be the result of a single one of these factors, but some kind of combination of factors. What matters is that the complex oral tradition associated with the moai, with all its multiple levels of initiation and lengthy training, would be difficult to sustain with a reduced population. It may also be that the Rapanui responded to the devastation with a loss of faith in the knowledge associated with the moai. By 1650 the stone quarrying stopped.

Quite suddenly, around 1770, the moai were deliberately toppled and destroyed, metaphorically and physically.

The first Europeans arrived on Easter Sunday in 1722. The Dutch crew only landed for one day, but noted that there were no big trees and that the statues were all standing. In 1770 a Spanish fleet mentioned the statues, but made no comment about any being fallen. In 1774 Captain Cook reported that many of the statues had been toppled from their platforms. By 1868 it seems that only one statue was still upright. European contact most certainly brought diseases for which the islanders had no resistance. Like indigenous cultures the world over, disease and unimaginably frightening death rates will have soon followed. It is likely that the islanders took out their anger on the statues, which were no longer serving the needs of the Rapanui. The moai had lost their power and meaning. Their knowledge was no longer effective.

The Birdman cult

One moai had very different images on it. A relatively small statue, it is now in the British Museum. On the back were images of the Birdman. A new tradition, referred to as the Birdman cult, is thought to have started around 1760, after the population decline. It lasted until the missionaries had converted the few remaining Rapanui to Christianity in 1868.

At the sacred area, Mata Ngarau, ritual leaders would chant and pray for success in the Birdman competition, held once a year at the spectacular Orongo village. A 300-metre cliff drops to the ocean on one side of the ceremonial centre. Each contestant would descend the sheer cliffs and swim with his provisions to the islet of Motu Nui, once the nesting grounds of thousands of seabirds, including the sooty tern. Many competitors died from drowning or falling from the cliffs. Some fell victim to the sharks. Once on Motu Nui, they waited in one of the 21 caves that were used as temporary residences and for burials. There they waited for the sooty terns to arrive. The goal was to be the first to bring an egg safely across the water and up the cliff. The winner would present the egg to his sponsor who would be declared Birdman for that year, an immensely powerful position.

In the caves and in some of the stone houses at the village of Orongo, there are well over a thousand images carved into the hard stone. Nearly half of these represent the Birdman, Make-make, who has a human form with a frigate-bird head. Make-make, the deity of the Birdman cult, is rarely represented anywhere else on the island. The Birdman motif is relatively abundant in Polynesian art and found in numerous petroglyphs around Orongo. The Birdman concept almost certainly arrived with the original settlers and was then raised in profile during this late stage in the island's pre-Christian life.

Art in many forms

Petroglyphs and rock paintings were widespread on Easter Island, although most of the rock art seems to date from the post-moai period. There is evidence of simpler designs, which have been covered by prolific images of a wide range of marine animals, roosters, canoes and even European ships. There are also over 500 vulvas and 400 fish hooks. Most of the artwork was associated with major performance sites, such as the ahu.

Portable art, a key aspect of the knowledge systems of non-literate cultures, is well represented in the Easter Island record. Wooden statuettes, 'moai kavakava', depict men with goatee beards and hooknoses, hollow cheeks, a spinal ridge and prominent emaciated ribs, which have been interpreted as indicators of famine. However, the bottom half of these figures are well-rounded and show no signs of starvation. Female figurines, 'moai papa', also display some male features, such as goatee beards, but are clearly female in their body forms. There are realistic male figures, 'moai tangata', and a range of animal forms. One of the few native animals, the lizard referred to in the local language as *moko*, is represented in lizardman figures, which also display aspects of humans and birds. Along with barkcloth images and feather work, it is likely the wooden ornaments date to the eighteenth and nineteenth centuries, the same time as the Birdman petroglyphs.

One of the most intriguing aspects of the prehistory of Easter Island is that of the rongorongo wooden tablets. Only about two dozen survive. According to Rapanui, most were destroyed on the order of the missionaries. Each tablet is incised with long sequences of abstract glyphs, along with humans, body parts, mythical and real birds, marine animals, plants, astronomical bodies, ships, boats, tools, weapons, ornaments and the frigate bird associated with Make-make. A line on the tablets is read from left to right and then the reader rotates the tablet 180 degrees to read the following line.

Oral tradition and records kept by the very first European observers are consistent: only a small elite was ever literate and the wooden tablets were restricted items used for chanting or recitation. The surviving fragments are probably only a hundred or so years old and post-date European contact. Some researchers believe that rongorongo is a full script that has yet to be deciphered. Katherine Routledge, however, concluded that rongorongo did not directly represent language but ideas that each scribe would interpret from memory to recall the island's history and mythology. This is proto-writing and hence acts as a memory aid only. Whether the Easter Islanders saw writing being used and then developed their own version, or developed the proto-writing totally inde- pendently is a topic of debate. Whichever is true, it is clear that these were intelligent people capable of adapting to new ways of storing information.

It was the extraordinary ability of the elders to memorise infor- mation and retain it accurately that enabled humans to reach even the remotest island and adapt to an alien environment in a way that no other species has ever done.

EPILOGUE

The memory code has been revealed. The method of loci is the universal driver for the construction of ancient monuments the world over. It is an ancient technique that has been used for millennia. Embedding knowledge in sequences of places in the landscape or on small devices was the fundamental technique for elders who were totally dependent on their memories to store all the knowledge of their cultures.

There is one factor that unites all the memory specialists who have ever used the method of loci in all its glorious variation—that is, the human brain. Our brains are hardwired to use structured spaces to store information.

The Nobel Prize in Medicine for 2014[1] was awarded to John O'Keefe, May-Britt Moser and Edvard I. Moser 'for their discoveries of cells that constitute a positioning system in the brain'. One of the researchers working with the Moser team, Charlotte Alme, described new research that demonstrates how the brain's enormous capacity for storage depends on small networks of brain cells in a structure called the hippocampus.[2] The research showed that rats stored a unique map or memory for each individual place in the array of rooms used in the experiments. We have so many different maps available in our complex brain structure that we can remember a huge number of similar places without mixing them up. The researchers concluded that this is why the method of loci works so well.

The hippocampus is found in every human brain. We can all store a vast array of knowledge by capitalising on the brain's capacity to remember locations and information associated with them. That is why monumental memory spaces have been a fundamental component in human communities all over the world for thousands of years.

Today we are just as capable of remembering vast stores of information as the elders of prehistory—we just need to bring to life our own memory spaces.

ACKNOWLEDGEMENTS

||||||||||||||||||||||||||||||||||||||||||||||||

There have been many people who have been an invaluable support during the past eight years of research and writing. I would never have gained the initial insight into the Indigenous way of memorising and organising knowledge if it had not been for my discussions with Australian Aboriginal colleagues, especially Nungarrayi (Warlpiri) and Daryl Pappin (Mutthi Mutthi) and staff at The Koorie Heritage Trust in Melbourne and the Ngarn-gi Bagora Indigenous Centre at La Trobe University.

The understanding of Australian Indigenous knowledge systems was also assisted hugely by correspondence with academics who work closely with Indigenous Australians, in particular Professor Iain Davidson and Dr Duane Hamacher, and the writings of many anthropologists, especially Professor Howard Morphy and Dr John Bradley.

In the United Kingdom, it was with great appreciation that I spent time in 2010 and 2013 with leading British Neolithic archae-ologist Dr Rosamund Cleal at The Alexander Keiller Museum at Avebury. I was privileged to be able to discuss the theory and application to the British and Irish Neolithic with experts, including

Dr Sally-Anne Coupar at The Hunterian at the University of Glasgow, Dr Alison Sheridan at the National Museum of Scotland in Edinburgh, and Adrian Green at The Salisbury Museum. Site director Nick Card and the members of the 2013 archaeological dig at the Ness of Brodgar, Orkney, gave me a very good hearing and wonderful feedback. It was a memorable experience to partake in such an extraordinary dig. Professor Mike Parker Pearson gave permission to examine the Grooved Ware, recently excavated from Durrington Walls, which was much appreciated.

I had a fortuitous meeting with American archaeologist Dr William D. Lipe at an archaeology conference in Australia late in 2009. Not only did Dr Lipe readily share his expertise on the archaeology of the Ancestral Puebloan world, but he also shared his extensive experience working with his Pueblo colleagues. He introduced me to the writing of Tito and Tessie Naranjo, and Rina Swentzell of Santa Clara Pueblo. It was Tito Naranjo who had indicated to Dr Lipe the need for archaeologists to engage with the research on primary orality.

Sociologist Dr Shing-Ling Chen from the University of Northern Iowa has been a valuable correspondent on primary orality. Her invitation to present the inaugural Marshall McLuhan Lecture at the National Communications Association Convention in Chicago, November 2009, enabled me to gain valuable feedback at an early stage, including that of the respondent, Dr Lance Strate.

With the assistance of a La Trobe University grant, I was able to undertake a research trip to the United States, during which I gained a great deal from meeting experts, including Larry Baker and Nancy Sweet Espinosa at Salmon Ruins archaeological site in New Mexico. Travelling with archaeologist Larry to Chaco Canyon is one of the most memorable experiences of my life. I gained hugely from discussions with Ron Shutiva and Berni

Keyope from the Acoma Pueblo, staff at the Indian Pueblo Cultural Center, Albuquerque, Sarah Margoles at Aztec Ruins, Diane Souder at the National Petroglyph Monument in Albuquerque and Patricia Jollie at the National Museum of the American Indian in Washington. In Louisiana, Dr Diana Greenlee was a very generous host at Poverty Point, while Dr Joe Saunders took me to Watson Brake. I spent three wonderful days in the bowels of the Peabody Museum of Archaeology and Ethnography at Harvard University with curatorial assistant Susan Haskell, and then three more with Dr David Curzon, sharing his extensive knowledge of a range of museums and art galleries in New York.

At La Trobe University, academic librarian Lisa Donnelly provided expert support, the value of which cannot be over-estimated. I valued the ongoing encouragement of my fellow postgraduate students in the English Program, in particular that of my co-supervisor Dr Alexis Harley. My research would never have reached fruition without the advice, expertise, diligence, patience and extraordinary flexibility of my PhD supervisor, Professor Susan Martin. She had no idea that the PhD she agreed to supervise on indigenous animal stories would end up in such uncharted waters.

I appreciate permission to use images from The Alexander Keiller Museum, Cahokia Mounds State Historic Site, Nic Chancellor, Ian Dennis, Michael Fox, Rudi Heitbaum, Peabody Museum of Archaeology and Ethnology, Thomas Q. Reefe, Mary Nooter Roberts, Museum of Native American History in Benton-ville, Pete Roberts, Ian Rowland, Julia Sorrell, Salisbury Museum, Weisman Art Museum, Hugo Whymark, and the many photo-graphs from Damian Kelly.

I greatly appreciated the enthusiasm, support and expertise of Elizabeth Weiss at Allen & Unwin throughout the development of this project. The book benefitted greatly from the meticulous editing by Meaghan Amor. Angela Handley also corrected many mistakes while she massaged all the elements to create this beautiful book. I am indebted to Philip Campbell for the cover and design.

I must thank my wonderful family and friends, too many to mention but so important every single day. I especially thank my daughter, Rebecca Heitbaum, and granddaughters, Abigail and Leah, for being such a precious reminder of the importance of today's endeavours for tomorrow's generations.

And finally, I must acknowledge the critical importance of the daily discussions of every aspect of this work with my husband, Damian Kelly, an educator, librarian, information technology expert and archaeologist. But more than that, without his gentle support and encouragement through the many times of intellectual and emotional turmoil, this book would not be in your hands now. Abigail and Leah often asked when we would be finished 'Grandma and Grandpa's book'. They got that attribution right.

ABOUT THE AUTHOR

IIIIIIIIIIIIIIIIIIIIIIIIIIIIIIIIIIIIIIIIIIIIIIII

Dr Lynne Kelly is a science writer and Honorary Associate at La Trobe University. She has spent most of her life teaching physics, mathematics, information technology and general science at secondary school level. Lynne has written popular science books about her investigations into claims of the paranormal, crocodiles and spiders. She started a PhD on indigenous animal stories, which led to a fascination with the way non-literate cultures manage to memorise a vast amount of practical information without writing. On Salisbury Plain one day, looking at Stonehenge, she realised that these ideas offered a new way of looking at archaeological sites around the world. So began the exciting journey leading to *The Memory Code*, her sixteenth book.

NOTES

▌ ▌

A detailed academic background for the way the control of knowledge was the primary source of power in small-scale indigenous cultures can be found in my book *Knowledge and Power in Prehistoric Societies: Orality, memory and the transmission of culture*, New York: Cambridge University Press, 2015. A detailed biography for the cultures, mnemonic devices and archaeological sites can also be found there and on my website: <**www.lynnekelly. com.au**>.

Chapter 1 Encyclopaedic memories of the elders

1. Sigmund Freud, *Totem and Taboo*, London: Routledge & Kegan Paul, 1960, pp. 1–2.
2. Quoted in John Bradley, *Singing Saltwater Country: Journey to the songlines of Carpentaria*, Sydney: Allen & Unwin, 2010, p. 29.
3. L.C. Wyman & F. Bailey, *Navaho Indian Ethnoentomology*, Albuquerque, NM: University of New Mexico Press, 1964.
4. C. Goddard & A. Kalotas, *Punu: Yankunytjatjara plant use: Traditional methods of preparing foods, medicines, utensils and weapons from native plants*, North Ryde, NSW: Angus & Robertson, 2002, p. iv.
5. S. Churchill, *Australian Bats*, 2nd edn, Sydney: Allen & Unwin, 2009, p. 22.
6. Bradley, *Singing Saltwater Country*.
7. Bradley, *Singing Saltwater Country*, p. 216.
8. Bradley, *Singing Saltwater Country*, pp. 81–2.
9. John Bradley, 'When a stone tool is a dingo: Country and relatedness in Australian Aboriginal notions of landscape', in B. David & J. Thomas (eds), *Handbook of Landscape Archaeology*, Walnut Creek, CA: Left Coast Press, 2008.
10. G. Bell, *The Desert and the Sown: Travels in Palestine and Syria*, New York: Dover Publications, 2008 [1907], pp. 48–9.

11. The best book I know on the world of modern memory champions is Joshua Foer's *Moonwalking with Einstein: The art and science of remembering everything*, New York: Penguin Press, 2011.
12. H.A. Tyler, *Pueblo Birds and Myths*, Norman, OK: University of Oklahoma Press, 1979, pp. 75–6.
13. J. Vansina, *Oral Tradition as History*, Madison, WI: University of Wisconsin Press, 1985, pp. 19–21.
14. J. MacDonald, *The Arctic Sky: Inuit astronomy, star lore, and legend*, Ontario: Royal Ontario Museum/Nunavut Research Institute, 1998, p. 168.
15. R.M.W. Dixon & G. Koch, *Dyirbal Song Poetry: The oral literature of an Australian rainforest people*, St Lucia, Qld: University of Queensland Press, 1996.
16. *Ceremony: The Djungguwan of Northeast Arnhem Land* (video recording), directed by Trevor Graham, Lindfield, NSW: Film Australia, 2006.
17. A. Ortiz, 'Ritual drama and the Pueblo world view', in A. Ortiz (ed.), *New Perspectives on the Pueblos*, 1st edn, Albuquerque, NM: University of New Mexico Press, 1972, p. 147.
18. A major source for my understanding of Pueblo culture is Alfonso Ortiz, *The Tewa World: Space, time, being, and becoming in a Pueblo society*, Chicago: University of Chicago Press, 1969.
19. R.M.W. Dixon, *The Dyirbal Language of North Queensland*, Cambridge: Cambridge University Press, 1972, p. 29.
20. B.J. Blake, 'Woiwurrung, the Melbourne language', in R.M.W. Dixon & B.J. Blake (eds), *Handbook of Australian Languages*, Canberra: Australian National University Press, 1979, vol. 4, p. 34. See also G.R. Holdgate, B. Wagstaff & S.J. Gallagher, 'Did Port Phillip Bay nearly dry up between ~2800 and 1000 cal. yr BP? Bay floor channelling evidence, seismic and core dating', *Australian Journal of Earth Sciences*, 2012, 58(2): 157–75.
21 W.R. Bascom, *Sixteen Cowries: Yoruba divination from Africa to the New World*, Bloomington, IN: Indiana University Press, 1980.

Chapter 2 Memory spaces, large and small
1. H. Morphy, *Ancestral Connections: Art and an Aboriginal system of knowledge*, Chicago, IL: University of Chicago Press, 1991, and H. Morphy, *Aboriginal Art*, London: Phaidon Press, 1998.
2. Buku-Larrngay Mulka Centre, *Saltwater: Yirrkala bark paintings of sea country: Recognising Indigenous sea rights*, Neutral Bay, NSW: Buku-Larrngay Mulka Centre in association with Jennifer Isaacs Publishing, 1999, p. 20.
3. M.N. Roberts & A.F. Roberts, *Luba: Visions of Africa*, Milan: 5 Continents Editions, 2007, p. 12.
4. W.R. Bascom, *Sixteen Cowries: Yoruba divination from Africa to the New World*, Bloomington, IN: Indiana University Press, 1980.
5. E.M. McClelland, *The Cult of Ifa among the Yoruba*, London: Ethnographica, 1982.
6. B. Tedlock, *Time and the Highland Maya*, rev. edn, Albuquerque, NM: University of New Mexico Press, 1992, p. 62.
7. Tedlock, *Time and the Highland Maya*, p. 80.
8. Alfonzo Ortiz's *The Tewa World: Space, time, being, and becoming in a Pueblo society*, Chicago: University of Chicago Press, 1969, and Richard I. Ford's revealing paper, 'The color of survival', *Discovery*, 1980: 17–29, should be read together.

Chapter 4 A journey through time

1. H. Morphy, *Aboriginal Art*, London: Phaidon Press, 1998, p. 48.
2. For example, see Charles C. Mann's article, 'Göbekli Tepe', in *National Geographic*, June 2011.
3. K.T. Lillios, 'Creating memory in prehistory: The engraved slate plaques of Southwest Iberia', in R.M. Van Dyke and S.E. Alcock, *Archaeologies of Memory*, Malden, MA: Blackwell, 2003.
4. D. Turnbull, 'Performance and narrative, bodies and movement in the construction of places and objects, spaces and knowledges: The case of the Maltese megaliths', *Theory, Culture & Society*, 2002, 19(5/6): 125–43.

Chapter 5 The ever-changing memory spaces at Stonehenge

1. Christopher Tilley wrote a hugely influential book on the importance of considering the role of the landscape in archaeological interpretations: *A Phenomenology of Landscape: Places, paths, and monuments*, Oxford: Berg, 1994. He pointed out that monuments were built in areas where there had been activity for millennia before, from the Mesolithic, which he linked, as I do, to control of knowledge and power.
2. There is a vast range of resources on the British Neolithic in general and Stonehenge in particular. A small sample of the most useful:
   - Richard Bradley's books, including: *The Prehistory of Britain and Ireland*, Cambridge: Cambridge University Press, 2007; *The Significance of Monuments: On the shaping of human experience in Neolithic and Bronze Age Europe*, London: Routledge, 1998; *An Archaeology of Natural Places*, London: Routledge, 2000
   - Burl, A., *A Brief History of Stonehenge: A complete history and archaeology of the world's most enigmatic stone circle*, London: Robinson, 2007
   - Cleal, R.M.J., Walker, K.E. & Montague, R., *Stonehenge in its Landscape: Twentieth-century excavations*, London: English Heritage, 1995
   - Many references by Mike Parker Pearson and his colleagues, including: Parker Pearson, M. & The Stonehenge Riverside Project, *Stonehenge: Exploring the greatest Stone Age mystery*, London: Simon & Schuster, 2012; Larsson, M. & Parker Pearson, M. (eds), *From Stonehenge to the Baltic: Living with cultural diversity in the third millennium BC*, London: Archaeopress, 2007
   - Pitts, M., *Hengeworld: Life in Britain 2000 BC as revealed by the latest discoveries at Stonehenge, Avebury and Stanton Drew*, London: Arrow Books, 2001
   - Ruggles, C., *Astronomy in Prehistoric Britain and Ireland*, New Haven, CT: Yale University Press, 1999
   - Thomas, J., *Understanding the Neolithic*, 2nd edn, London: Routledge, 1999.
3. Parker Pearson & The Stonehenge Riverside Project, *Stonehenge*. The stages quoted replace Phases I, II and III as used in earlier literature.
4. Mike Parker Pearson, Richard Bevins, Rob Ixer et al., 'Craig Rhos-y-felin: A Welsh bluestone megalith quarry for Stonehenge', *Antiquity*, 2015, 89: 1331–52.
5. Burl, *A Brief History of Stonehenge*, p. 19.
6. O. Williams-Thorpe, C.P. Green & J.D. Scourse, 'The Stonehenge bluestones: Discussion', in B. Cunliffe & C. Renfrew (eds), *Science and Stonehenge*, Oxford: published for the British Academy by Oxford University Press, 1997, pp. 315–18.

7. M. Parker Pearson, Josh Pollard, Colin Richards, et al., 'Materializing Stonehenge: The Stonehenge Riverside Project and new discoveries', *Journal of Material Culture*, 2006, 11(1–2): 227–61; M. Parker Pearson, 'The Stonehenge Riverside Project: Excavations at the east entrance of Durrington Walls', in Larsson & Parker Pearson (eds), *From Stonehenge to the Baltic*, pp. 125–44; Parker Pearson & The Stonehenge Riverside Project, *Stonehenge*.

8. Parker Pearson, 'The Stonehenge Riverside Project', p. 140.

9. Caesar, as quoted in P.B. Ellis, *Caesar's Invasion of Britain*, New York: New York University Press, 1980, p. 30.

Chapter 6 The megalithic complexes of Avebury and Orkney

1. Dating in the Avebury landscape is approximate due to dating difficulties, but the chronology is reasonably confidently established. Dates given here are taken from the National Trust's guidebook, *Avebury: Monuments and landscape,* by Dr Ros Cleal, 2008. The major references used for the Avebury section are:
   - Burl, A., *Prehistoric Avebury*, 2nd edn, 2002
   - Pitts, M., *Hengeworld*, 2001
   - Pollard, J. and Reynolds, A., *Avebury: The biography of landscape*, 2002.

2. I.F. Smith (ed.), *Windmill Hill and Avebury: Excavations by Alexander Keiller, 1925–1939*, Oxford: Clarendon Press, 1965, p. 7.

3. Lynda J. Murray, *A Zest for Life: The story of Alexander Keiller*, Swindon, UK: Morven Books, 1999, p. 54.

4. Caroline Wickham-Jones, *Between the Wind and the Water: World Heritage Orkney*, Cheshire: Windgather Press, 2006, p. 83.

Chapter 7 Newgrange and the passage cairns of Ireland

1. G. Stout & M. Stout, *Newgrange*, Cork, Ireland: Cork University Press, 2008, p. 4.

2. A great deal of extreme speculation based on little or no archaeological evidence has been written about the Irish monuments. References which were of particular use for this chapter were Stout & Stout, *Newgrange*, along with:
   - Brennan, M., *The Stones of Time: Calendars, sundials, and stone chambers of ancient Ireland*, Rochester, VT: Inner Traditions International, 1994
   - Bradley, R., *The Prehistory of Britain and Ireland,* Cambridge: Cambridge University Press, 2007
   - Jones, A., *Memory and Material Culture,* Cambridge: Cambridge University Press, 2007
   - O'Kelly, M.J., *Newgrange: Archaeology, art and legend*, London: Thames and Hudson, 1982
   - Ruggles, C., *Astronomy in Prehistoric Britain and Ireland,* New Haven, CT: Yale University Press, 1999
   - Thomas, J., 'Monuments from the inside: The case of the Irish megalithic tombs', *World Archaeology,* 1990, 22(2): 168–78.

3. Stout & Stout, *Newgrange*, p. 50.

4. O'Kelly, *Newgrange*, p. 122.

5. Stout & Stout, *Newgrange*, p. 19.
6. See, for example, M. Patton, *Statements in Stone: Monuments and society in Neolithic Brittany*, London: Routledge, 1993, pp. 69, 131.
7. Stout & Stout, *Newgrange*, pp. 53, 55.
8. Stout & Stout, *Newgrange*, p. 53.
9. Stout & Stout, *Newgrange*, p. 58.

Chapter 8 The tall stones and endless rows of Carnac

1. The major references used for Brittany were:
   - Burl, A., *From Carnac to Callanish: The prehistoric stone rows and avenues of Britain, Ireland and Brittany*, New Haven, CT: Yale University Press, 1993
   - Patton, M., *Statements in Stone: Monuments and society in Neolithic Brittany*, London: Routledge, 1993
   - Scarre, C., *Landscapes of Neolithic Brittany*, Oxford: Oxford University Press, 2011.
2. Scarre, *Landscapes of Neolithic Brittany*, p. 100.
3. Patton, *Statements in Stone*, p. 62.
4. Scarre, *Landscapes of Neolithic Brittany*, p. 241.
5. See for example, Scarre, *Landscapes of Neolithic Brittany*, p. 243. The interpretation is not only quoted by Chris Scarre. I found the breasts in a great deal that I read on Brittany.
6. Patton, *Statements in Stone*, p. 120.
7. Patton, *Statements in Stone*, p. 156.

Chapter 9 The unparalleled architecture of Chaco Canyon

1. There is a great deal of excellent literature on the American southwest archaeology. The major references used for this chapter were:
   - Frazier, K., *People of Chaco: A canyon and its culture*, New York: Norton, 2005
   - Kantner, J., *Ancient Puebloan Southwest*, Cambridge: Cambridge University Press, 2004
   - Lekson, S.H., *The Chaco Meridian: Centers of political power in the ancient Southwest*, Walnut Creek, CA: AltaMira Press, 1999
   - Lekson, S.H., *Great Pueblo Architecture of Chaco Canyon, New Mexico*, Albuquerque, NM: University of New Mexico Press, 1986
   - Noble, D.G. (ed.), *In Search of Chaco: New approaches to an archaeological enigma*, Santa Fe, NM: School of American Research Press, 2004
   - Sebastian, L., *The Chaco Anasazi: Sociopolitical evolution in the prehistoric Southwest*, Cambridge: Cambridge University Press, 1992
   - Van Dyke, R.M., *The Chaco Experience: Landscape and ideology at the Center Place*, Santa Fe, NM: School for Advance Research Press, 2007
   - Van Dyke, R.M., 'Memory and the construction of Chacoan society' in R.M. Van Dyke and S.E. Alcock, *Archaeologies of Memory*, Malden, MA: Blackwell, 2003.
2. Lekson, *The Chaco Meridian*, p. 80.
3. L.J. Kuwanwisiwma, 'Yupköyvi: The Hopi story of Chaco Canyon', in D.G. Noble (ed.), *In Search of Chaco*, pp. 41–8.

4. Contemporary Pueblo resources include:
   - Ortiz, A., *The Tewa World: Space, time, being, and becoming in a Pueblo society*, Chicago: University of Chicago Press, 1969
   - Reyman, J.E., 'Priests, power, and politics: Some implications of socioceremonial control', in J.B. Carlson & J.W. Judge (eds), *Astronomy and Ceremony in the Prehistoric Southwest*, Albuquerque, NM: Maxwell Museum of Anthropology, 1987: pp. 121–47
   - Titiev, M., *The Hopi Indians of Old Oraibi: Change and continuity*, Ann Arbor, MI: University of Michigan Press, 1972
   - Titiev, M., 'The story of Kokopele', *American Anthropologist*, 1939, 41(1): 91–8
   - Varien, M.D., Naranjo, T., Connolly, M.R. & Lipe, W.D., 'Native American issues and perspectives', in W.D. Lipe, M.D. Varien & R.H. Wilshusen (eds), *Colorado Prehistory: A context for the Southern Colorado River Basin*, Denver, CO: Colorado Council of Professional Archaeologists, 1999, pp. 370–404.
5. S.H. Lekson, T.C. Windes & J.R. Stein et al., 'The Chaco Canyon community', *Scientific American*, 1988, 259: 100–9.; Van Dyke, *The Chaco Experience*, p. 114; K.R. Durand, 'Function of Chaco-Era great houses', *Kiva*, 2003, 69(2): 141–69.
6. R.G. Vivian, D.N. Dodgen & G.H. Hartmann, *Wooden Ritual Artifacts from Chaco Canyon, New Mexico: The Chetro Ketl collection*, Tucson, AZ: University of Arizona Press, 1978.
7. A. Kenward, 'Artifact: Mimbres bowl', *Archaeology*, 2008, 61(3): 72.
8. A. Sofaer, *Chaco Canyon Astronomy: An ancient American cosmology*, Santa Fe, New Mexico: Ocean Tree Books, 2008.

Chapter 10 Giant drawings on the desert floor at Nasca

1. Luis Briones-M, 'The geoglyphs of the north Chilean desert: An archaeological and artistic perspective', *Antiquity*, 2006, 80(307): 9–24.
2. The major references used for this chapter were:
   - Aveni, A.F., *Between the Lines: The mystery of the giant ground drawings of ancient Nasca, Peru*, Austin, TX: University of Texas Press, 2000
   - Aveni, A. & Silverman, H., 'Between the lines: Reading the Nazca markings as rituals writ large', in A.F. Aveni (ed.), *Foundations of New World Cultural Astronomy: A reader with commentary*, Boulder, CO: University Press of Colorado, 2008, pp. 621–33
   - Curry, A., 'Rituals of the Nasca Lines', *Archaeology*, 2009 (May/June): 34–9
   - Silverman, H., 'The archaeological identification of an ancient Peruvian pilgrimage center', *World Archaeology*, 1994, 26: 1–18
   - Silverman, H., *Cahuachi in the Ancient Nasca World*, Iowa City: University of Iowa Press, 1993.
3. Aveni, *Between the Lines*, p. 138.

Chapter 11 Memory spaces across the Americas

1. References on the archaeological sites and cultures across the Americas are numerous and not always consistent. The big picture was pretty much the same, but details and dates varied greatly. References listed below are those that I took as the final arbiter when I was unable to resolve the differences.

Maya:
- Coe, M., *The Art of the Maya Scribe,* New York: Harry N. Abrams, 1998
- Coe, M., *Breaking the Maya Code,* London: Thames & Hudson, 2012
- Coe, M.D. & Houston, S., *The Maya,* 9th edn, London: Thames & Hudson, 2015

Olmec, Zapotec, Aztec:
- Coe, M.D. & Koontz, R., *Mexico: From the Olmecs to the Aztecs*, 7th edn, London: Thames & Hudson, 2013.

Inca:
- Aveni, A.F., *Between the Lines: The mystery of the giant ground drawings of ancient Nasca, Peru*, Austin, TX: University of Texas Press, 2000, has a good summary despite the title indicating that it is about the Nasca
- Silverman, H. & Isbell, W., *The Handbook of South American Archaeology*, Dordrecht: Springer, 2008.

2. Coe, *Breaking the Maya Code*, p. 13.
3. J.W. Saunders, R.D. Mandel, C.G. Sampson et al., 'A mound complex in Louisiana at 5400–5000 years before the present', *Science,* 1997, 277: 1796–99.
4. I devoted an entire chapter to Poverty Point in *Knowledge and Power in Prehistoric Societies.*
5. J. Abel, J. Rick, P. Huang et al., *On the Acoustics of the Underground Galleries of Ancient Chavín de Huántar, Peru*, Paris: Acoustics-08 Paris, 2008.
6. Barbara Tedlock, *Time and the Highland at Maya*, Albuquerque, NM: University of New Mexico Press, 1992.
7. Tedlock, *Time and the Highland at Maya*, p. 80.
8. Excavation reports by archaeologist Robert Riordan and the Masters thesis of Katherine Lynn Rippl, 'Examination of two post circles found in the Ohio Valley', Michigan State University. From personal contact.
9. The major references on the Mississippian mound-builders were:
    - Leary, J., Darvill, T. & Field, D. (eds), *Round Mounds and Monumentality in the British Neolithic and Beyond*, Oxford: Oxbow Books, 2010
    - Pauketat, T.R., *Ancient Cahokia and the Mississippians*, Cambridge, UK: Cambridge University Press, 2004
    - Pauketat, T.R. & Alt, S.M., 'Mounds, memory, and contested Mississippian history', in R.M. Van Dyke and S.E. Alcock (eds), *Archaeologies of Memory*, Malden, MA: Blackwell, 2003.
10. The most important of the resources on the khipu and ceques were:
    - Brokaw, G., *A History of the Khipu*, Cambridge: Cambridge University Press, 2010
    - Dearborn, D.S.P., Schreiber, K.J. & White, R.E., 'Intimachay: A December solstice observatory at Machu Picchu, Peru', *American Antiquity*, 1987, 52(2): 346–52
    - Niles, S.A., *The Shape of Inca History: Narrative and architecture in an Andean empire*, Iowa City: University of Iowa Press, 1999
    - Silverman, H., 'The archaeological identification of an ancient Peruvian pilgrimage center', *World Archaeology*, 1994, 26(1): 1–18
    - Urton, G., *Signs of the Inka Khipu: Binary coding in the Andean knotted-string records*, Austin, TX: University of Texas Press, 2003.

Chapter 12 Polynesian navigators create a unique world on Easter Island
1. The major references on Easter Island were:
   - The Easter Island Foundation website: <http://islandheritage.org/wordpress/>
   - Flenley, J. & Bahn, P., *The Enigmas of Easter Island: Island on the edge*, 2nd edn, Oxford: Oxford University Press, 2003
   - Hunt, T. & Lipo, C., *The Statues that Walked: Unraveling the mystery of Easter Island*, New York: Free Press, 2011
   - Routledge, K., *The Mystery of Easter Island*, Rapa Nui: Rapa Nui Press, [1919] 2005 (facsimile edn).
2. The major references on the Pacific navigators were:
   - Gladwin, T., *East is a Big Bird: Navigation and logic on Puluwat atoll*, Cambridge, Mass.: Harvard University Press, 1970
   - Goodenough, W.H. & Thomas, S.D., 'Traditional navigation in the Western Pacific: A search for pattern', *Expedition*, 1987, 26(3): 3–14
   - Hage, P., 'Speculations on Puluwatese mnemonic structure', *Oceania*, 1978, XLIX(2): 81–95
   - Lewis, D., *We, the Navigators: The ancient art of landfinding in the Pacific*, Canberra: Australian National University Press, 1972
   - Turnbull, D., *Masons, Tricksters and Cartographers: Comparative studies in the sociology of scientific and indigenous knowledge*, Amsterdam: Harwood Academic, 2000.
3. Flenley & Bahn, *The Enigmas of Easter Island*, p. 69.
4. M. Campbell, 'Memory and monumentality in the Rarotongan landscape', *Antiquity*, 2006, 80 (307): 102(116).
5. Campbell, 'Memory and monumentality', p. 115.
6. The major references on New Zealand were:
   - Catton, P., 'Philosophy, Matauranga Maori, and the meaning of NZ biculturism', paper presented at the Nga Kete a Rehua—Inaugural Maori Research Symposium, Christchurch, New Zealand, 4–5 September 2008
   - Goldman, I., *Ancient Polynesian Society*, Chicago, IL: University of Chicago Press, 1970
   - Haami, B., *Pūtea Whakairo: Māori and the written word*, Honolulu: University of Hawaii Press, 2006.
7. Goldman, *Ancient Polynesian Society*, p. 40.
8. Haami, *Pūtea Whakairo*, p. 16.
9. Routledge, *The Mystery of Easter Island*, p. 171.
10. Routledge, *The Mystery of Easter Island*, p. 196.
11. Hunt & Lipo, *The Statues that Walked*.

Epilogue
1. See <www.nobelprize.org/nobel_prizes/medicine/laureates/2014/>.
2. The Norwegian University of Science and Technology, 'Eleven maps for eleven rooms: Probing the brain's extensive capacity for storing memories', *ScienceDaily*, 8 December 2014, <www.sciencedaily.com/releases/2014/12/141208152518.htm>. The academic paper is C.B. Alme, M. Chenglin, J. Karel et al., 'Place cells in the hippocampus: Eleven maps for eleven rooms', *Proceedings of the National Academy of Sciences*, 8 December 2014, <www.pnas.org/cgi/doi/10.1073/pnas.1421056111>.

INDEX

▌▌▌

References to illustrations are in *italics*; references to colour section plates
are abbreviated as *Pl.* and refer to individual plate numbers.